MANAGEMENT
21C

PRAISE FOR MANAGEMENT 21C

"Excellent!" Chowdhury has gathered together under one roof, so to speak, a remarkable group of thinkers who give us their best bets on how our organizational futures will look. I found it enlightening and useful."

WARREN BENNIS

Distinguished Professor of Business, *Univ. of Southern California*
Co-author of *Organizing genius* and *Co-leaders*

"You only have to take a look at the list of contributors to know the kind of book you're going to be reading. It's extremely stimulating and is fabulous at guiding the reader through the minefield of management.

ANITA RODDICK O.B.E.

Founder, *The Body Shop*

"In the fast-moving information age what managers and business leaders need most is perspective. Subir Chowdhury provides us an excellent perspective to better utilize the gigabytes of information that are thrust upon us 24 hours a day."

J.D. POWER III

Chairman, *J.D. Power and Associates*

"Subir Chowdhury has collected a 'who's who' of thinkers and writers about leadership. In addition to his own thought-provoking chapter, 'Towards the Future of Management', the book opens a window on the challenges for leadership in the new millennium.

The book has the *fascination of a good novel* – plus exposure to the ideas of many of our best 'futurists'. I recommend it to organization leaders, consultants and academics working on this critical issue for all of us."

RICHARD BECKHARD

Principal, *Richard Beckhard Associates*
Emeritus Professor, *Sloan School of Management, MIT*

"Remarkable thought leaders have produced a remarkable guide for the leader in the new century."

FRANCES HESSELBEIN

Chairman of the Board of Governors, *Peter Drucker Foundation*

"Each chapter will kick start the brain to deal with the 21st century. A very thoughtful collection."

PHILIP B. CROSBY

Author, *Quality & Me*

"If you read only one management book this year, make it *Management 21C*. A provocative future-orientated book that offers a dramatic and convincing view of what leaders and organizations will need to be successful in the next century."

JOHN A. QUELCH

Dean, *London Business school*

"Winning will require continuous change and Chowdhury's menu provides one of the best thought templates for competing in the 21st century."

E.A. BLECHSCHMIDT

President & CEO, *Olsten Corporation*

To my wife, Malini

and to all the great minds

who made this book possible

MANAGEMENT 21C

SOMEDAY WE'LL ALL MANAGE THIS WAY

SUBIR CHOWDHURY

FINANCIAL TIMES

Prentice Hall

PEARSON EDUCATION LIMITED

Head Office:
Edinburgh Gate
Harlow CM20 2JE
Tel: +44 (0)1279 623623
Fax: +44 (0)1279 431059

London Office:
128 Long Acre, London WC2E 9AN
Tel: +44 (0)171 447 2000
Fax: +44 (0)171 240 5771
www.business-minds.com

———————————————

First published in Great Britain 2000

© Subir Chowdhury 2000
Chapter 14 © Peter Senge and Katrin Käufer 2000
Chapter 18 © Rosabeth Moss Kanter 2000
Back cover photograph © Pat Seiter

The right of Subir Chowdhury to be identified as author
of this work has been asserted by him in accordance
with the Copyright, Designs, and Patents Act 1988.

ISBN 0 273 63963 3

British Library Cataloguing in Publication Data
A CIP catalogue record for this book can be obtained
from the British Library.

10 9 8 7 6 5 4 3 2

Typeset by M Rules
Printed and bound in Great Britain by
Biddles Ltd, Guildford & King's Lynn

*The Publishers' policy is to use paper manufactured
from sustainable forests.*

MANAGEMENT 21C

SUBIR CHOWDHURY

MOREEN ANDERSON	CHRISTOPHER A. BARTLETT
HAMID BOUCHIKHI	DAVID CONKLIN
PAUL DAINTY	PAUL A.L. EVANS
CAELA FARREN	J. WIL FOPPEN
ROBERT M. FULMER	SUMANTRA GHOSHAL
MARSHALL GOLDSMITH	LINDA A. HILL
INGALILL HOLMBERG	ROSABETH MOSS KANTER
KATRIN H. KÄUFER	JOHN R. KIMBERLY
JAMES M. KOUZES	STUART R. LEVINE
PETER LORANGE	PETER MORAN
BARRY Z. POSNER	C.K. PRAHALAD
JONAS RIDDERSTRÅLE	PETER M. SENGE
LAWRENCE TAPP	DAVE ULRICH

CONTENTS

ACKNOWLEDGMENTS

I gratefully acknowledge a large debt to 26 distinguished thinkers and authors who have contributed to this book. *Management 21C* would never have materialized without the generous support of Moreen Anderson, Christopher A. Bartlett, Hamid Bouchikhi, David Conklin, Paul Dainty, Paul A.L. Evans, Caela Farren, J. Wil Foppen, Robert M. Fulmer, Sumantra Ghoshal, Marshall Goldsmith, Linda A. Hill, Ingalill Holmberg, Rosabeth Moss Kanter, Katrin H. Käufer, John R. Kimberly, James M. Kouzes, Stuart R. Levine, Peter Lorange, Peter Moran, Barry Z. Posner, C.K. Prahalad, Jonas Ridderstråle, Peter M. Senge, Lawrence Tapp, and Dave Ulrich. I very much appreciate the time and effort each of them has put into this project. Their dedication and invaluable insights to their work have been a great inspiration to me.

Special thanks to Richard Beckhard for his support from day one, and to Marshall Goldsmith, a great colleague and a true friend who has inspired me from the infant stage of the project.

I owe a great deal to Peter F. Drucker, a pioneer and the greatest management thinker of our time. His writings inspire me every day.

A great friend of mine and a constant supporter of my work who daily puts aside his own requirements in order to help me is Robert MacLeod. Harriet Levine is a true friend whose enthusiasm and support on this project has been so valuable to me. And another very special friend in the publishing business, Cynthia Zigmund, is always beside me on any of my writing ventures.

I am also grateful to all the personal assistants and research associates who have been the links to *Management 21C* contributors. They include Ginger Bitter, Lisa Cohen, Nathalie D'Aboville, Barbara Devine, Kristin C. Doughty, Judy Ellis, Catherine Fitzsimons, Annette Forbes, Amy Hungerford, Barbera Kooijman, Jean Macdonald, Claire Manefield, Cappy Reed, Willa Reiser, Rita Kaulesar Sukul, Amélie Theorell, Andrea Truax, Sharon Wilson and Meg Wozny.

I am very lucky to have had the chance to work with an energetic editor at Financial Times Prentice Hall, Pradeep Jethi. His encouragement is valuable to any author. I would also like to thank Amelia Lakin, Martin Drewe, Angela

Lewis, Kate Jenkins and Claudia Orrell of FT Prentice Hall for their constant assistance.

Most of all, my heartfelt thanks go to my wonderful wife, Malini, who supports me totally in every venture I undertake.

SUBIR CHOWDHURY
Novi, Michigan

PREFACE

While the revolution in information technology is bringing us all closer together, globalization is challenging our language skills, and a new generation is reshaping our business strategy. Is business changing or is managing changing? Will the success of manufacturing industry depend upon their embracing IT? Will individuals target employers or will organizations target employees? These were some of the questions which inspired me to create *Management 21C*.

The book you are reading reveals the collective thoughts and visions of some of the world's great minds. It is a truly global pioneering venture. From Australia to America, from France to the Netherlands, Britain to Canada, Sweden to Switzerland, the very best contemporary management thinkers are here at your fingertips. *Management 21C* brings together visions for the new millennium in one concise book, allowing you to understand the changes happening now and what changes you can expect. The future of business *will* be different: whose versions are you reading?

With a detailed description of the global emergence and rise of new businesses and cultures, *Management 21C* will intrigue, provoke, encourage, and, above all, change the attitudes of everyone who reads it. Each chapter is unique and valuable. In chapter 1 I introduce new concepts including Return on Talent (ROT), Fire Prevention, and the Talent Mangement System.

In the first part, discover the Janusian leader, the dualistic leader, the value-based Edu-leader, sensational leadership, the power of collective genius, mastery, and mindset. Part two, "21C processes," describes the actions, skills, and strategies that leaders and managers will need to be able to compete in the future. In the final part, the customized workplace, the creative web, and kaleidoscope thinking inspire you to reconsider the 21C organization and help you prepare for it.

Management 21C is for those who believe in creative war, for those who inspire other people, for those who believe in others and not just themselves, for those who celebrate diversity, for those who constantly search for a dream, for those who want to reshape the world of tomorrow. Someday we'll all manage this way.

Management 21C was created by inspiration. Its aim is to inspire others. *Management 21C* is the ultimate inspiration.

SUBIR CHOWDHURY
Novi, Michigan
Easter 1999

1

TOWARDS THE FUTURE OF MANAGEMENT

SUBIR CHOWDHURY

The art of managing is changing, and at a rapid pace. In the corporate world, managers are continually discussing the evolving nature of business and its effects on them. But very few properly focus on managing itself. Ford is an example of how the style of managing is changing, against a background of a US auto industry generally known for its resistance to change and for its bureaucratic leadership. Each Friday, via email, Ford chief executive officer Jacques Nasser reaches the group's 100 000 plus employees and updates them on its successes and failures.

When I first read Alfred P. Sloan's book, *My Years with General Motors*, I discovered that his extraordinary success was due mainly to his information-focussed leadership. Sloan, a visionary, effectively gathered information from GM's dealers and used it to his advantage. Half a century later, managing information is still instrumental in business success. It was as necessary in Sloan's time as it is in ours. But the fundamental difference between his day and Nasser's is the method of managing information. This makes us think about managing and about the future of managing too.

Management in the 21st century will depend on its fundamentals. These rely on leadership, processes, and organizations. In this chapter I discuss all three vital parts of 21st century management.

THE 21ST CENTURY LEADER

Search the dream, act the dream, and make the dream real. That's what we must do. In the summer of 1998, while I was roaming Silicon Valley in the company of twenty something CEOs, an idea struck me – "Dream-Searching Leadership". Twentieth century leaders have been evolving into 21st century leaders by adopting this way of thinking. The 21st century leader's most valuable asset will be the ability to dream, just as it is for entrepreneurs. These leaders will seek the dream, nurture it, and strive to make it real. But dream is just another word unless the idea is implemented effectively. Successful leaders act on their dreams using good communication, inspiring everyone in the organization to believe in their dream too. As soon as one dream becomes real, these leaders go for the next one. The constant search for new dreams and taking effective action to make them real is at the heart of dream-searching leadership.

> *The 21st century leader's most valuable asset will be the ability to dream, just as it is for entrepreneurs.*

Peoplistic communication

Rather than becoming individualistic, become peoplistic. You can have the best communication systems, but if you are individualistic as a leader the organization suffers. Peoplistic communication is the key. Internet and Intranet are effective communication systems, and management spends large amounts of money to make such communication systems better. This is fine, but most of the time managers make the mistake of not identifying the difference between the art of communication and its medium. I have seen CEOs of several large and mid-sized US companies introduce the Internet to make sure there is effective communication from the top to the bottom. The Internet does not communicate with people; people communicate with people. The Internet is only a medium, and even a wonderful Internet system does not by itself guarantee effective communication. Everyone knows the Internet makes communication faster, yet 70 percent of e-mail receivers do not respond immediately. How many of them are using the Internet as a fully effective communication tool?

A peoplistic communicator provides a friendly atmosphere in which everyone communicates quickly. In large organizations, communication can fail due to layers of bureaucracy and people might receive only 10 percent of the information intended for them. Effective communication helps to break down traditional organizational hierarchy. It also encourages communication of both good and bad news, so that any type of news can travel from one end of the company to the other, and through all levels. The 21st century leader will be a firm believer in such peoplistic communication, which is fast and all-enveloping.

Emotion and belief – inseparable twins

You should touch the heart, touch the mind, touch the emotion. While I was working at a General Motors' plant as a consultant, my first assignment was to solve a complex paint problem. From the start, I realized the root cause of any such problem would lie beneath the surface, and the solution would be known to the workers who have daily involvement in that area. Generally, management ignores such workers' recommendations, does not value their judgement, and does not even try to understand them. Management questions their capability, and believes in outsiders rather than insiders. Furthermore, it does not consider how detrimental an outsider's presence may be to an insider. I was one of those outsiders, and, alas, I solved the problem. The only thing I did was, rather than focussing on the problem, I focussed on the workers who had been involved with it. I touched their hearts, I touched their minds, and I created an emotional bond with them. I assured them they would not be penalized for giving me information. Whatever they told me, I told the management. Based on my recommendation, immediate action was taken to solve the problem.

Management must understand that employees' emotional commitment is extremely valuable to an organization. To get them committed to a new strategy, the challenge that management typically faces is to reduce the time between the conception of an idea and its implementation. One way of increasing that commitment is to get people throughout the organization fully involved in creating the strategy. This can be a great challenge, but a visionary CEO will succeed if people are emotionally committed to achieving a common goal.

Believe. That should be the 21st century leader's watchword. There is a big difference between accepting and believing. Most of the time, management creates the sort of culture that workers accept rather than believe in. Imposing something on employees is a sign of management arrogance; people may accept it through fear but won't believe in it. This is relevant to change. Any attempt to change may fail; but if people believe in change it will succeed. In the 21st century, leaders must create an atmosphere in which people believe in strategy, believe in management decisions, and believe in their work. Once people believe in management decisions, there is excitement within an organization. Such an atmosphere makes an organization prosper. Successful leaders always create this sort of environment both inside and outside the organization.

Creating a fearful atmosphere is another major management blunder. Most of the time management fails to recognize the fact that it creates such an atmosphere within an organization. I have seen this almost everywhere, from Delhi to Detroit, Stockholm to Seoul. Fear badly affects an organization's strength and success. When I was in Seoul, a city trying to recapture a successful economy, I found in one major conglomerate or chaebol fear in everyone. Workers, engineers, junior managers – all were reporting positive information and data to senior management because of fear. I found that practically every chart reporting healthy progress was a lie. I asked them why they did this and the typical answer was: "My job will be eliminated if I report the truth." These workers do not trust the management, and they do not believe in the management's method of managing. Management can create a better working environment within an organization by eliminating fear and creating an emotional bond with the workforce.

Multi-skilled

Twenty-first century leaders will become more multi-skilled than their 20th century predecessors. Knowledge of languages, cultures, and a wide range of subjects will be vital to achieve success. Unless they are subject matter experts, they cannot effectively use their potential. Tomorrow's leaders will be experts in several fields because if they have the desire for knowledge, they can obtain it. Any skills can be learned. Ignorance will be no excuse.

One of the important characteristics of a multi-skilled leader is the ability to encourage diversity. A true commitment to this begins with a clear vision and strategy. Valuing diversity creates an environment that thrives on excitement, and it encourages everyone to reach their full potential. As Hewlett-Packard chairman, Lewis Platt points out:

> "We believe our diversity represents a tremendous strength for Hewlett-Packard. It allows us to tap a broad range of human potential. HP's diversity is a competitive advantage for our customers, our employees, and our company."

The true challenge facing the organizational world is not geographic distance but cultural distance. Diversity has always been the USA's greatest challenge, but it is also its greatest strength. If organizations can embrace and manage diversity as a business strategy, they will be successful. Many organizations make fashionable statements about diversity, but how many actually do something about it? Diversity is a business imperative. Consolidation and the Internet have been challenging companies to become more diverse every day, and in today's knowledge-rich world of competition, you never know where the best idea will come from.

> *The true challenge facing the organizational world is not geographic distance but cultural distance. Diversity has always been the USA's greatest challenge, but it is also its greatest strength.*

Next mentality

Twenty-first century leaders will hunger for the next goal. They will strive for almost anything that increases their organization's success. Traditionally, management often rests on its laurels when it has achieved something, instead of looking for the next achievement. This attitude damages their organization. Good leaders celebrate a success but immediately set about achieving the next one. "What's next?" will be the widespread attitude of tomorrow's leaders. I call them the "next mentality breed." They will be:

- hard working
- never satisfied
- idea-centric
- curious
- persistent.

In every business sector there is a constant race going on, whether it is in innovation, competition, or other fields. The winner gains most competitive advantage. But to come first you must act fast, and to react quickly you must have next mentality attitude.

A friend in Silicon Valley started an Internet company and two years later sold it for an amazing $80 million. Still living in an apartment, he is working on his next goal rather than spending his time celebrating his success.

General Electric CEO Jack Welch always demonstrates next mentality leadership, and creates the next mentality attitude in those around him. In a nationwide satellite broadcast, he said: "We want people who get up every morning with a passion about finding a better way: finding from their associate in the office, finding from another company. We're constantly on the search."[1]

21ST CENTURY PROCESSES

Management must realize the importance of lessons learned. Failures teach how to be successful in future. When a desired goal fails to materialize, many leaders look for a magic formula rather than accepting the reality. Twenty-first century leaders and managers must rethink 20th century processes.

These processes must focus on core practices, and in this chapter I have concentrated on four critical areas which I believe will have significant impact on a 21st century organization. These are:

- grass-root education
- fire prevention
- direct interaction
- effective globalization.

Grass-root education

Grass-root education, not merely education, is management's killer strategy. Grass-root education involves the training of the entire staff, without discrimination, from the chairman to the worker on the factory floor. Often, management neglects to provide any kind of training at the lower levels. At one US manufacturing facility, managers were changing the spreadsheet analysis software from Lotus to Excel. I noticed that while they were trained in using Excel, none of the lower level employees was, despite the fact they would be the main users. Six months later, the trained managers were no longer using the new program, and passed it down the line to those employees who had never been trained in the first place. This type of management practice is worrying.

Grass-root education helps to bring about proper implementation, whether it is of a new computer system or company strategy. Training without implementation means an organization is throwing away money. I have seen organizations spend millions of dollars training employees in the use of specific tools, yet in many cases these employees will not be using these tools in their normal jobs. Managers then wonder why no benefit comes from the money spent on training.

Every training program must have a strategic implementation plan and managers must always monitor these plans to make sure the training has not been a waste of time. Every year hundreds of multinational companies spend billions of dollars on leadership training. I know some middle managers of these corporations who have attended this training, and I have never seen any real change in their skills or way of working. Top management must monitor the results of such training at every level of their organization.

Bringing about change is far more difficult without grass-root education. Unless everyone really tries to make it happen, it will lose its momentum. So many initiatives fail because management forces change on employees rather than educating them about what the organization plans to do. Change takes time but many of us don't realize it.

Before introducing change it is important to find colleagues to embark on the journey of change with you. Find those individuals who support you over change, and this will help persuade others, who at first may not be convinced by your plans, that the change will benefit them. And remember, to achieve this goal you should be flexible and creative. Management talks about change in regular meetings, but most of the time it cannot convince its people how that change will benefit them.

Ford has taken a major initiative to change the company's traditional mindset through teaching. In a *Harvard Business Review* interview, CEO Jacques Nasser said: "You can't reinvent a company like Ford overnight; we have too much tradition. But there is no question that we have to change our fundamental approach to work – we have to change our DNA. And teaching does that better than any other way I know." Thanks to the teaching programs Ford has used, its people have added some $2 billion to the bottom line. Rather than pushing its people to accept change, Ford has created a culture that helps implement it.[2]

Fire prevention

Fire prevention, not fire fighting, must be practiced. Most corporations still reward highly those managers who act as fire fighters. In a survey, 75 percent of US managers said good fire fighters get fast promotion. But there is no reward for fire preventers. Two years ago I was having a discussion with a General Motors executive who was extremely proud of his fire-fighting teams, and he was telling me how one team had solved a difficult problem. "What my team did was disassemble the complex product completely and put those pieces back together again. Problem solved, and money saved for the organization." I asked him what the root cause of the problem had been, but he could not reply. I then asked how his team could guarantee that the problem would not come back. Again, there was no answer. This way of operating, curing rather than preventing, is common in many organizations, from North America to Asia, and from Europe to Australia.

Prevention does not bring immediate glory. Very few leaders reward their managers for the ability to prevent problems. Yet defect-prevention keeps customers satisfied and loyal. That is why the US consumer's love affair with Japanese products continues. In 1996, for example, the Honda Accord outsold all other automobiles in the US, setting an all-time sales record. And for the past 18 years, Honda has ranked number one in owner loyalty, according to a survey by R.L. Polk & Co. Furthermore, Honda announced in May 1999 a third successive year of record profits, helped in no small part by its sales in the USA. Toyota, too, earned customer loyalty around the world by focussing on prevention.

In the 21st century customers will demand perfection and uniqueness in products, and superior service in connection with these products. To bring out better products faster, successful 21st century organizations will focus on upstream engineering, with a lot of attention paid to "fire prevention." In November 1998, *Fortune*'s Gene Bylinsky reported that a remarkable machine, DC265, produced by the Xerox Corporation, had captured 70 percent of the market for high-priced, digitally controlled copiers by employing fire-prevention tools like Robust Engineering. The machine's touch screen – an improvement over the buttons on rival Japanese copiers – illustrates how some areas of American industry have begun to deliver superior products after years of trailing Japan.[3] It will not be new technology alone that

> *In the 21st century customers will demand perfection and uniqueness in products, and superior service in connection with these products.*

will determine marketplace success; how managers effectively harness this technology will be crucial in the 21st century.

Direct interaction

Interact with your customer – that will be the slogan of the year 2000 and beyond. Twenty-first century organizations will strive for customer enthusiasm instead of customer satisfaction. Customer enthusiasm means excitement and loyalty on the part of the customer, fuelled by the service and products available to them exceeding their expectations. The way to make an organization profitable is not just to find customers but to keep them. Surprisingly, the means of creating and keeping customers is changing every day. Twenty-first century organizations will create new and loyal customers through direct interaction with them. Customers need attention at all times. IBM's CEO, Lou Gerstner, spends more than a third of his time visiting and interacting with the group's customers.

Customers are smarter than they used to be, partly thanks to the revolution in information technology. They do not care about management structures, strategic planning, the financial perspectives, or the leader of the organization. What they do care about are products and services available to them. Customers value quick and easy access to products, and they demand a lot of information before making a decision on whether to buy. The Internet is fulfilling many customers' information needs, and a company might find it useful to gather feedback from present and future customers by setting up an Internet "forum." If introduced effectively, it could greatly enhance customer monitoring, and customer input would influence product-related decisions.[4] I believe 21st century organizations will introduce virtual customer interaction centers. Due to increasing competition, managers have to react quickly to improve products and services. Centers like these would provide the necessary data to allow quick reaction to customers' needs.

Effective globalization

Countless organizations are expanding internationally, and this is the biggest business trend in the USA, Asia, and Europe. Yet many CEOs do not properly understand how to globalize effectively or how it helps them compete with others. Just because a company is globally present does not guarantee global success, and neither does having lots of national flags flying in the entrance hall of a corporate headquarters.

Five years ago, American and European companies became fanatical about China and India, and invested heavily to become leaders in those countries. Without any prior cultural, social or political research, they introduced their high-priced products to Indian and Chinese consumers. The automobile in

India is a prime example. Gradually every large automobile manufacturer in the USA and Europe was beaten off by the locally produced model, the Maruti, not because of quality but because of the price consciousness of Indian consumers. Managers have to understand the market and its customers before introducing a product. Nicholas Trivisonno, the chairman and chief executive of A.C. Nielsen, the US-based international market research company, says: "There is no global customer. Each country and the consumer in each country has different attitudes and different behaviors, tastes, and spending patterns." The company has a presence in more than 90 countries across three continents, and works for more than 9000 clients.[5]

Organizations must respond to different markets by adapting products, services, and processes to local requirements. McDonald's offers burgers made from lamb rather than beef in India because of religious considerations, and Baskin-Robbins offers green-tea flavored ice cream in Japan. But they must also realize when local adaptation can hamper customer acceptance of a product. For example, US restaurant chain TGI Friday incorporated many local dishes into its menu when it opened in South Korea. Analysis of the reasons behind poor market performance revealed that customers anticipated a visit to America and were disappointed at finding the same old local dishes.[6]

Globalization may be a benefit or a drawback to an organization, depending on a country's political and economic situation. Three years ago companies did well by investing in Asia, but recently these investments have been suffering badly. On the other hand, Asian companies that invested in the west have benefited. Globalization will always entail risk, which will vary from country to country. The key is how quickly a company can react to this dramatic change. To create consistent growth and wealth in this volatile atmosphere, management must:

- study local culture, local market, and local competition;
- prepare a business model that effectively serves the market needs;
- select the right strategic local partner or group with the best local market knowledge;
- encourage employees by maintaining the local values;
- introduce new and innovative product, with local flavour.

THE 21ST CENTURY ORGANIZATION

Over the winter of 1999, as I was writing about 21st century management, several mega mergers were shaking up corporate America, Europe was anticipating the introduction of a common currency, and the economic breakdown in Asia was continuing. My scattered thoughts merged into a new idea: the talent-centered organization. A 21st century organization's success will depend on the effective use of talented people. Talent-centered organizations will constantly search for new talent, keep them by satisfying their needs, use them effectively, and create a challenging environment for them to work in.

People create organizations, and people can destroy them. The most valuable commodity in business is not technology or capital but people. The driving force behind a 21st century organization will be its people. While the virtual organizations are celebrating their success in financial markets and breaking the ground rules of the stock exchange, it should be remembered that they owe their success not to the technology they embrace, but to what lies behind it: people – old, young, women, men, black, white. In his 1998 book *The Human Equation*, Stanford Business School professor Jeffrey Pfeffer predicted that: "Companies that manage people right will outperform companies that don't by 30 percent to 40 percent."[7] People manage people, inside and outside an organization. Effective management of people is a challenge managers will increasingly face in the 21st century.

> *People create organizations, and people can destroy them. The most valuable commodity in business is not technology or capital but people.*

Return on talent

For decades, organizations have utilized key metrics like ROI (Return on Investments) and ROA (Return on Assets). Twenty-first century organizations will utilize a measurement called ROT (Return on Talent). Current business measurement equations merely measure the use of capital, but ROT is expressed as follows:

$$\text{ROT} = \frac{\text{knowledge generated}}{\text{investment in talents}}$$

ROT measures the payback from investment in people. It shows if managers are hiring the right people, and how effectively they use them to achieve business success. ROT can be a quantitative or qualitative measurement based on management's viewpoint. Are managers getting the maximum payback every minute of the day on their investment? If management wants to see quantitative results, it must put a price tag on knowledge generated, based on results.

Effective managers put ROT measurement metrics in place to monitor performance and forecast opportunities. This determines whether the investment is profitable or not. To make the investment profitable, management must:

- constantly measure ROT
- continuously improve ROT
- re-shuffle talents.

Knowledge generated

The value of knowledge generated increases with its effective deployment. Effective knowledge generated means high ROT. It leads to creative work-forces, innovations, smooth processes, continuous product improvements, and proper communications. It helps management to be flexible, to capitalize on opportunities, and keep pace with the rapidly changing business environments.

Talented people influence those around them, and their knowledge will be shared over time. Good knowledge generators at all levels of the organization should be rewarded. If 21st century managers expect them to achieve their potential maximum performance, and potential maximum return, they must not place them in routine jobs.

Investment in talents

Without investment in talents, an organization becomes stagnant. I have seen organizations invest in technology, machines and people. But in the 21st century, the most valuable out of the three will be the investment in people. However, management must also be careful to invest in the right people, whose capability must match the organization's needs.

Knowledge generated and investment in talents lie at the heart of ROT, which I believe will be the key to 21st century organizational success. High ROT depends on an effective talent-management system.

Talent-management system

A talent-management system (TMS) is an effective tool in an organization. By using it, managers can properly deploy the skills of talented employees. You may come across plenty of talented people working for an organization that cannot produce significant results. This is due to the lack of proper TMS. The same people working in an organization which uses a TMS will produce good results. The TMS has four elements:

- attracting talents
- keeping talents
- managing talents
- identifying talents.

Attracting talents

The relentless pursuit of talent should be a main management strategy. More and more companies simply cannot recruit talented people fast enough. This talent shortage is the biggest obstacle to a company's growth, and overcoming it can be a huge strategic advantage. But money alone won't do it. Talented people want to be part of an organization they can believe in, one that excites them at all times. All organizations should create a flexible working environment that attracts the most talented people to create the knowledge an organization needs.

Keeping talents

The successful 21st century organization will not take the loyalty of talented people for granted. It will constantly try to recruit and keep them, and will have think-tanks at every level. The mutual commitment of an employer and an employee will be one of the most important factors for a 21st century organization. Joe Liemandt, CEO of Trilogy Software, a rapidly growing software firm based in Austin, Texas, says Trilogy treats its employees like "they're all managers, they're all partners, they're all shareholders." And he firmly believes that is why Trilogy is so successful. But his biggest worry is holding on to his talented people. He knows they can go anywhere. "There's nothing more important than recruiting and growing people. That's my number one job."[8]

Barb Karlin, director of great people at Intuit, boldly says: "If you lose great people, you lose success. It's that simple." The organization must foster an atmosphere which makes its talents want to stay.

Managing talents

Managing talents is a different skill, one that has to be learned. Managers must know how to get the best out of people, and how to strategically place them in the right position where they are not dragged down by routine work. Managers must provide the setting in which they can produce maximum knowledge, maximum innovation, and have maximum impact. In fact, talent strategically managed will generate maximum return. I strongly believe that 21st century organizations will have chief talent officers (CTOs), who manage talent effectively inside and outside the organization. The CTO must hire the best, use the best, and keep the best.

> *Managers must provide the setting in which they can produce maximum knowledge, maximum innovation, and have maximum impact. In fact, talent strategically managed will generate maximum return.*

Identifying talents

Talents are a scarce resource, and also frequently an untapped one. Year after year I have come across management that does not know how to identify talented people. General Motors is a prime example. I have met so many bright men and women there but I believe the management fails to use them effectively. These people are untapped talents. They are frustrated talents, and are therefore unproductive talents. In the 21st century, if GM management does not use these talents properly, someone else will. Management must identify the hidden talents of current employees before hiring new talent.

Relentless search for innovation

The 21st century organization will reinvent its product daily. In the *Wall Street Journal*, soft drink manufacturer Snapple's CEO Michael Weinstein, who turned the company around, said: "We're not in the soft drink business; we are in the fashion business. It is a constant whirl of new products, flavors and packaging, pitched to consumers who want the latest thing."[9]

The creative process is always chaotic, but innovative organizations always have persistent people who make things happen. Twenty-first century organizations will support persistent people and encourage them to believe in their dream. For consecutive years, Enron has been named the most admired Fortune 500 company in the innovativeness category. On its web site, Enron chairman and CEO Kenneth L. Lay says: "We are a strong believer in competition. Virtually every industry opened up for competition sees tremendous innovation almost immediately. Enron is a laboratory for innovation."[10] This kind of top management commitment to innovation permeates to every level at Enron.

There may be failures, but that is all part of the game. You should accept failure and learn from it. Albert Yu, senior vice president of Intel's Microprocessor Products Group and the person responsible for stoking the innovative engines of the world's semiconductor superpower,[11] says:

> "There is a tremendous power in a glorious failure. The infamous Pentium flaw in 1994 was devastating and we went through all the stages of grief – denial, anger, and acceptance. It was incredibly painful to the company, and to me personally. But we managed to become better as a result. It marked a real transition. I'm a different person today. I've beefed up the way we validate our technology before it gets out the door. We went from having a product-engineered orientation to a consumer orientation . . . We all recognised that the problem threatened the image of Intel. We had real teamwork and came through the crisis together. Now we know that we can respond to any crisis ten times faster than before."

CONCLUSION

In this chapter I have introduced concepts that I believe will have a profound impact in the 21st century and they could apply as easily to the non-profit making company as to the profit maker, and to a government-backed organization as to a multinational.

What would happen if a country wanted to operate under "talent management system" or "dream-searching leadership?" Interestingly, these concepts do not have any boundaries. For example, India has a tremendously talented workforce and plenty of leaders. But what the country lacks is a talent-management system.

Cyberspace has been breaking down geographic walls since its inception, but still most cyberspace ventures originate in the United States. It is not due to lack of wealth elsewhere, or a talent shortage. It is due to the lack of dream. Young men and women from all over the world want to come to the USA because it is the nation which shows them how to dream, which encourages ideas, and which creates success. The USA has always been a global leader practicing dream-searching leadership.

I

21C

LEADER

So what exactly are the implications for the 21st century leader? What does it take to inspire others to achieve success? Leadership experts and teachers James M. Kouzes and Barry Z. Posner open the first part of the book and introduce *The Janusian leader* – the leader with the capacity to look forward and back, to preside over endings and beginnings, sunsets and daybreaks – who asks: "What have I learned about leadership throughout my career that will serve me well into the future? What have we collectively learned about leadership that we can teach others so they can benefit from our experience?" Kouzes and Posner present seven key lessons that stand the test of time. They confidently declare that when the 22nd century arrives, these lessons will still be as valid as they are today.

Preparing for a digitized, globalized future has shown the need for a new and different leadership – innovative, passionate, sensational. These are leaders who have a dream and unique ideas that constitute true competitive advantage. Average traditional leadership will not survive in the next millennium. To be competitive we must embrace the last taboo – building on emotion and imagination. Sensational leadership thrives on unleashing this imagination and emotion. Stockholm School of Economics Professors Ingalill Holmberg and Jonas Ridderstråle predict that future leaders and organizations will be forced to come up with innovative ways to increase the pace of *creative destruction*.

Twenty-first century world-class corporations will make use of ever-evolving *collectives* of talented, passionate and diverse individuals. The leaders of these will shape what is, in essence, *collective genius*, defined by Harvard Business School Professor Linda A. Hill. Since the competitive environment has fundamentally changed, strategic management of talent is the key to competitive advantage. Managing how people fit and operate within the organization is fast becoming the fundamental leadership dilemma. In this chapter the author has also profiled a selection of new CEOs of young ventures. Hill helps us to understand the process necessary to develop and unleash the power of highly interactive talents and teams.

Leadership has become the task of creatively harnessing the tension between opposite forces. This is already apparent, and as we move into the new millennium the implications of leading and living in a world of duality, dilemma and paradox will become more obvious. That is the underlying prediction in renowned thinker Paul A.L. Evans' chapter. In a very powerful way, INSEAD Professor Evans helps the reader to recognize the dualities in life today and provides the example of L'Oréal, the world's leading cosmetics firm and the most consistently profitable firm in France. Evans also provides lessons and insights on how to survive in a world of paradox and dualities.

Stuart R. Levine believes that value-based leadership skills will help leaders to learn, adapt, and respond positively in the new millennium. He also points out the most admired individual will be defined as an *Edu-leader* – a person driven by core values who builds trusting relationships through effective communication. By nature of these skills, the Edu-leader focusses on moving people and organizations forward by teaching and increasing the competency of their employees. In his chapter, Levine introduces seven principles which define the elements of successful transition from the 20th to the 21st century.

Caela Farren believes that mastery of a profession or trade will be the critical advantage or even a necessity for 21C leaders and managers. Farren takes us through the six critical areas affecting an organization and invites you, the management of today, to become the masters of tomorrow.

In future, managers who are able to learn and adapt will continue to command a premium. Paul Dainty and Moreen Anderson predict that central to the success of these managers will be the capacity to understand and manage one's mental approach or "mindset." They have argued that complexity and constant change will characterize people's work environments and that to succeed, individuals need to think more broadly about the capabilities and mindsets they bring to their jobs. Melbourne Business School Professors Dainty and Anderson also predict that for many companies the corporate battles of the millennium will be more about changing mindsets than about changing technology.

2

THE JANUSIAN LEADER

JAMES M. KOUZES AND BARRY Z. POSNER

As we pass through the portal that opens on to the 21st century, the ancient Roman deity Janus presides. Ever since 153 B.C., January has been Janus' month, and on 01/01/00 Janus welcomes not only the beginning of a new year but the dawn of a new millennium. Janus, most often depicted with two faces – one to see into the past and one to see into the future – best represents the spirit of this moment.

The capacity to look ahead and to look back is critical to learning and to leadership. In fact, research strongly suggests that the ability to look first to our past before we march blindly forward actually strengthens our capacity to see the future more clearly.[1] Yet today's global leaders have to operate at Internet speed, and even a nanosecond's pause to reflect on past lessons seems to many like a waste of time, today's scarcest resource. Remembering Janus, however, we must resist that temptation, especially at this moment of great symbolic significance.

The Janusian leader – the leader with the capacity to look forward and back, to preside over endings and beginnings, sunsets and daybreaks – pauses and asks: "What have I learned about leadership throughout my career that will serve me well into the future? What have we collectively learned about leadership that we can teach others so they can benefit from our experience?"

For more than two decades we have been on a continuing quest to discover what it takes to become and serve as a credible leader. We have been driven by a desire to uncover the common practices of ordinary men and women when they are carrying out their leadership. And knowing that the portrait of leadership drawn from personal-best cases is only a partial picture, we have also explored the expectations that constituents have of leaders. Strategies, tactics, skills, and practices come to life only when we more fully understand the fundamental human aspirations that connect leaders and their constituents.

Our analysis of thousands of cases, surveys and empirical studies reveals a consistent pattern of exemplary leadership practices and fundamental constituent expectations. While there is still much to be learned, in this chapter we present seven key lessons that stand the test of time and are worthy of being carried with us from one millennium to another. When the 22nd century arrives, we assert, these lessons will still be as valid as they are today. So, what does it take to lead others to get extraordinary things done in organizations, and what are the implications for the 21st century leader?

LESSON 1

CREDIBILITY IS THE FOUNDATION OF LEADERSHIP

Many people around the globe are fed-up, angry, disgusted, and pessimistic about their future. In many places alienation is higher than it has ever been. Loyalty to institutions – and institutions' loyalty to people – is sinking like a stone. No longer would we rather fight than switch; we just switch. Free-agentry has migrated from the world of sports to the world of work. In such a climate, how can a leader possibly mobilize a seemingly unwilling constituency toward some unknown and even more uncertain future?

For the answer to this question, we turned to the constituents, the followers. We asked people from over 30 countries representing every conceivable sector and function what they "look for and admire in a leader, in a person whose direction they would willingly follow." Consistently people have told us since 1980 (and still tell us today) that they want leaders who exemplify four qualities: they want them to be honest, forward-looking, inspiring, and competent.[2] In our research our respondents strongly agree that they want leaders with integrity and trustworthiness, with vision and a sense of direction, with enthusiasm and passion, and with expertise and a track record for getting things done.

What makes these findings compelling is that the characteristics are essentially the same ones that form the basis of what communication experts refer to as "source credibility." In assessing sources of information – whether the sources are newscasters, salespeople, managers, physicians, politicians, or priests – audiences are more likely to believe individuals whom they rate high on being trustworthy and honest, having expertise and competence, and being dynamic and inspiring. In our research we discovered that constituents expect the very same thing from their leaders as they do from any other believable source of information. They want a leader who is credible. Credibility is the foundation of leadership.

We want to believe in our leaders. We want to have faith and confidence in them as people. We want to believe that their word can be trusted, that they are personally excited and enthusiastic about the direction in which we are headed, and that they have the knowledge and skill to lead. Credibility is the foundation on which leaders and constituents build the grand dreams of the future. Without credi-bility, visions will fade and relationships will

> *If people don't believe in the messenger, they won't believe the message.*

wither. If people don't believe in the messenger, they won't believe the mes-sage. Our findings have been so consistent for so long that we have come to call this the First Law of Leadership.

So how do leaders overcome cynicism and restore the faith and confidence necessary to attract and retain the best people? The first action leaders must take is to establish and sustain personal credibility. Leadership is, after all, a relationship between those who aspire to lead and those who choose to follow. The quality of this relationship strongly influences members' commitment to the organization, its people, its products, and its customers.

Values and beliefs are at the core of personal credibility. In fact, credibility derives from the Latin word credo, meaning "I believe." People expect their leaders to stand for something and to have the courage of their convictions. If leaders are not clear about what they believe in, they are much more likely to change their position with every fad or opinion poll. The first milestone on the journey to leadership credibility, therefore, is clarity of personal values. And it is essential to note that those leaders who are clearest about their personal values are the most committed to the organization's goals and objectives.

Implications for the 21st century leader

To be a leader, no matter the year, one must first engage in a process of self-discovery. The capacity to win the personal credibility jackpot depends on how well we know ourselves. To be credible, leaders must know who they are and what they stand for. They must develop and articulate a clear set of guiding principles, a leadership philosophy. The better they know themselves the better they can align words and deeds.

We can all expect much more massive and wrenching changes in the 21st century. The efficacy of any change initiative is inextricably linked to the cred-ibility of the person(s) leading the efforts. Constituents will become willingly involved to the extent that they believe in those sponsoring the change. It is wise, therefore, for leaders to begin every significant change with a "credit check." It is not just "Do they believe that the new SAP system will improve our performance?," it is also "Do they believe in me and my ability to lead this change effort?"

_____ LESSON 2 _____

LEADERSHIP IS EVERYONE'S BUSINESS

Myth associates leadership with superior position. It assumes that leadership starts with a capital "L," and that when you're on top you are automatically a leader. But leadership isn't a place, it's a process. It involves skills and abilities that are useful whether one is in the executive suite or on the front line, on Wall Street or Main Street. And the most pernicious myth of all is that leadership is reserved for only a very few of us. The myth is perpetuated daily whenever anyone asks, "Are leaders born or made?" Leadership is certainly not a gene, and it is most definitely not something mystical and ethereal that cannot be understood by ordinary people. It's a myth that only a lucky few can ever decipher the leadership code. Of all the leadership myths, this one has done more harm to the development of people and more to slow the growth of countries and companies than any other.

Our research has shown us that leadership is an observable, learnable set of practices. In nearly two decades of research we have been fortunate to hear or read the stories of over 7,500 ordinary people who have led others to get extraordinary things done. There are millions more. If there is one singular lesson about leadership from all of the cases we have gathered, it is this: leadership is everyone's business.

_____

Just ask Melissa Poe of St. Henry's School in Nashville, Tennessee.[3] As a fourth-grade student fearful of the continued destruction of the earth's resources, Poe wrote a letter to the then-U.S. president, George Bush, asking for his assistance in her campaign to save the environment for the enjoyment of future generations. After sending the letter, Poe worried that it would never be brought to the president's attention. After all, she was only a child. So, with the urgency of the issue pressing on her mind, she decided to get the president's attention by having her letter placed on a billboard. Through sheer diligence and hard work, the nine-year-old got her letter placed on one billboard free of charge and founded Kids for a Clean Environment (Kids F.A.C.E.), an organization whose goal is to develop programs to clean up the environment.

Almost immediately, Poe began receiving letters from youngsters who were as concerned as she was about the environment. They wanted to help. When Poe finally received the disappointing form letter from the president, it didn't crush her dream. She no longer needed the help of someone famous to get her message across. Poe had found in herself the person she needed – that powerful someone who could inspire others to get involved and make her dream a reality.

Within nine months more than 250 billboards across the country were displaying her letter free of charge, and Kids F.A.C.E. membership had swelled. As the organization grew, Poe's first Kids F.A.C.E. project, a recycling program at her school, led to a manual full of ideas on how to clean up the environment. Poe's impatience and zest motivated her to do something and her work has paid off. Today there are more than 300,000 members and 2,000 chapters of Kids F.A.C.E. (www.kidsface.org)

––––––––

Poe is proof that you don't have to wait for someone else to lead. You don't have to have a title, you don't have to have a position, and you don't have to have a budget. By viewing leadership as a fixed set of character traits or as linked to an exalted position, a self-fulfilling prophecy has been created that dooms societies to having only a few good leaders. It is far healthier and more productive for us to start with the assumption that it's possible for everyone to lead. If we assume that leadership is learnable, we can discover how many good leaders there really are; that leadership may be exhibited on behalf of the company, the government, the school, the religious organization, the community, the volunteer group, the union, or the family. Somewhere, sometime, the leader within each of us may get the call to step forward.

Of course, we should not mislead people into believing that they can attain unrealistic goals. Neither should we assume that only a few will ever attain excellence in leadership or any other human endeavor. Those who are most successful at bringing out the best in others are those who set achievable but stretching goals and believe that they have the ability to develop the talents of others.

From what we observed in our research, as more and more people answer the call, we will rejoice in the outcome. For what we discovered, and rediscovered, is that leadership is not the private reserve of a few charismatic men and women. It is a process ordinary people use when they are bringing forth the best from themselves and others. Whether you are in the private or public sector, whether you are an employee or a volunteer, whether you are front line or senior echelon, whether you are a student or a parent, we believe you are capable of developing yourself as a leader far more than tradition has ever assumed possible. Liberate the leader in everyone and extraordinary things happen.

Implications for the 21st century leader

When you think about it, isn't exemplary leadership really all about liberating the leader in everyone? Aren't leaders supposed to reach inside the organization and release the capacity of everyone to excel? Leadership development is not the same as executive development. If we want more leaders, we had better follow the lead of companies that involve leaders in teaching leaders throughout the organization. We must broaden our concept of leadership to include those on the front lines as well as those in the executive suites. When everyone in our organizations behaves as leaders – when everyone challenges, inspires, enables, models, and encourages – commitment is far greater and success is more likely. The secret of high-performing organizations is that everyone within them knows that leadership at all levels is expected and rewarded, and that individuals everywhere are responsible for making extraordinary things happen.

LESSON 3

CHALLENGE IS THE OPPORTUNITY FOR GREATNESS

When Dr Charlie Mae Knight was appointed the new superintendent for the Ravenswood School District in East Palo Alto, California, she was the 12th superintendent in ten years. She encountered a district in which 50 percent of the schools were closed and 98 percent of the children were performing in the lowest percentile for academic achievement in California. The district had the state's lowest revenue rate. There were buckets in classrooms to catch the rain leaking through decrepit roofs, the stench from the restrooms was overwhelming, homeless organizations were operating out of the school sites, and pilfering was rampant. Gophers and rats had begun to take over the facilities. As if this weren't challenging enough, Knight had to wrestle with a lawsuit that had gone on for ten years, whose intent was to dissolve the district for its poor educational quality and force the children to transfer to schools outside their community.

These challenges would discourage almost anyone. But not Knight. After assuming the post, she immediately enlisted support from Bay Area companies and community foundations to get the badly needed resources. The first project she undertook was refurbishing the Garden Oaks School. Volunteer engineers from nearby Raychem Corporation repaired the electrical wiring and phone systems. A volunteer rat patrol used pellet guns to eliminate the rodents. The community helped paint the building inside and out, and hardware stores donated supplies. Before long, local residents began calling to find out what color paint was used for the school so they could paint their houses in a matching shade. They went out and bought trees and sod and planted them in front of their homes. New leadership came forth from parents who began to demand more of a say. In response, an "Effort Hours" program for parents was set up so that they could volunteer time at the school. Teachers began to notice that something was happening, and they wanted to be part of it too. The district was on a roll.

Within two years of Knight's arrival, the children exceeded the goal of performing in the 51st percentile on academic achievement scores. (Today one of the district's schools has climbed to the 68th percentile, miles above the percentile where it had started.) The district had one of the first schools in the state to use technology in every discipline, outdistancing every school in California technologically, and it was the first elementary school to join the Internet. The lawsuit was dropped. Revenues rose from $1,900 per student to $3,500. And for the first time, East Palo Alto received the state's Distinguished School Award, based on its improved test scores and innovative programs.

If we are going to have a future, let alone thrive in one, we learn from Knight that leaders don't wait – in fact can't wait – for grand strategic plans to be completed, new legislation to be passed, or consensus to be built. Like other leaders who achieve extraordinary results, Knight knew she had to produce some early victories. "It's hard to get anybody excited just about a vision. You must show something happening," she told us. "Winning at the beginning was so important because winning provided some indication of movement. I had to show some visible signs that change was taking place in order to keep up the momentum, and in order to restore confidence in the people that we could provide quality education."

Leaders seize the initiative. Starting an organization, turning around a losing operation, greatly improving the social condition, enhancing the quality of people's lives demands a proactive spirit. Waiting for permission to begin is not characteristic of leaders. Acting with a sense of urgency is. If you're going to lead now or in the future, the first thing to do is launch a voyage of discovery.

> *Waiting for permission to begin is not characteristic of leaders. Acting with a sense of urgency is.*

Implications for the 21st century leader

Make something happen. In our well-intended efforts to thoroughly diagnose the situation, to craft artful change programs, and to build broad consensus, we stall progress. By all means be true to intervention theory and practice, but also get things moving. Focus on small wins – things like fresh paint and clean school yards. Set up little experiments instead of grand transformations. Transformation is a scary word. It may even discourage people. It may also fuel cynicism. Little successive victories earn leaders a lot of credit, and they inspire confidence.

——— LESSON 4 ———

LEADERS FOCUS ON THE FUTURE

At 3:29 pm on 15 October 1978, a team of ten women accomplished something that no other group had ever done. The American Women's Himalayan Expedition was the first American climbing team to reach the summit of Annapurna I, the tenth-highest mountain in the world. Arlene Blum was the leader of the expedition. Her stirring account of that adventure, *Annapurna: A Woman's Place* (reissued by Random House in October 1998) is a highly acclaimed adventure story.[4] But why should someone, whether man or woman, want to do something like that?

"For us, the answer was much more than 'because it is there,'" says Blum. "We all had experienced the exhilaration, the joy, and the warm camaraderie of the heights, and now we were on our way to an ultimate objective for a climber – the world's tenth-highest peak. But as women, we faced a challenge even greater than the mountain. We had to believe in ourselves enough to make the attempt in spite of social convention and 200 years of climbing history in which women were usually relegated to the sidelines."[5] Blum talks about how women had been told for years that they were not strong enough to carry heavy loads, that they didn't have the leadership experience and emotional stability necessary to climb the highest mountains. After a climb of Mount McKinley in 1970, her personal faith in the abilities of women climbers was confirmed. "Our expedition would give ten women the chance to attempt one of the world's highest and most challenging peaks, as well as the experience necessary to plan future Himalayan climbs. If we succeeded, we would be the first Americans to climb Annapurna and the first American women to reach 8,000 meters (26,400 ft)."[6]

Being forward-looking is what differentiates leaders from other credible people. While credibility is the foundation of leadership, the capacity to paint an uplifting and ennobling picture of the future is that special something that truly sets leaders apart.

Blum saw what others had not seen. She imagined something for her group that went far beyond the ordinary, far beyond what others thought possible. For Blum, it was proving that women are capable of doing things that others had thought impossible. She, and the other leaders in our study, shared the characteristic of "envisioning the future," of gazing across the horizon of time and imagining that greater things were ahead. They foresaw something out there, vague as it might appear from the distance, that others did not. They imagined that extraordinary feats were possible, or that the ordinary could be transformed into something noble. As Blum puts it, "To get anywhere – in climbing or in business – you have to know where you are headed. I'm not talking about 'corporate vision.' I'm talking about a clear picture that depicts where you, the individual, want to go."[7]

The overwhelming consensus is that without vision, little can happen. All enterprises or projects, big and small, begin in the mind's eye. They begin with imagination and with the belief that what is merely an image can one day be made real. Without a clear view of the future, constituents will be as nervous as tourists anywhere in the world driving along a mountainous route in the fog.

Implications for the 21st century leader

Climbing a mountain is a wonderful metaphor for organizational change leadership. The summit is the vision. You always keep that pinnacle in mind as you prepare for and make the ascent. Don Bennett, the first amputee to climb Mt Ranier, told us he imagined being on top of the mountain 1,000 times *a day*.

Leaders have to do the same thing – keep their eyes focussed on the summit and their minds concentrated on getting there.

Leaders must do at least two other fundamental things to increase their capacity to enlist others in an uplifting image of the future. First, they must spend more time thinking, reading, studying, and reflecting on the future. Whether it's visiting their own research labs or the labs of a nearby university, whether it's talking to colleagues in other parts of the world, or whether it's going on-line and surfing the web for the latest trends, leaders must devote themselves to being futurists.

They must also engage their constituents in a dialogue about the future. They must enthusiastically communicate exciting opportunities because when others can clearly see how they fit into an ideal and unique image of the future they are significantly more inclined to want to go there. It's like trying to put together a jigsaw puzzle. It's a lot easier when we can see the picture of the completed puzzle on the box top before we start trying to put the pieces in place. Leaders must be able to vividly paint that picture.

LESSON 5

LEADERS ARE TEAM PLAYERS

Early in our research, and very early in his career, we asked Bill Flanagan (now group president for Amdahl Corporation) to describe his personal best. After a few moments of reflection, Flanagan said he couldn't do it. Startled, we asked him why. Flanagan replied: "Because it wasn't my personal best. It was our personal best. It wasn't me. It was us."

Leadership is not a solo act. In the thousands of personal-best leadership cases we have studied we have yet to encounter a single example of extraordinary achievement that occurred without the active involvement and support of many people. We don't expect to find any in the 21st century either. Leadership is a dialog, not a monolog.

If the goal is superior performance, the winning bet will be on co-operation over competition and individualistic achievement every time. Competition almost never results in the best performance. Pursuing excellence is a collaborators' game. And this is even more true if conditions are extremely challenging and urgent, as they are likely to be throughout most of the early parts of the 21st century. Author and university lecturer Alfie Kohn explains it this way: "The simplest way to understand why competition generally does not promote excellence is to realize that trying to do well and trying to beat others are two different things."[8] One is about accomplishing the superior, the other about making another inferior. One is about achievement, the other about subordination. Rather than focussing on stomping the competition into the ground, true leaders focus on creating value for their customers, intelligence and skill in their students, health in their patients, and pride in their citizens. In a more complex, wired world, the winning strategies will always be based upon the "we" not the "I" philosophy.

> *In a more complex, wired world, the winning strategies will always be based upon the "we" not the "I" philosophy.*

At the heart of collaboration is trust. Without trust you cannot lead. Exemplary leaders are devoted to building relationships based on mutual respect and caring. In a recent PricewaterhouseCoopers study on corporate innovation in companies listed on the *Financial Times 1000*, the researchers report that trust was "the number one differentiator" between the top 20 per cent of companies surveyed and the bottom 20 per cent. "The top performers trust empowered individuals to communicate and implement change in order to turn strategic aims into reality," say the investigators.[9]

Long before "empowerment" was written into the popular vocabulary, credible leaders knew that only when their constituents felt strong, capable, and efficacious could they ever hope to get extraordinary things done. Constituents who feel weak, incompetent, and insignificant consistently underperform, want to flee the organization, and are ripe for disenchantment, even revolution.

If we examine the times when people feel powerless and the times when they feel powerful, we are struck by the clear and consistent message: feeling powerful – literally feeling "able" – comes from a deep sense of being in control of our lives. When we feel able to determine our destiny, when we believe we are able to mobilize the resources and support necessary to complete a task, then we will persist in our efforts to achieve. But when we feel we are controlled by others, when we believe that we lack the support or resources, we may comply but we show no commitment to excel. Credible leaders choose to give away their own power in service of increasing another's sense of self-confidence, self-determination, and personal effectiveness. Making others more powerful is truly what enhances the possibilities of success.

Implications for the 21st century leader

Bonds have to be strengthened between leaders and constituents. This may be a networked world, but virtual trust is an illusion. Trust develops when we get to know each other, and there is no substitute for spending time with people face to face. To build strong teams we must talk with each other about the things about which people care deeply. The leader's job, however paradoxical it may sound, is to turn constituents into leaders themselves. This requires a deep commitment to the personal and professional development of others. It means sharing, and even giving away, resources to others, and making certain that people always feel they have the power of choice in their hands. Serving and supporting, rather than commanding and controlling, are the watchwords for the 21st century's leaders.

LESSON 6

THE LEGACY YOU LEAVE IS THE LIFE YOU LEAD

Antonio Zárate knew that Metalsa, an automotive metal stamping company in Monterrey, Mexico, needed a major overhaul. The turnaround at Metalsa began in earnest after Zárate, then director of operations, visited Japan in 1985. "The Japanese firms were a little bit different from Metalsa, not only in tools, but also in values," observes Zárate. "The people I saw seemed to care for each other; the team was more important than the individual, and the people were very honest."

Zárate believed that Mexican people shared these values – but that they were somehow inhibited from expressing them at work. He suspected that the bureaucratic and autocratic nature of traditional Mexican business practices prevented tapping into the best efforts and the will of the people. This would have to change if Metalsa was to become competitive in world markets.

In 1986 Zárate started promoting a new philosophy within operations at Metalsa. Then in 1988 he was appointed CEO – that is, to the outside world he is the chief executive officer, but internally he goes by "co-ordinator of the guiding team" – and spread the credo to all parts of the company. Zárate summarizes the Metalsa way with this formula:

$$QWL = TPQ + TQC + LDS$$

Everyone there knows what it means: "Quality as a Way of Life" results from "Total Personal Quality" plus "Total Quality Control" plus "Leadership." As Zárate says: "We believe that quality products and services can be produced only by quality people."

The overarching philosophy is elaborated in a set of corporate-wide cultural values, such as trust, solidarity, service, and training, and a set of individual personal values, such as responsibility, punctuality, honesty, humility, austerity, patience, service, and seeking "total personal quality."

To spread the change, Zárate knew he had to take his message directly to each member. "I felt the people needed to see that I was taking time to talk to them personally about quality, philosophy, and how we were going to go ahead," he explains. He implored employees to concentrate on improving the quality of the person within themselves. He knew that if they did so, and if they adopted a high spirit of service, their actions would surely reflect their own quality as people. He assured them that if they practiced the right attitude every day on little things, then all things would get a little better every day. Throughout his discussions, Zárate also conveyed his belief that service to the customer was as important as the physical quality of the product.

He was equally adamant about solidarity, asking rhetorically: "When you want to conquer your enemy, you try to divide them; so why divide our own company?"

Things began to change. Executives started serving the customer and stopped being bureaucrats. They stopped wasting time on needless paperwork. Time clocks were ripped out, and work teams now keep their own attendance records. Quality control inspectors and supervisors were eliminated; their roles have been assumed by the team members. In the process Metalsa went from seven layers of management to only four – including Zárate.

Beyond layers of management, social layers have been eliminated as well. Status has been central to all hierarchies, and it was quite pronounced in Mexico. So the first thing Zárate eliminated was status. It was typical, for instance, that attendance at a meeting was listed according to position. Now everything is alphabetical. There are no reserved parking spots for executives; all parking spaces are open to everyone. People don't have job titles; everyone is a co-ordinator.

Upon the foundation of clear values, Zárate has guided Metalsa's workers from a questionable future into worldwide recognition as a manufacturer of quality products for the automotive industry and a model of an enlightened Mexican employer. When Zárate joined as a manager in 1978, Metalsa operated just one plant, had $23 million in domestic sales, sold only $23,000 per employee, produced no exports, employed 1,000 workers and had a 10 percent rejection rate. By 1995, after seven years under Zárate's leadership, Metalsa operated six plants, increased sales to over $150 million with 40 percent exports, had over 2000 employees, had sales per employee of up to $75,000, improved productivity by 200 percent, and reduced the reject rate to one-tenth of 1 percent. Metalsa had also won numerous supplier awards for quality, including the prestigious QSP award in 1994, given by General Motors to only 171 out of its 30,000 suppliers worldwide.

The future of Metalsa is far brighter today than a decade ago, and it is clearly positioned to compete in the global marketplace. "Quality at Metalsa is a way of life," Zárate says proudly, "based upon the conviction that in order to compete in the marketplace it is necessary to serve. We say that people have to live to serve instead of living to be served."

In our extensive research on leader credibility, we asked people to tell us how they would know if someone was credible. The most frequent response was: "They do what they say they will do." Example-setting is essential to earning credibility. When it comes to deciding whether a leader is believable, people first listen to the words, then watch the actions. A judgement of "credible" is handed down when the two are consonant. How you lead your life is how people judge whether they want to put their lives in your hands. If you dream of leaving a legacy, you had better heed the Golden Rule of Leadership: DWYSYWD – Do What You Say You Will Do.

Implications for the 21st century leader

The truest test of credible leadership is what leaders pay attention to and what they do. Leaders are judged by how they spend their time, how they react to critical incidents, the stories they tell, the questions they ask, the language and symbols they choose, and the measures they use. Every organizational assessment should include an audit of these dimensions for leaders. They need to become conscious of the messages they are sending with their actions. Nothing fuels the fires of cynicism better than hypocrisy, and leaders will need to be constantly vigilant about aligning what they practice and what they preach so that they set the example for others. Like Antonio Zárate, leaders must first clarify what they stand for and believe in and then take actions that are consistent with these beliefs.

LESSON 7

CARING IS AT THE HEART OF LEADERSHIP

We have all been misleading ourselves for years. We have been operating under some myths about leadership and management that have kept us from seeing the truth. First, there is this myth of rugged individualism. There is this belief that individualistic achievement will get us the best results. "If you want something done right," we hear, "do it yourself." We seem content to believe that we don't need other people to perform at our best. The fact is we don't do our best in isolation. We don't get extraordinary things done by working alone, with no support, no encouragement, no expressions of confidence, and no help from others. We don't make the best decisions that way, we don't get the best grades, we don't run faster, we don't achieve the highest levels of sales, we don't invent breakthrough products, and we don't live longer. And even if we did, what difference would it make?

We have also operated under the myth that leaders ought to be cool, aloof, and analytical; they ought to separate emotion from work. We are told that real leaders don't need love, affection, and friendship. "It's not a popularity contest," is a phrase we've all heard often. "I don't care if people like me. I just want them to respect me." Nonsense. At the heart of effective leadership is a genuine caring for people.

One of the most uplifting interviews we conducted in the course of writing our third book, *Encouraging the Heart*, was with Tony Codianni, director of the Training and Dealer Development Group for Toshiba America Information Systems. Codianni told us: "Encouraging the heart is *the* most important leadership practice because it's the most personal."[10] Codianni believes leadership is all about people, and if you are going to lead people you have to care about them.

The Center for Creative Leadership (CCL) has taken a look at the process of executive selection, and their results support Codianni's observation. In examining the critical variables for success for the top three jobs in large organizations, they found that the number one success factor is "relationships with subordinates."[11]

In an even more startling study, CCL found something that should forever put to rest the myth of the purely rational manager. Using a battery of measurement instruments, CCL researchers looked at a number of factors that could account for a manager's success. CCL found that only one factor significantly differentiated the top quartile of managers from the bottom quartile. (They found it on an assessment instrument called FIRO-B developed by William C. Schutz. The FIRO-B measures two aspects of three basic interpersonal needs – the extent to which we express and we want inclusion, control, and affection.[12])

The popular assumption about managers is that they are high on a need to express control. So you might think that is the factor that distinguishes highest from lowest-performing managers. But that is *not* what CCL found. The single factor that differentiated the top from the bottom was *expressed affection*. Contrary to the popular myth of the cold-hearted boss who cares very little about people's feelings, the highest performing managers show more warmth and fondness toward others. They get closer to people, and they are significantly more open in sharing thoughts and feelings than their lower performing counterparts. These managers were not without their rational sides. In fact, they all scored high on "thinking," and they all scored high on their need to have power and influence over others. It is just that these factors didn't explain why managers were higher performers.

When the CCL researchers examined their findings more closely, they found that the highest performing managers' subordinates two levels down in the organization were significantly more satisfied overall with their co-workers, supervision, top leaders, organization planning, ethics, and quality. Clearly, openness and affection pay off.

Because the evidence tells us that expressing affection is important to success, and we need it, it is as if we are all trying to hide something we all want. It is a secret we are afraid to reveal because it might make us look soft or wimpy or who knows what. That secret is this: we all really do want to be loved.

It is impossible to escape the message here, that when people work with leaders who care about them and encourage their hearts, they feel better about themselves.

> *When people work with leaders who care about them and encourage their hearts, they feel better about themselves. These leaders set people's spirits free, often inspiring them to become more than they ever thought possible.*

Their self-esteem goes up. These leaders set people's spirits free, often inspiring them to become more than they ever thought possible. And that, indeed, may be our ultimate mission as leaders.

Implications for the 21st century leader

Appreciation, acknowledgement, praise, thank yous. Some simple gesture that says, "I care about you and what you do." That's how we start. Encouragement, whether in the form of a simple thank you or an elaborate celebration, is feedback – positive feedback. It is information that communicates "You're on the right track. You're doing really well. Thanks." To deny each other this gift of positive feedback is to deny increased opportunities for success.

BELIEVING YOU CAN MAKE A DIFFERENCE

In our classes and workshops we regularly ask people to share a story about a leader they admire and whose direction they would willingly follow. From this exercise we hope they will discover for themselves what it takes to have an influence on others. We have another objective: we want them to discover the power that lies within each one of us to make a difference.

Virtually everyone we have asked has been able to name at least one leader whose compelling impact they have felt. Sometimes it is a well-known figure from the past who has changed the course of history. Sometimes it is a contemporary role model who serves as an example of success. And sometimes it is a person who has personally helped them learn – a parent, friend, member of the clergy, coach, teacher, or manager.

Veronica Guerrero made us realize just how extraordinary those around us can be. Guerrero chose her father, José Luis Guerrero, as the leader she admired. Guerrero told the story of her father's leadership in the Union Nacional Sinarquista (UNS) in the early forties. She related in detail what her father did and summed it up with this observation from José Luis: "I think the work that I did back then helped me extend myself and others to levels that I didn't know I could reach . . . If you feel strongly about anything, and it is something that will ultimately benefit your community and your country, do not hold back. Fear of failing or fear of what might happen does not help anyone . . . do not let anyone or anything push you back."

Veronica Guerrero closed her description of her father (who was dying of pancreatic cancer) with this observation: "As I heard his story and I saw a sick, tired, and weak man I could not help thinking that our strength as humans and as leaders has nothing to do with what we look like. Rather, it has everything to do with what we feel, what we think of ourselves. . . Leadership is applicable to all facets of life."

That is precisely the point. If we are to become 21st century leaders, we must believe that we, too, can be a positive force in the world. It has everything to do with what we feel, and what we think of ourselves.

3

SENSATIONAL LEADERSHIP

INGALILL HOLMBERG AND JONAS RIDDERSTRÅLE

We must all prepare for a world characterized by the simultaneous impact of digitization and globalization. This is an excess economy with markets for absolutely everything, from raw material and financial resources to patents and people. In such a place, the sources underlying competitiveness will gradually shift toward things that we cannot touch. Instead, both potential customers and prospective employees will cry out for leaders, strategies, organizations, products and services that touch them. The new dominant source of competitiveness will rest with our ability to understand, develop, and profit from emotions and imagination. In such unconventional times we cannot have conventional leadership. We need different leadership. We need innovative leadership. We need passionate leadership. We need sensational leadership.

THE SURPLUS SOCIETY

This is the age of abundance, and competition as we know it has gone totally mad. How else can we explain the fact that the average US citizen is exposed to 247 ads per day? Or that he or she has encountered 350000 commercials before turning 18? No wonder Mercedes Benz used a woman having an orgasm in one of its TV commercials, or that Miller's magician in a recent beer commercial makes hair grow in the armpits of the women surrounding him. Extreme times call for extreme measures, and the excess economy is developing everywhere across the globe.

In 1996, 1000 new types of soda were introduced on the Japanese market – less than 1 per cent are still for sale. The same year, Sony launched 5 000 new products – more than two new products per work-hour. Maybe this is necessary in a market where the average product life cycle for consumer electronics products is down to three months. Still, compared to Walt Disney, Sony's innovation record is a mere breeze. Disney CEO Michael Eisner claimed that the company develops a new product – a film, a comic book, a CD, or whatever – every five minutes. In Norway, a country with 4.5 million inhabitants, the average consumer can choose from 200 newspapers, 100 weekly magazines, and 20 TV channels.

Knowledge is also exploding. There are currently 140 000 IT engineers at work in Bangalore, India, the world's second largest city for software development. So what is the average salary of an Indian engineer? It ranges from US$500–1000 per month depending on experience. In the light of this, why should you hire anyone from Germany, Sweden, the UK, or the US in future?

This has truly been the century of geniuses. Some 90 percent of all the scientists who have ever walked the face of the earth live right now. In 1960, US schools saw 5000 MBAs graduate; last year that figure was 75 000. In the UK, the number of MBA courses has risen from 2 to 130 in the past 30 years. Welcome to the age of more – more fear, more fun, more uncertainty, more competition.

There is no doubt about it. In the near future there will be a surplus of similar companies, employing similar people with similar skills, launching similar products and services, with similar quality, price, and performance, and they will all be competing. As consumers, you will learn to love it – once you have become used to being condemned to freedom . . . the freedom to choose. As executives, you will hate it. Once supply exceeds demand in your industry, you too will have to deal with the demanding customer, and the demanding customer is a dictator. There is nowhere to run and nowhere to hide. In a surplus society on the verge of friction-free capitalism, they are all out to get you. Perhaps Intel Chairman Andy Grove is right when he argues that only the paranoid survive.

How do you create sustainable competitive advantages in a surplus society? The answer is, you can't. We will argue that future success is dependent on the development of conditions that facilitate the continuous (re)creation of customer value. In our minds, this process increasingly calls for co-creation of competitive advantage, involving everyone and everything, going on everywhere and non-stop. As Austrian economist Joseph Schumpeter once said, success will depend on the ability to constantly engage in creative destruction.[1] At least this is what many Silicon Valley companies communicate to their employees when telling them: "Obsolete your own products."

WHY MANAGERS LOVE MONOPOLIES

In a market economy, business basically boils down to making money, at least enough money to secure survival of the firm. Now, this is not the reason why people start successful companies – remember that Ford was founded to democratize the automobile and Disney to make people happy, not to make money – but showing a profit is still necessary. Therefore, despite all the talk about the superiority of the capitalist system and the criticality of cutthroat competition, it is our experience that all managers, regardless of age, gender, and geographical origin, share the same secret dream. The dream that keeps them all sweating and turning over in bed at night revolves around the only way to make money. It is their private little dream about the creation of temporary monopolies. Why do all executives share this fantasy? It is really quite simple. Unless the firm is in a monopoly position, competition will force it to engage in ruthless price wars resulting in zero profits.

All managers share the same secret dream. It is their private little dream about the creation of temporary monopolies.

As little as managers would admit that their secret dream is about the creation of temporary monopolies, most executives would never acknowledge that the ultimate aim of their strategic intentions and actions is to kill the spirit of free enterprise. Yet, doing this trick over and over again is what they are paid for, and often quite handsomely, one might add. To create a temporary monopoly, the company needs to be different. The product offering must add unique value to a specific set of customers – a niche. In the case of Progressive Corp., the sixth largest car insurance company in the USA and one of the more successful ones, this focus means targetting customers that are criminals, alcoholics, and drunkards. Anyone want to argue with the fact that competition has gone berserk? To cut a long story short, in a surplus society, strategy is about revoking the customers' right to freedom. In the age of abundance, strategy is about choosing the customer, and then choosing for the customer. In an excess economy, strategy is about not leaving the customer any choice – it is about being the only natural choice.

FROM CORE COMPETENCIES TO CORE COMPETENTS

Any company has a tremendous need for individuals who can come up with unique ideas. In many organizations, these "core competents," e.g. individuals who embody the skills necessary to create temporary monopolies, rather than the core competencies, which Gary Hamel and C.K. Prahalad introduced a few years back, constitute the true source of competitive advantage.[2] Whereas competents personify prospective cores, it is our experience that competencies, at least as popularly defined, often represent retrospective cores. Naturally, most companies, and particularly those managers who are not core competents themselves, hate this fact and would never acknowledge it. To fight back, firms are trying to become less dependent on these "walking monopolies." One of the main objectives of the renowned knowledge management system "Navigator" used by the Swedish insurance company Skandia is thus to turn human capital into structural capital. Skandia hopes the corporation is worth a bit more than the bricks and mortar when people leave the offices around 5 pm. Still, someone like Bill Gates admits that if 20 people were to leave Microsoft, the company would risk bankruptcy. Nathan Myhrwold, Chief Technology Officer there, claims that in the new economy, the difference between the average and the good is no longer a factor of 1:2; it is a factor of 1:100 or 1:1,000! At Nintendo, the computer games company, management argues that an ordinary person cannot design a really good game no matter how much he or she tries.

Do not kid yourselves. You cannot hire these people. Provided you are attractive enough, maybe they will hire you – if you are lucky. What is even worse, these core competents are often more than a little strange. We usually refer to them as entrepreneurs, a nicer word for oddballs. These individuals thrive on constantly questioning the existing ways of operating, the norms and regulations. They are the people you would hate to have as your son- or daughter-in-law. Entrepreneurs are people who look into the world with totally open eyes, with the mind and curiosity of a newborn child. They are mavericks who get a kick out of taking personal risks. How many such individuals do you have at your company, on your board, or in the room next to you? What is the "weird-factor" at your firm? Is it high enough? Somehow we doubt it.

The average never wins

Unfortunately, our heritage from the industrial age dictates that standardization and de-personalization of individuals does work. Consequently, most firms are so inbred that you sometimes expect the next person to show up with a huge head, red curly hair, and an extra eye in the middle of the forehead. We should not expect too much innovation at a company where 95 percent of the employees look and think exactly the same. And if people want to change, they only want to become even more like the boss. In the inbred firm, repetition dominates at the expense of renewal, and the exploitation of givens crowds out the creation of novelty. Innovation, on the contrary, is contingent on variation, and on individuals who refuse to take part in the look-and-act-alike competition. True, you can say a lot of things about people such as Richard Branson, Anita Roddick, Ross Perot, Luciano Benetton, and Bill Gates, but you can't say they are normal. Normal people do normal things, with normal results. And one thing is for sure, the average has never won, and it never will.

The main difference in a surplus society is that the average is getting an addition of some 3000 million people in other parts of the world, a large number of start-up companies, and a plethora of new customer offerings, and they all want to share the new wealth. And guess what – a lot of these people are no longer only good at producing plastic flowers and cheap toys. Economies such as those of Taiwan or Hong Kong are already knowledge-based, where more than 65 percent of gross domestic product is generated by service-related activities. On the west coast of the USA, some of the more prestigious universities, such as Stanford, Berkeley, and UCLA, are using a quota system to limit the number of students from southeast Asia. Competing on grades, many Americans would not stand a chance. A country like Singapore, which author William Gibson once described as "Disneyland with death penalty," spends 25 percent of its GDP on research, development, and education. It does not take a genius to figure out who they are sentencing right now.

COMPETITIVE ADVANTAGE:
FROM LOCATION TO EMOTION AND IMAGINATION

In what ways can you create temporary monopolies in the age of abundance? To answer this question, we need to look at the historical evolution of the bases of competitive advantage. In the beginning, competitive advantage was primarily derived from location. It was the access to raw materials that pro-vided the specific advantages necessary to create and exploit temporary monopolies. The successful company of the 19th century profited from access to oil, forests, mines, etc. Families such as the Rockefellers became incredibly rich. However, the capitalist economy is ruthless. Soon, free markets for raw materials made it increasingly difficult to use location as the single source of competitive advantage.

As this happened, technology and innovation, together with the access to capital, became the new differentiator. The key to competitiveness was creat-ing more value out of the same input. At the turn of the century, the business community was thus dominated by a number of well-known capitalists, a few entrepreneurs, and their innovations – Thomas Alva Edison, Alfred Nobel, Otto Diesel, the separator, the automobile, and the ball-bearing. Competitive edge was based on ingenuity. However, once again the market struck back. Products were imitated and patents were sold or acquired. When these inno-vations were turned into everybody's property, competitive advantage could no longer be based on a former technological monopoly.

Consequently, we entered the organizational age. In the USA, pioneers such as Alfred Sloan and Henry DuPont designed the multidivisional firm, an architecture which later came to dominate the structure of most large, complex firms.[3] The new organization allowed a continuous upgrading of previous technological advantages. Progressively, throughout the latter half of the 20th century, consequent types of organizational innovations have given rise to new temporary monopolies; JIT, BPR, MBO, MBWA, Kanban, matrix management, outsourcing, downsizing, lean production, etc. The list could go on ad infinitum.

Gone are the days of the bureaucratic firm that Max Weber outlined almost a century ago. Jack Welch at General Electric even characterizes the hierarchical firm as an organization that has its face toward the CEO and its ass toward the customer. Today, if you belong to the in-crowd, your organization is supposed to look like a blueberry pancake, a fishnet, a shamrock, gazelles, or even boiling spaghetti. Most modern firms still base their competitiveness on developing organizational solutions that enable them to uphold a fruitful balance between exploiting givens and creating novelty. However, as we see it, there is reason to believe that this source of competitive advantage is also soon to be overshadowed.

Right now, international consulting companies are conducting arbitrage on diffusing identical organizational solutions around the world. McKinsey & Company, Andersen Consulting, Boston Consulting Group, and Cap Gemini to name but a few, all contribute to the current global homogenization of organizational solutions. A cadre of MBA students from all continents read the same books, learn the same recipes, and go to work for competing firms. These people contribute to more rapid imitation and similar solutions. Moreover, the introduction of IT, to enable increased customization, co-ordination, communication, etc., will certainly give a number of companies some initial advantages. However, as nearly all firms become virtual and wired, we foresee that information technology will act as a homogenizing force, making company structures even more similar.

Naturally, given variations in values and institutional settings in different parts of the world, certain differences will probably never disappear. Still, it is worth noting that even something as accepted as lifetime employment in Japan appears to be giving way to arrangements involving more flexibility. Currently, as much as 25 percent of the Japanese workforce is made up of part-timers and temps. Nevertheless, as a consequence of increasing global organizational homogenization, we predict that it will become increasingly difficult to base temporary monopolies on purely organizational innovations.

So what do we do if competitiveness can no longer be based on location, technological innovation, or the structuring of our organization? In our view, it is time to start exploiting the last taboo – to build competitiveness around and on something we all know exists but which is seldom discussed in business situations. We must start basing our temporary monopolies on emotions and imagination. Exploiting the last taboo means departing from the tradition that people are to be treated as just another factor of production, a human resource. It is our experience, and, we suspect, yours too, that few people enjoy being treated as human resources: they want to be seen as individuals.

ECONOMIES OF SOUL

Love, lust, joy, wildness, and a touch of the zany – why is it that at many companies these are frowned on? Still, we know that the best (and worst) things in life are associated with strong feelings. The company that aspires to be competitive in the future cannot deprive itself of the strengths associated with what we would like to call "economies of soul." Scale and skill economies will still matter. But as Professor Manfred Kets de Vries at INSEAD puts it, unless the resources that make people mad, sad, and glad, can be put to good use, knowledge is not used, it is abused. This is one of the main reasons why so many executives admit that as little as 10–15 percent of the intellectual capital at their companies is used properly. Most seem a bit embarrassed when confessing it, but somehow the average manager has gotten used to it and accepted that this is how it is and should be. To survive in a surplus society, we believe it is vital to escape from a situation in which employment actually means "competence castration." Henry Ford allegedly once said: "Why is it that I always get a whole person, when what I really want is just a pair of hands?" Today, we need whole persons – head and heart, body and soul. Feelings and fantasy go hand in hand. Without soul, there can be only limited skill.

In relation to our customers the new trend means focussing on the extended experience, trying to look and think beyond the actual parts. As a Hewlett-Packard executive once remarked, sushi is cold, dead fish, but that isn't how it should be marketed. So why, then, do so many companies persist in selling cold, dead fish to consumers so much more interested in sushi? Think about when you last bought a PC. What were the sales arguments – price, performance, or power? We claim that in a true excess economy, all those are given. From a strict price/performance view it will not really matter which vacuum cleaner, TV set, VCR, or microwave you buy. They are all more or less equally good. Getting that stuff right only buys you a ticket to take part in the game. In the future, your company will win by appealing to the feelings and fantasies of the customer. Otherwise, you will have to deal with the demanding customer on a purely economic basis, which will inevitably result in zero profits as you will compete globally with an infinite number of other similar firms. In the age of affection, the only way to create real profit is to attract the emotional rather than the purely rational consumer or colleague.

Most people, consumers as well as colleagues, already are, or at least could be, driven by a rationale that extends far beyond the purely economic one. Alberto Alessi, CEO of the company with the same name, said people have an enormous need for art and poetry that industry does not yet understand. He can charge some $80 for a toilet brush, so he must be doing something right. You just don't pay this ridiculous sum of money because Alessi's toilet brush has superior functionality: you buy something more – an extended experience. Creating this extended experience calls for the hidden treasures of the organization and its members to be tapped.

SENSATIONAL LEADERSHIP

How do we unleash the potential for emotional competitiveness and corporate imagination? At least in the West, the preferred approach for handling increased organizational complexity or new organizational dimensions is to add yet another box to the organizational chart. So let's set up a department for emotions and imagination, and appoint a manager, male and aged 46, to run it. As much as this procedure may seem ridiculous, it very much resembles the way in which we have gone about handling issues such as quality and knowledge during the past 20 years. It totally misses the point.

Why? Not that long ago we did some consulting for a major retailer in Sweden. The company had experienced tremendous problems with shoplifting. Finally, management decided to do something. They

> *"Emotion and imagination" is not a department, it is a frame of mind.*

appointed a head of security to take care of the problem. The result: more things disappeared. The reason: by making this issue a big thing for a selected few, the others stopped caring. Instead, true sources of competitive advantage, such as knowledge, quality, and "human resources," must be turned into a small thing for the majority of people in the organization. "Emotion and imagination" is not a department, it is a frame of mind.

It is time for management to stop constantly rearranging boxes and arrows and refocus its efforts on other tasks – to practice sensational leadership. By sensational we mean spectacular enough to capture the attention of those we want to influence. But sensational also means leadership that appeals to all five senses. Can people see you, hear you, smell you, taste you, feel you? All this starts with being available – it's time to start living leadership. Sensational leadership calls for a shift in what managers do, and in how they do it. Sensational leadership is about thriving on imagination and emotion.

From originators of order to creators of chaos

The first challenge has to do with the fact that most executives have grown accustomed to changing only in reaction to outside forces. The pervasiveness of a reactive stance is evident in the fixation on solving problems. Many managers and also great academic thinkers still believe that leadership is truly about problem-solving. We beg to differ. In our minds, successful leadership will have more to do with generating problems – uncertainty production, rather than reduction.

No matter the type of organization, exploitation of givens over time tends to crowd out the creation of novelty. In the former case, learning is less ambiguous and it is much easier to see the results of our efforts.[4] Therefore, the role of the true leader is not to ensure that the firm is an efficient exploiter; all our organizational innovations are pretty good safeguards of that. Instead, leadership is about fostering and protecting imagination and experimentation. It is the task of management to challenge the organization, not to control it. Sony's instruction to employees to "make it the size of a pocketbook" when developing the Walkman is a well known example. The use of stretch goals also serves a similar purpose. Toshiba's instruction to "make it with half the parts, in half the time, and at half the cost" when developing a new VCR may be a telling example too. You challenge the people to perform at their utmost by generating the problem, but you do not hand them ready-made solutions or tell them what to do. The problem is that the typical executive is handsomely paid for looking and acting like a walking garbage-can, matching problems with solutions, as organizational scholars James March and Johan Olsen might have put it.[5]

Much current thinking on management is built on the assumption that the absence of leadership results in chaos. Therefore, it is the role of the leader to bring order into chaos. We would like to challenge this view by suggesting that the absence of leadership mostly results in repetition and reproduction. The organization becomes static and constipated. Under this assumption, it becomes the task of leaders, anywhere and everywhere, to infuse chaos into order – to challenge the others to depart from the patterns of the past and to creatively destroy the present profit-makers, by creating new ones. In our minds, sensational leadership is about stirring the pot rather than putting on the lid. The future leaders are creators of chaos just as much as originators of order.

In order to survive, companies must learn to tap the intellectual and emotional capacity of core competents and teams working on the edge of chaos. Yet most efforts at fostering team-building and collective learning seem to backfire. One problem revolves around the impact of the management fads of the eighties, such as visionary leadership. By introducing concepts like visions, corporate culture, and management of meaning, the focus is shifting from the action level of innovation to all the layers of management, a shift including yet another powerful instrument in stereotyping leadership and leadership activities.

A dangerous paradox is at hand. Even though it is argued that the future organization must be based on the principles of decentralization and empowerment, it is still the task of the top management team to develop all the instruments to realize the full potential of the firm. Instead of fostering a climate of imagination and creativity, diversity is often replaced by a single-minded vision and ideal images picturing the goals and dreams of senior management. Quite often, the only thing created is a range of colored pamphlets, inspiring no one, except maybe the board of directors.

We would argue that sensational leadership is about developing the capacity for collective experimentation and opening the door to chaotic action. The leader's role is to cultivate autonomy, individual opportunity, and competition, but also co-operation and the sharing of ideas – to provide global garbage-cans, i.e. platforms for knowledge creation and transfer, rather than acting as a garbage-can himself. Chaos can be promoted by creating a much more diverse organization, mixing men and women, and the old and young. However, we are not saying that firms should move from hierarchy to anarchy. Sensational leadership is about articulating and communicating these principal principles that keep the organization together. As noted by creativity guru John Kao, to improvise you need a tune.[6] With one small common denominator, whether it be attitudes, shared ownership, or something else, we can afford to vary in all other dimensions. The modern organization is not homogeneous or heterogeneous, it is both. In essence, leadership is about striking this delicate balance, whether it is about time, place or people. But by striking a balance, we mean going for extremes, not trying to attain the average.

Creative insights rarely come to us in finished form. They are more like a hunch, ideas with unknown consequences. Lack of creativity has never been a true problem. The main problem is getting rid of the old and making room for the new. Old mental structures and outdated organizational arrangements effectively hinder and block new ways of thinking and new ways of doing things. Creativity requires the reframing of our mental models and the restructuring of all the assumptions behind these models. And remember, no one has a monopoly on creativity, not even a temporary one. Not even Microsoft.

From reasoning with people to AID-ing them

We will not succeed, however, in turning this new mindset into organizational action by merely reasoning with people. Instead it is time to start AID-ing them. What do we mean by this? As we see it, there are four different ways in which you can communicate with people; you appeal to their Affection, Intuition, Desire or you appeal to their reason. Most managers are masters in the last category. This is where most of them got their training and experience, and this is what the average leader is typically rewarded for. But eventually the analytical side of the brain becomes so dominant that some executives find it difficult to avoid going round in circles.

The challenge has to do with the fact that in an age of affection, success will depend less and less on our reasoning skills: there are millions of other super-smart people out there. Instead, in the new economy, it will be the task of leaders throughout an organization to take people on a journey into an uncertain and chaotic future – every day, week after week, year after year. And as noted by Professor Noel M. Tichy at the University of Michigan: "The best way to get people to venture into unknown terrain is to make it desirable by taking them there in their imagination."[7] Succeeding in this means exploiting the opportunities connected with the A, the I and the D – affection, intuition and desire – and not relying on simply more reasoning.

We must move from the head to the heart and go after people's affection, intuition and desire. The Apple team that developed the first Mac believed their computer would not only change computing but the whole world. They had a purpose. The team had a soul. The members were driven by the desire to make a difference. No surprise that when Steven Jobs was trying to recruit John Sculley from Pepsi, he just asked him if he wanted to spend the rest of his life selling sugared water or if he wanted a chance to change the world.

> *We must move from the head to the heart and go after people's affection, intuition and desire.*

Ken Alvares, head of worldwide human resources at Sun Microsystems, says the goal "is to keep people so busy having fun everyday that they don't even listen when the headhunters call."[8] Sensational leadership is about harmonious people, not harmonious organizations. We all suspect happy people do a better job. But then just how many companies have words such as fun and happiness included in their vision or mission statements? It is our experience that the best predictor of performance is the average number of laughs per employee per day. Companies should use that relationship to their advantage.

Of course, any time we communicate with someone our message is a blend of A, I and D. If you have a few minutes to spare, take a look at the latest slogan created by your organization – a new mission statement or an ad – and rank it in terms of these dimensions. Let your spouse or a friend go through the latest speech you gave, and do the same with that. In an age of abundance and information overload, where time is a scarce resource, are you really getting through? Is something lacking? If you don't change, will you stand a chance in this age of attention? We suspect most managers could load their messages with many more feelings. The sensational leaders already do. Herb Kelleher at Southwest Airlines says: "We are not afraid to talk to our people with emotions. We're not afraid to tell them, 'We love you.' Because we do."[9]

CONCLUSION

The coming years will bring a transition to a surplus society, in which all firms will have to deal with fierce global competition and increasingly demanding customers. In this age of abundance, the need to be unique and to continuously create new temporary monopolies will peak. Consequently, leaders and organizations will be forced to come up with innovative ways to increase the pace of creative destruction. No longer can temporary monopolies be based on merely location, innovation, or organization. The new era will call for exploiting the last taboo – unleashing the *emotions* and *imagination* of the organization and its customers.

In our opinion, sensational leadership is a prerequisite for successfully competing through feelings and fantasy. Sensational leadership is not about developing a hypermodern way of rearranging the chairs; it is about instituting a different mindset. This new paradigm calls for recognizing that modern management is about infusing chaos, rather than introducing order; providing platforms for collective experimentation, rather than individually planning for all organizational actions; and AID-ing people, rather than just reasoning with them. In the emotional enterprise, the traditional master becomes a servant – a servant to the future of the firm, not to his self-interest. In the age of affection, sensational people will demand sensational leadership.

4

LEADERSHIP AS COLLECTIVE GENIUS

LINDA A. HILL

What will world-class companies look like in the 21st century? They will act, look and feel like the most successful entrepreneurial ventures. Corporations, no matter how large and established, will need to behave with the agility and creativity that characterize small, aggressive startups. They will be ever-evolving collectives of talented, passionate and diverse individuals. What will the leaders of these world-class companies look like? Leaders will be the architects of these collectives. They will sit at their center, shaping what is, in essence, collective genius.

With more and more companies having access to the same technology, markets, methods of production and channels of distribution, the competitive environment has fundamentally changed. As disparities across these have shrunk, the strategic management of talent has become the key to competitive advantage.

In this chapter, I will profile a selection of leaders for the future, individuals who fully appreciate that the final frontier of organizational leverage is employee motivation and talent.[1] For these individuals, collective genius is not an oxymoron, but rather the reality they strive to create in their organizations. This will be a tale not simply of what they do and how they do it but perhaps more importantly who they are and how they think. Most of these individuals will be unfamiliar. Many are new CEOs of young ventures. They are unassuming and have shunned the trappings of power. As we will see, they represent some of the best-kept secrets in the business world. I suspect that, before long, we will be reading about them and their exciting enterprises in the pages of business magazines and journals.[2]

WHERE IS GENIUS?

When we think of genius, we usually think of extraordinary individuals. We imagine prodigies creating, often in isolation. The reality is quite different from the myth. Creativity is an interactive and a developmental process for even the most gifted. In his seminal book on the genius of individuals such as Freud, Einstein and Picasso, Howard Gardner made the following admission: "As a psychologist interested in the *individual* creator, I was surprised by this discovery of the intensive social and affective forces that surround creative breakthroughs."[3]

Although prodigies are born, they are then *made* through their social interactions. Significant creative breakthroughs represent years of sustained activity with others. Creative individuals need both independence and engagement to do their best work. On one hand, they crave intellectual and emotional space and solitude. To master a field demands a discipline and focus that is often all-consuming. On the other hand, the creative process thrives on the tension that arises as individuals with widely different but complementary abilities or points of view grapple with one another. With this tension comes vulnerability and anxiety, and so individuals need social support to sustain them through what can be a highly charged and taxing experience.

When we think of genius and creativity, we most often think of artists and scientists. But of course genius and creativity can be found in many of life's domains. In business, we think of entrepreneurs, especially in the "new technology industries." The successful ventures are truly creative collaborations of talented people committed to beating the odds.

> *The successful ventures are truly creative collaborations of talented people committed to beating the odds.*

WHY COLLECTIVES?

Much has been written about the new organization and what it will look like. Companies are breaking down traditional boundaries to create lean, adaptive, global organizations. Horizontal networks and inter-functional teams that cut across national boundaries are taking their place alongside, and sometimes even replacing, functional, hierarchical organizational structures. Companies are forming strategic alliances to acquire important capabilities with suppliers, customers, and even competitors. Small companies are looking for the financial wherewithal and vast distribution networks that big partners can offer. Large companies are building strategic alliances and acquiring small companies to gain access to their innovative research and entrepreneurial energy. In

order to compete in a turbulent, demanding and global business environment, an organization's boundaries will need to be permeable and flexible.
Organizations will continually revitalize and reconfigure themselves as their
needs shift.

To capture these realities, I prefer the metaphor of companies as collectives
to the more popular one of companies as networks. The notion of the collective
captures the duality inherent in the creative process. A collective can be treated
as singular when the collective is thought of as a whole and as plural when the
individual members are thought of as acting separately. The creative process
involves the struggles of talented individuals and the collective as a whole to
establish a meaningful identity that is an integral part of the other. Managing
this paradox is fast becoming *the* fundamental leadership dilemma. To address
it, leaders have three primary responsibilities:

- to articulate why the collective exists
- to determine who should be part of the collective
- to at once unleash and harness the genius of the collective.

Articulating why the collective exists

Virtually all conceptions of leadership begin with the assumption that a critical
role for the leader is to set direction: craft and communicate a mission or
vision. Traditionally we have focussed on vision's role as helping people understand the organization's direction and how they can contribute to it. But the
vision has a more elemental function. It defines what binds the individuals
together in the first place. We cannot even talk about a collective of people
without referring to what makes them a collective, or why they exist.

Leadership is about providing the moral and strategic vision that defines the
collective's *identity*. As the leadership profiles that follow will demonstrate, the
vision addresses the human search for being a part of something larger than
one's self and finding meaning in work – the engagement side of the inde-
pendence/engagement duality in the creative process. People, especially the
gifted, want to be part of something that is truly visionary and enduring – to
identify and be part of the future before it happens. The vision needs to tap into
people's professional pride, the engine for the extraordinary motivation and
commitment demanded by creativity.

As organizations become increasingly diverse and their boundaries flexible
and amorphous, the notion of what brings people together to act as one body
becomes ever more critical. Being clear about the vision is especially important
for answering the questions of who should be "in" and who should be "out" as
companies make decisions about strategic alliances, outsourcing and acquisitions. It takes time and energy to nurture the kind of partnerships required to

do collective work with those who are different. It is not easy to integrate new members into a collective and still retain the integrity of the collective.

Determining who should be part of the collective

Collective genius can occur only if the right members are in the collective, i.e. the multiple and diverse geniuses or expertise required to live the vision. World-class companies need world-class people. In this section, we will consider examples of leaders who have been able to discern genius in all of its guises, wherever it might be located.

Perhaps the experiences of Felix Racca and Emilio López, co-founders of the Argentine software company InterSoft, best illustrate the relentless dedication to drawing on a broad base of talent and perspectives. Racca and López named their company InterSoft because, as they explain, they were not going to be just multinational, they intended to be interplanetary! "We wanted to be the Argentine dream – proving to Argentina and the world that we could hold our own and be successful. We wanted to be revolutionaries doing what the big boys did, for about a tenth of the cost." Trailblazing has become InterSoft's hallmark. Although they have yet to become interplanetary, they are now multinational. To the surprise of their colleagues and competitors, InterSoft has become a virtual company made up of programers in Argentina and some of the top software engineering talent in Russia.

In the early nineties, InterSoft had difficulty finding the programing talent it needed locally. The company created a cadre of top-notch programers from across Latin America with whom they used no formal arrangements or contracts, but instead created relationships based on trust. In 1992, Racca and López traveled to Moscow. They regarded going to Russia like going to Japan or Germany right after World War II in search of opportunity. They met with over 50 software professionals before discovering Orgland, whose programers were graduates of the Moscow Institute of Physics and Technology. López explained:

> "As soon as I met the Orgland people I had a good feeling about them. I was especially impressed with their experience in graphic user interfaces (GUI), something that InterSoft was just beginning. Their spirit and attitude towards work reminded me of InterSoft when we were starting out. We spent time getting to know them, talking about religion and history. We discovered that Argentines and Russians have a lot in common. As Roman Catholics we shared some Russian Orthodox beliefs about the family and certain moral principles. Both cultures have romantic and socialist tendencies. They have the steppes and we have the pampas. Both cultures appreciate a good drink! We thought that since their company had so many young people, they would get along with us."

Despite potential barriers of distance and language (English would generally be their common language), InterSoft decided to acquire Orgland after a joint trial project. The inevitable complexities of the collaboration would be managed largely via e-mail.

Even with this acquisition, InterSoft was in need of additional talent. They began to proactively develop it, offering advanced programing courses to which the most able university students flocked. What started informally eventually became an extensive and renowned internship program. To use a phrase coined by Morgan McCall, their strategy was not merely selection of the fittest, but rather *development* of the fittest.[4]

As Racca and López found out, more often than not leadership entails recognizing potential genius and then cultivating it. According to Randy Haykin, the founder of Interactive Minds, a Silicon Valley "venture catalyst" firm, his competitive edge comes from being able to spot talent before his competitors do. Many of the individuals with whom he works in the interactive software field have little or no track record. Haykin's calling is to find people who have great ideas and provide them with the resources they need to nurture the ideas into a successful business.

Haykin founded Interactive Minds in January 1995 as a consulting company. Over time it has evolved into what he describes as a venture catalyst organization with the following mission:

> "Interactive Minds provides the three things entrepreneurs are always seeking: strategic or hands-on assistance, people, and money. We provide strategic support to assess, define and plan a successful business. In addition, we take hands-on management roles to help clients address marketing, sales, business development, and operations issues. Interactive Minds helps clients assess and define their management requirements and then undertakes systematic searches to find, screen, and attract leading talent. Finally, the company supplies seed and early-stage venture capital to high-potential companies."

The first start-up opportunity Haykin worked with through Interactive Minds was Greenhouse Networks, a new division of America Online. In this role, Haykin looked through hundreds of business plans, which allowed him to gain a sense of what would and would not work, while also forming relationships with people he would return to in the future. Haykin subsequently rotated through many interim positions, including Vice-President of sales and marketing of the founding team of Yahoo! He sees his role as helping others take their ideas and build something extraordinary: "I want to create *multiple* billion dollar companies. I want to have been part of *several* Yahoo!s in my life, whether I'm the CEO or the VP of sales and marketing, or even just the person who put the money into them."

Like Haykin, Franco Bernabè, once the CEO of a Fortune Global 500 company, understands better than most about the power of recognizing and unleashing untapped talent. Bernabè, former CEO of Eni, Italy's large energy-focussed industrial group, led the company through a successful turnaround and privatization against tremendous odds.[5]

––––––––

When a new government swept into power in Italy in 1992 and appointed Bernabè CEO of Eni (at that time ranked twenty-first in the Fortune Global 500 in terms of revenues), many were shocked. Until then, his nine-year career with the company had been behind the scenes, where he worked as a planner and financial controller. From those positions, Bernabè had developed strategic plans for Eni that were not particularly popular with the company's senior management. In fact, his tireless advocacy for change had prompted the board of directors to demote him once and call for his ousting twice. Yet Bernabè was undeterred, and when he was designated CEO, he made change his top priority. He was determined to "create a company of entrepreneurs, where people felt like partners in a professional service firm – a global company that is so free of bureaucracy that all that is left are people who create value." He worked relentlessly to "liberate the Eni group from the public arena" because he believed privatization was in the best interests of both the company and the country. His idealism and his patriotism were perhaps his more important sources of power.

In his tenure, Bernabè was able to transform the company from a debt-ridden, government-owned and politically controlled entity into a competitive and profitable publicly traded corporation focussed on energy production. Several months after Bernabè took power, much of Eni's senior management team was arrested and jailed on corruption charges. Bernabè ended up selling off 200 companies, dismissing hundreds of managers, and installing radically new business systems and procedures. He explains what kept him going through trying times: "My basic motivation was moral; 85 percent of the people were paying for the wrongdoings of 15 percent of the people, who were responsible for the corruption and misuse of politics. Their image as good, honest, hard-working people was being stolen from them. I had to right that inequality."

––––––––

While many of the changes he made were not atypical of turnarounds, he made one significantly different move: to fill the empty executive positions, he believed that the talent needed to revive the company was already inside. Bernabè explained his rationale:

> "With the head of human resources, I pored over hundreds of resumés from people within Eni. A lot of people – consultants and investment bankers – told me to look outside the company. But I believed there was plenty of talent inside the company that only needed to be nurtured and given the right tools to succeed. We would choose people according to their experience and performance. I wanted them to be professionally sound, naturally, but that was the easy part. More difficult was finding people who would give me guarantees of integrity and show signs of independence. One person I chose, for instance, had once left Eni because he found the company too bureaucratic and cumbersome. I asked him to become chief financial officer."

Bernabè himself at one time was "untapped talent." Early in his career, when he was the chief economist for Fiat, Bernabè began to feel that his work was becoming "dangerously routinized and specialized." He recalls: "At that time, the consensus was that devising strategy and running the company were complete opposites. I was told that there was not any possibility of evolving my career by taking on direct operating responsibilities." At this juncture he was enticed to join Eni. Ironically, in November 1998, Telecom Italia, Italy's second largest company, offered Bernabè the position of CEO. The request purportedly came from the Agnelli family, influential shareholders on both the Telecom Italia and Fiat boards. Bernabè is an example of how stretch leadership experiences can unlock talent.

As these leaders know, the disparity in creativity and productivity between top performers and average performers is tremendous.[6] A company can be only as strong as its weakest member. When people and their relationships are key business drivers, wrong moves in hiring people and selecting partners and investors can be ruinous. The talented and ambitious want to associate only with others who are talented and ambitious. Who is in the collective will largely determine who else is willing to join in the future. The trade-offs between quality, cost and expediency must be carefully weighed.

Deciding who should be in the collective is not simply a matter of evaluating the talents of each potential member. After all, the whole is more than the sum of its parts. To be creative, individuals need to interact with both those who can support them and with those who can provide them with creative abrasion, to use a term coined by Dorothy Leonard.[7] In other words, the collective must include a diversity of talent, people of different backgrounds, expertise and contrasting perspectives. But with that diversity come challenges. Relationships with those who are dissimilar in many ways (e.g. in expertise, career history, nationality) can be difficult to establish.

A significant portion of leaders' time will be spent on locating, assessing, attracting and, when necessary, developing the needed talent. They will have to think holistically about their choices: who needs to be involved to leverage the individual talents into collective genius? What chemistry is needed among the members if they are to sustain the intense, long-term relationships required in a creative endeavor? Leaders must ascertain not just technical expertise but also personal qualities and "cultural fit."

A recurrent theme is that leaders look for people who show the potential to be leaders themselves. They are eager to surround themselves with people who are more talented than they are. They seek self-directed learners, problem-finders and problem-solvers who like to grapple with matters of considerable scale and scope. They want initiative-takers, people who are sent out to fish for a flounder and come back with a whale; those who are willing to make the big bets.

These leaders have learned to cope with, and even be invigorated by, the stresses of ambiguity, conflict, overload, and risk. Hirschhorn suggests that a promise often associated with the new model of flat and lean corporations in which the boundaries (of hierarchy, function and geography) have been eradicated is that these companies will become "one big happy family."[8] This notion is not only unrealistic but undesirable. Just because work roles are no longer defined by the formal organizational structure does not mean that differences in authority, skill, talent, and perspective disappear. In the boundaryless organization, new challenges arise: "Who is in charge of what? Who does what? What's in it for us? Who is and isn't us?" Conflict among the different constituencies in an organization can be healthy and productive; indeed, diversity and conflict are essential ingredients for creativity and innovation.

> *Conflict among the different constituencies in an organization can be healthy and productive.*

Not everyone, however, can thrive in such environments. People who can make it in these organizations of collective genius have learned how to maintain their independence while also learning how to collaborate. They are people with the talent of a soloist, but the temperament of an orchestra player – in the opinion of many, a rare breed.[9] Finally, they must be builders, individuals who can commit and persevere, "push and push to see the vision through" and go the unexpected extra mile.

Unleashing and harnessing the collective genius

Once leaders know what they want to build (have clarified the vision), once they have acquired the right building blocks/materials (collected the talent), they have to actually put up the building (execute the vision). This is largely a process of shaping the collective or the soft side of an enterprise: the culture and processes, and the structure.

Shaping the culture and processes: The creative process as managing paradox

Unleashing and harnessing the genius of the collective is hard work because it is a process of managing paradox. Four conflicting tensions – or paradoxes – at the heart of the process of collective genius must be understood, accepted, and as much as possible balanced:

(i) embrace individual differences *and* collective identity and goals (the one outlined earlier in the discussion of the creative process);

(ii) foster support *and* confrontation among members of the collective;

(iii) focus on performance *and* learning and development;

(iv) balance the leader's authority *and* the discretion and autonomy of the members of the collective.[10]

i) Embrace individual differences and collective identity and goals

The first paradox is the need to embrace individual differences while pursuing collective identity and goals. As discussed earlier, the creative process demands a mix of diverse individuals. For the collective to benefit from this diversity by drawing on each individual's talents, there needs to be a process that allows for varied perspectives, priorities, and styles. The only way these voices can be expressed and heard is to treat people fairly, which means to treat people differently. To the extent that these different voices are in fact brought out into the open and adaptations made, there will inevitably be conflict and perhaps competition among team members. Too much conflict and competition can lead to a "win/loss" mindset instead of a problem-solving collaborative approach to working out issues. Thus, the leader's task is to integrate the individual differences and mobilize them in pursuit of the common vision. Creative collectives allow for individual difference and freedom, yet have in place super-ordinate goals to which all members are committed.

ii) Foster support and confrontation among members

If member diversity is to be acknowledged and differences of opinion encouraged, the collective must develop a culture of trust in which members will want to support one another. In such a culture, members are cohesive. They are genuinely interested in what others think; they are willing to listen to and clarify what is being said. They are open to accepting the leadership and influence of others whose expertise, information, or experience are relevant to the decision or task at hand. Members inquire of each other as much as they advocate, adopting a more Socratic method of mutual coaching and learning.

However, if the members become *too* supportive of one another, they may stop confronting each other. In very cohesive groups, strong norms to preserve harmonious and friendly relationships can evolve and "groupthink," as opposed to critical thinking, can occur. Members will stop giving their opinions on each other's decisions and actions, suppressing their thoughts and feelings, sometimes at considerable personal cost. They will end up making decisions with which some individuals privately disagree because no one wants to be responsible for creating conflict. Creativity cannot happen when groups move to a "weighted average" approach.

If such behavior persists, the collective will over time demand narrow conformity from its members, which will inhibit the free exchange of ideas and the team's ability to adapt. If and when a dispute finally comes out into the open, members are likely to become polarized around the particular issue; because of their pent-up frustration, they will just want to "get their way" instead of problem-solving the matter constructively. Creative collectives will find a way to allow conflict to be expressed without it being too disruptive.

iii) Focus on performance and learning and development

The third paradox is focussing simultaneously on current performance, and learning. Producing results today, while equally stressing innovation for tomorrow, is not easy, given the pressures of the competitive environment. Start-ups are all too aware of the need to be frugal with their resources as they make trade-offs between short-term financial goals and long-term investments.

With the most important investment, people, the trade-offs are especially difficult. Leaders must frequently choose between the short-term solution of filling a position with someone who already knows how to do a task, versus the longer term solution of providing someone else with the opportunity to learn it. Mistakes have to be treated as sources of learning rather than reasons for punishment if risk-taking and hence development and innovation are to be encouraged. "Supportive autonomy" is the name of the game. Individuals are held accountable to high standards, but a joint problem-solving approach is adopted when the inevitable missteps occur. Moreover, people are encouraged to take charge of their own development and become "perfect protégés" whom others will want to mentor.[11]

iv) Balance the leader's authority and member discretion and autonomy

The fourth paradox involves achieving a delicate balance between the authority of the leader and the discretion and autonomy of the other members of the collective. Leaders cannot delegate final accountability for the team's performance, and delegation does not mean giving up control. The more autonomy members have, the more important it is that they be committed to a common vision. More creative collectives will tend to be flexible, balancing authority between the leader and the other members in ways best suited to the issue at hand. Some decisions are made by consensus. Some are made through negotiations between the leader and others most directly affected. Others are made in a consultative manner, with the leader getting input from the members and discussing alternatives with them, while retaining the role of ultimate decision-maker. And, finally, some decisions are made by the leader without consultation with members.

What is crucial is that the leader has enough credibility that others are comfortable with whatever process is chosen. In fact, in well-functioning collectives in which there is a high degree of mutual trust, leaders are given more latitude to decide things without having to explain or justify their actions. By contrast, in collectives where there is little trust, members will question even the most innocent or innocuous suggestion the leader makes.

Shaping the structure: An action orientation

Along with the culture and processes, another part of the collective to be shaped is structure. Historically, structure has not been thought of as the soft side of an organization. But leaders involved in the architecture of collective genius do see it that way. They have an action-orientation to structure. To paraphrase Nitin Nohria, who has written extensively on the structure of global organizations and knowledge management, they have moved from structure to structuring.[12] Based on two questions, leaders continually adapt the shape and size of the collective:

- What vital decisions must be made or activities carried out for the company to flourish?
- Where does the necessary expertise reside?

Based on the answers to these questions, organizations put together semi-permanent groupings of the appropriate individuals.

Many companies are beginning to adopt a model rather similar to that of independent movie production companies. Their structures are chameleon-like as they adapt to the needs of the ever-changing line-up of insiders and outsiders (freelance artists and technicians) involved in a particular production. Positions often cut across traditional boundaries. Work assignments are more project-like, flexible, and involve multi-tasking (qualities that, research shows, make the position intrinsically motivating). They often reflect shared accountabilities because the scale or scope of the task is bigger than one person.

Suzanne de Passe, the CEO of de Passe Entertainment and Creative Partners, who is respected for both her creative vision and business acumen, wanted to create an "artist's company." Unlike most production companies, executives in her organization had both development and production responsibilities. Although this practice sometimes slowed them down, de Passe believed the bottlenecks forced them to take the time to consider carefully those issues relevant to artistic quality. As de Passe explained: "We're like a bowl of spaghetti. Given our small size, we have to tap into one another's varied strengths." De Passe wanted her organization to operate more like a "tennis-doubles team" or an "improvisational jazz ensemble," to use Peter Drucker's analogy for self-managed work teams.[13] Only the team performs; individual members contribute. Team members cover their teammates, adjusting as necessary to their teammates' talents and weaknesses and to the changing demands of the task – a common feature of early-stage companies when resources of all types are tight. As de Passe and her colleagues can attest, the requirements for tennis-double type teams are quite stringent, demanding intense commitment, mutual expectations, mutual trust, and mutual influence.

More and more, even large multinational companies are moving toward organizational structures and job designs analogous to those found in de Passe's company. At companies like Intel, Monsanto and Nickelodeon Latin America, people are placed in "two-in-a-box" arrangements – two people with complementary skills (e.g. a marketing and a production specialist; a futurist and a details-oriented pragmatist) share the responsibilities of one role. This form is used at all levels, among other things to start up a new product or service requiring a broad bandwidth of skills and styles, or to smooth managerial transitions and groom successors. Indeed, we are even seeing more examples of co-CEO arrangements like that of John Reed and Sandy Weill at Citigroup.

James Kralik and Hamilton Tang at Lark International Entertainment Ltd. are ideal examples of leaders who have structured their organization to tap into collective genius. Lark operates 18 multiplex cinemas in Hong Kong, Taiwan, Singapore, Malaysia, and the People's Republic of China. In addition to operating cinemas, Lark is involved in automated tele-ticketing, Chinese-language film production and distribution, and family amusement centers. With revenues of more than US$50million, the company has produced a 30+ percent annual return for its shareholders since Kralik joined Lark in 1993. Tang, a fellow graduate of Harvard Business School who was working at Morgan Stanley in Hong Kong, joined in 1996.

As he thought about building an executive team that would allow Lark to expand throughout Asia, Kralik imagined the following:

> "I wanted to build a close-knit corporate team that could function effectively in a wide variety of roles. It's a challenge to bring good people together who can operate without a great deal of support. The chemistry had to be perfect. I had always been convinced that only groups of people could accomplish great things. You can break one stick, but not a bunch tied together. I wanted to create an environment that everyone would find rewarding while giving them responsibilities that would benefit their long-term development. This meant finding the best people who would bring out the best in each other and have fun together. As I met each potential hire, I explained that whatever we did, we would do it well. I wanted the company to become a leader – a model organization. We were not going to be satisfied with mediocrity."

Although it would take Kralik three years to convince Tang to join his entrepreneurial adventure officially, Kralik knew that Tang was the one. Kralik wanted a partner in the fullest sense of the word; Tang would have the same economic stake in the company. Over the years he kept Tang abreast of his activities, the good and the bad, and even set aside an office for him. He felt Tang would fit into the company, and that they were on the same wavelength and had different types of expertise.

In the first week of working together, Kralik hired a contractor to tear down the wall between his and Tang's offices and replace it with glass. He asked that, in addition, a sliding glass window be installed between his desk and Tang's. He shared his reasoning:

> "It is important not to have a closed environment. We are like two trains going full-steam with a tenuous link between us. Having a wall between us just does not work. This sliding glass window helps us to make sure that we do not go off in

different directions . . . Most of the time the window is open, and we just try to function. We give each other space, but we are also co-dependent since we hand things back and forth. That dynamic works very well, and we try to pass it on to the rest of the team. While they do not do it as often because they tend to be focussed on one project for longer periods of time, they still need to work together in a seamless, organized way."

As they both admit, their partnership, like strong marriages, is not without fireworks at times. Some of the best marriages are made up of "the odd couple of ego equals," in which the partners have complementary talents and styles and are secure enough to accept their weaknesses and let their partners compensate as necessary.

Building the corporate culture of their dreams as they work across nations has been a complicated process. Some employees have been uncomfortable with the level of freedom and ambiguity, and have chosen to leave. Others, like Kralik's assistant, have been attracted to Lark for precisely these reasons, and have grown to find it a wonderful place to work:

> "In most Chinese companies, there are endless rules and ceilings that prevented me from taking on new responsibilities. But that is not true here. Jim wanted me to take initiative. He was kind and when we quarreled or I made a mistake, we talked about it as friends. From the Chinese point of view, this was very unusual because it ignored the strict guidelines that should exist between colleagues. If subordinates speak too directly to a boss, they could be fired. However, with Jim there are no boundaries. He expects me to share all my opinions frankly so things can get done. Work here is not just about pay, but also fun and spiritual support."

A PRIME EXAMPLE OF EXECUTING COLLECTIVE GENIUS

Creating collective genius is such a formidable task that it is not surprising that most new ventures fail. Their leaders are simply not up to the challenge. In my travels around the globe I have had the good fortune to meet some of those leaders who are determined to rise to the occasion. Thus far we have seen collective genius in the software, investment, oil, and entertainment industries. Let us now turn to Mark Levin, the CEO of Millennium Pharmaceuticals, the leader who most readily springs to my mind as a practitioner of collective genius. What better industry than biotechnology to represent the result of collective genius in our recent history and how it will continue to unfold in the 21st century? Biotechnology is a new industry just coming into its own, but the risks and the rewards are already legendary.[14] Of the 1300 biotechnology companies today, 350 are public, and approximately ten have been able to deliver products to the marketplace.

Although Levin and his colleagues are not among that select group, many experts believe they are in an unparalleled position to commercially exploit their hot scientific ideas in the near future. This is because, as Levin explains, Millennium is a magic combination of a "great place with great people who do great things." Levin unhesitatingly outlines the matters to which he devotes his attention and the drivers of the company's success – "our vision, our people talent and our creative environment." These parallel exactly the three leadership responsibilities we have been exploring throughout this chapter. To illustrate just how difficult leadership as collective genius is, let us look in some detail at Levin and Millennium. We must consider not just what they are doing, but also how they are doing it; that is, shaping the soft side of the company to unleash and harness collective genius.

MARK LEVIN AND MILLENNIUM PHARMACEUTICALS

In 1993, Millennium was formally founded on the premise that technologies developed to elucidate the human genome could, at the same time, be applied to the discovery of previously unknown genes and corresponding proteins that would be targets for novel disease therapies. Levin and his founding scientific advisors began to work out both the vision and Millennium's particular competitive advantage. As Levin said:

> "Our vision is to go beyond genomics. Genomics has spawned a transformation of the biological sciences involving parallel revolutions in information sciences, micro-miniaturization and automation. This powerful combination of technologies is allowing scientists to understand life and disease processes at the molecular level in a way never before possible. Millennium will be a leader in this revolution with a high throughput, integrated science and technology platform that could transform discovery across the life sciences and enable Millennium to realize its ultimate vision of transcending the limits of medicine."

Execution: A management quagmire

To execute this vision, Millennium has become a "small complex company," as are most of the organizations designed to cope with the four paradoxes of collective genius. Levin described the company and its structure by making a series of drawings that are reproduced in Fig. 4.1. The "vision structure" is meant to reflect Millennium's business model to leverage its gene-to-patient technology platform, in order to generate a diverse portfolio of therapeutic and diagnostic products, at minimal expense to shareholders.

Defining the "collective" at Millennium is not easy. With an abundance of partners and projects under development, Millennium's organizational structure is understandably complex and ever evolving. Counting over 900

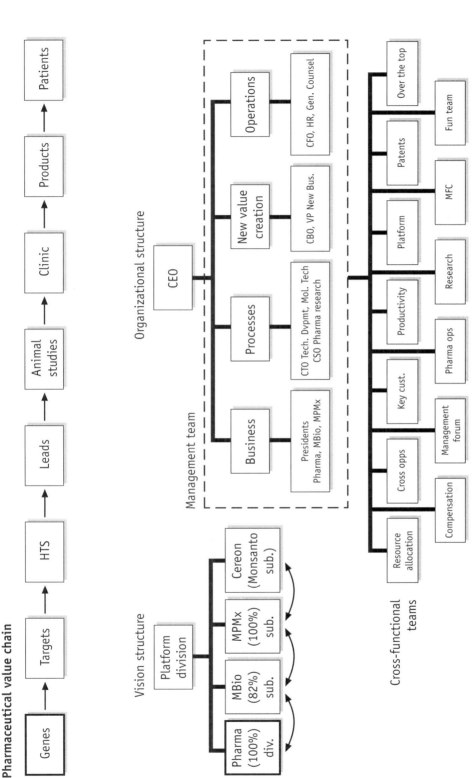

Fig. 4.1 Levin's drawings to describe Millennium's task, vision, and organization

employees by the end of 1999, Millennium is arranged as a "family of innovative companies" that focus on different aspects of the pharmaceutical value chain. As shown in Fig 4.1, the platform and Pharma form the basic divisions of Millennium, while MBio, and MPMx are subsidiaries with their own presidents and company stock, independent of the parent company. Cereon is a wholly-owned Monsanto subsidiary that is located within Millennium. To further complicate who is "in" the collective, Millennium has a series of strategic alliances, which, in an industry characterized by long development cycles and high failure rates, are an important way to acquire capabilities and much needed capital. These "over-the-top" alliances, with funding commitment that far surpasses Millennium's nearest rivals, testify to the perceived quality and depth of Millennium's technology platform.

The company depends on knowledge and technology transfer among talented specialists, and is therefore very team/matrix-oriented to channel individual and collective expertise where it is needed. Because of the nature of the work, Millennium has evolved a highly personalized strategy of knowledge management.[15] Managers rely heavily upon face-to-face interactions and work hard to create the appropriate forums to facilitate dialog and debate, exchange both explicit and tacit knowledge, and achieve the deeper creative insights that come from the give and take of talented colleagues struggling with a problem. Their best meetings take on the tenor of a laboratory seminar in which substance, not style, matters, and junior and senior people offer ideas, raise the fundamental questions and engage in hard-nosed but constructive critique. The "organizational structure" illustrates the cross-functional teams that report to the management team on a regular basis. These teams, each with its own charter and goals, are critical to cross-organizational communication, collaboration and delegation. The teams are often large; more than 30 people from across the company might be working on one alliance at a given time. To encourage people to think about what is best for the company and not simply about their immediate project, people are encouraged to "wear multiple hats:" As Levin says:

> "We allow people to participate in cross-functional teams across the company in a very, very complicated and integrated matrix organization. Every scientist, clinician, business person is on a variety of different teams that are responsible for developing products, developing technology or managing partnerships. So they get a tremendous breadth of experience quickly and a day-to-day understanding of how the company works. We have active internal transfers across the divisions and subsidiaries."

Levin strives to create an inclusive learning environment in which very little is confidential (except for the proprietary information that cannot be shared across corporate partners). The arrows in Fig. 4.1 indicate the permeable boundaries that ensure that all the specialized knowledge individuals have is shared and mobilized toward the collective vision. Some of their partners (who are also competitors) have full-time people who live and work inside the Millennium walls. Levin never refers to "insiders" and "outsiders" in his discussions of the company and its many partners. But he is not naïve; he fully understands that his approach is risky, that these individuals represent their companies and are monitoring and reporting back what and how well Millennium is doing. But he also knows that he has to accept this trade-off since information-sharing and knowledge management across the company are critical to Millennium's success. This approach will keep Millennium on the cutting edge, aware of disruptive technologies[16], and it will make it better, faster, and cheaper than its competitors in the drug development race.

The nuts and bolts of investing in people

Finding and enabling people to pursue such an audacious vision in such a complex structure requires a great deal of time and energy. It is not surprising that Levin spends 40 percent of his time on what he refers to as "organizational development:" selection, development, and empowerment of people.

As we saw with Haykin, Bernabè, and the InterSoft and Lark partners, Levin searches out talent and builds his collective carefully and deliberately. Levin has recognized the importance of strong people from the very beginning, and built the company around a core of four leading scientists he knew would not only provide the scientific expertise for the company but would help to attract other leading talent. Around this core, Levin and his colleagues remain actively engaged in attracting talent, both strategic partners and individuals: scientists, clinicians, and business people. More than 30 countries are represented on the Millennium staff, and three of its partners are non-US based companies. What he is trying to build is a mosaic, not a melting pot; both the whole and the pieces are evaluated and assessed at once. Everyone, from the junior research associate to the general manager of a division, goes through a rigorous hiring process in which Levin tries to participate. Technical talent is not enough; recruits have to have a "good culture match." Although Millennium looks for people with diverse backgrounds and perspectives, they are not open to people with different core values. As Levin explains: "We let people be who they really are, so we have to make sure that who they are really fits the mission." Millennium, therefore, does extensive reference checks to assess people's leadership skills, how they interact with others, and how they have worked with and motivated others in the past. "We look for people who have created environments that have allowed others to excel and to do great things."

Again, like the successful leaders we have seen earlier, Levin understands that leaders and creators are born, then made. He is prepared to make the investment in their development. Among the clinicians and scientists he interviews, he has difficulty finding "people who are willing to commit a significant part of their time to building a great company" (as opposed to scientific matters). In addition, like most new technology companies, Millennium suffers particularly from a shortage of people with the kind of business acumen and execution skills that come with extensive operating experience usually gained in large companies. But many individuals from large companies find it difficult to thrive in Millennium's entrepreneurial culture. As a consequence, Millennium has a cadre of organizational development experts who teach, coach and bring in outside experts to offer a mini-university. They design programs and processes such as town meetings and frequent off-site visits to encourage open communication and dialog about the company vision and what is happening in the larger business and scientific environment.

Finally, and perhaps most importantly, people at Millennium are empowered. Levin learned the importance of delegation while working in large companies. Although he might be viewed by some as "hands-on," he is eager to share the potential to have influence with all the members of the Millennium collective. Talented people are always pushing for that next challenge and opportunity to grow. Levin understands that the more talented the people are, the more they want to contribute and the more they desire personal leadership opportunities. Career development, making sure people continually grow and stretch themselves, is a corporate priority.

Even very young people have the opportunity to make some significant commitments and decisions for the company. Their career aspirations and developmental needs have to be carefully balanced with shorter-term performance objectives. The human resource staff make sure that performance appraisals are done to help people develop appropriate career expectations and get the developmental experiences they need. Needless to say, the talented do not always take kindly to learning of their personal limits, and that they are not quite ready for that next big assignment.

You cannot have empowerment without controls. It is clear at Millennium that duties and obligations come with the rights and privileges of empowerment. People are held accountable, and scientific integrity is key. Millennium's partners expect them to deliver and to deliver big. Millennium's controls are communicated mainly through the soft stuff such as vision and culture (although efforts are made to make sure the hard stuff, such as compensation and information technology, are appropriately aligned). People know what their priorities are. Thanks to the rigorous selection, development and knowledge management processes, they have very high personal standards and the information and expertise they need to make important judgement calls. With rapid growth and a constant influx of new projects, however, it is becoming harder and harder to hold people accountable for their promises.

Millennium is an invigorating – but not necessarily an easy – place to work. Biotechnology is a very unforgiving, competitive industry. Managing rapid internal growth and a complex set of multinational alliances, with all the attendant travel, can lead to burnout. And as described earlier, the creative process is inherently emotionally charged, with peaks and valleys. Life at Millennium can be stressful. Company-wide surveys are done regularly to discern commitment to core values, perceived culture, and views on career development. It is imperative that Millennium acknowledges and addresses the anxieties that come with working in such an entrepreneurial, creative setting, and makes sure the appropriate balances are being struck with regard to the four creativity paradoxes. The "Fun Team" is always busy, planning scavenger hunts and weekly company parties, among other events. The company attracts the best in a very competitive labor market, not only because it does great science, but also because it has a reputation as a great place to work. The company vision, structure, and environment all combine to unleash the entrepreneurial power of creativity. The challenge ahead for Levin and Millennium will be to know when and in what ways to reconstitute and reconfigure the shape of the enterprise to maintain the collective genius at the heart of their competitive advantage.

WHERE ARE THE LEADERS OF THE FUTURE?

John Kotter declared that in the latter half of the 20th century many companies were overmanaged and underled; management is about coping with complexity while leadership is about coping with change.[17] Global competitiveness has raised the stakes and leadership and management have become ever more crucial and ever more difficult. Leaders must be able to synthesize diverse ideas and share their vision and values with diverse others across the world. Great vision and strategy without great execution will kill an enterprise. Even young, small companies present significant management challenges, given their complex flexible architectures.

The biggest obstacle to launching a successful company is no longer attracting financial capital but attracting intellectual capital. Ann Winblad, an influential entrepreneur and venture capital leader in technology, looks for three things when deciding whether or not to invest in a company – market opportunity, the capacity to deliver product, and the ability of the entrepreneur to sustain excellence and grow new leaders.[18] Leaders who can manage talent and grow a company are so hard to

> *The biggest obstacle to launching a successful company is no longer attracting financial capital but attracting intellectual capital.*

find. She and her partners see their job as simultaneously building leaders and building companies around significant market opportunities.

In this chapter I have introduced you to some of those leaders in the making. They are translating their personal values into calculated and sustained action by building collective genius. None claims to have it completely right, but they are determined to get it right. What qualities do they have in common that give them the wherewithal to transform their dreams into reality?

As we have seen, they are visionaries. They can take in the opportunities and challenges associated with being in a global social, economic and political world. They are 360-degree thinkers who can cope with cognitive complexity and can unravel complex issues to their core. It is probably not accidental that Levin, whom *The Economist* declares to be the leading practitioner of biotechnology, is not really a biotechnologist at all, nor even a bench scientist. He was a chemical engineer and worked in process control for companies as varied as Miller Brewing, Eli Lilly, and Genentech, one of the first and most successful biotechnology companies. Before starting Millennium, Levin spent seven years at the Mayfield Fund, a venture capital firm. Based on his generalist background and cross-disciplinary web of relationships, Levin could imagine and communicate a new direction based on a unique combination of scientific and technological innovations. Interestingly, having served many times as interim CEO of other start-ups, Levin found himself even seduced by the opportunities Millennium represented. It was, he explained, the "breadth of the vision, ultimately going into the genome to find out the causal pathways of many human diseases – what could be more exciting scientifically?"

These leaders can cope with the dualities of leading collective genius because they see the world in shades of gray, not black and white, and yet can be decisive and take big risks. Their awareness of their personal values – what Bernabè referred to as his "inner compass" – lets them navigate and make the exacting trade-offs associated with collective genius. Because they are committed to their values, they are builders and investors. They are not interested in the "get rich quick" approach, but in sustainability, thus they take the time to lay a solid foundation for their companies. While riding on a train across China when he was in his early 20s,

> *Leaders can cope with the dualities of leading collective genius because they see the world in shades of gray, not black and white, and yet can be decisive and take big risks.*

Kralik wrote down his personal goals, which included making a substantial impact on international co-operation and making a positive difference in the daily lives of those with whom he came into contact. He keeps a list of these goals, to which he refers almost weekly, on his desk at Lark.

In meeting with the leaders discussed here, I was struck by their inquisitiveness, the vivacity of their imagination, and their reflective nature. Most are voracious readers (from history and philosophy to the popular press) and travelers, always scanning the world for great ideas and seizing opportunities to observe and interact with talented people. Bernabè told the story of how one of his colleagues asked him why he was always wasting his time thinking about the capabilities of his laptop. Shouldn't he be leaving that to his chief technology officer? Bernabè told him that understanding how a laptop worked was part of his job in creating Eni's culture. "How should people in our organization connect with one another? What could be more important than finding the answer to that question?"

If these leaders have one trait in common, it is that they are insatiable learners. There is a humility about them; they feel privileged to lead. As de Passe put it: "I am here to serve and remove impediments." Bernabè often walked to work or rode his bicycle, and people frequently commented that he was rather shy. Levin has one of the smaller offices in the company, wears jeans to work most days, and interacts freely with people at all levels in the company.

Fundamentally, they are comfortable with sharing power. Despite all the talk about empowerment, many people are too afraid to give up the control it implies. These leaders are secure in themselves; they know their strengths and weaknesses. They know they don't have to have all the answers. They surround themselves with great people who can cover for them when necessary. They are committed to work on themselves and improve their talents. They have the psychological and emotional maturity to weather the entrepreneurial storm. They are often calm when others would be overwhelmed.[19]

The bottom line is these leaders are an inspiration to be around because they truly believe in people. For them, leadership is about humanity, getting the very best out of people to make progress. They see the extraordinary in people whom most see as only ordinary. Let me quote one last leader, the legendary South African President Nelson Mandela, who has dedicated his life to unleashing the collective genius of his country's diverse population. He has been a leader in the 20th century whose wisdom and humanity will continue to be relevant in the next millennium:

> "A leader . . . is like a shepherd. He stays behind the flock, letting the most nimble go on ahead, whereupon the others follow, not realizing that all along they are being directed from behind."

THE DUALISTIC LEADER: THRIVING ON PARADOX

PAUL A.L. EVANS

Ten years ago, I was struggling late at night with a speech to conclude a conference on trends in human resource management in multinational corporations. Doodling the themes of the discussions on paper, a pattern suddenly jumped out. For every business leader talking about the need for vision, someone else emphasized with equally potent logic the necessity for bottom-line business pragmatism. There were companies that were decentralizing, arguing for customer-oriented entrepreneurship. But they were counterbalanced by an equal number arguing for centralized business control in order to exploit economies of scale. If the arguments on the need for accountability were appealing, there was a reminder in one firm of what happens when accountability drives out teamwork – as the senior executives watched one of their major businesses go down the tube to the lament of "What a pity that Joe's messed it up . . . but he's accountable."

The Eastern Tao had recognized this many centuries before, Hegel and Jung had wrestled with the implications, and Toynbee had seen this in the decline and fall of empires throughout history. But this was my own recognition that we have moved into a world where the leadership challenge is that of navigating between opposites.

Robert Quinn at the University of Michigan had a similar experience when trying to make sense out of data on organizational effectiveness, a domain that had perplexed researchers. Once again, the pattern jumped out at him. Effectiveness is difficult to understand because it is inherently paradoxical. To be effective, an organization must possess attributes that are contradictory, even mutually exclusive. He called these attributes competing values – control and flexibility, internal and external focus, means and ends orientation.[1] Today they are becoming institutionalized in the shape of balanced scorecards for measuring performance which portend the shape of 21st century management.

Most senior executives today recognize these dualities, as I call them, when they talk about the difficult balancing acts in their roles. Charles Hampden-Turner calls them dilemmas and they create the paradoxes that Charles Handy has also described.[2] In our own studies, we have found most of the problems and frustrations that people experience are the consequence of such dualities. The new century will be an era where we learn how to harness the tensions that they create rather than being subject to them.

STEERING THROUGH THE PENDULUMS

Opposite forces create paradoxes, seemingly contradictory statements that are more or less true. You cannot make these paradoxes disappear, you cannot resolve them or solve them, they do not go away.

In the past, they have expressed themselves as leisurely swings of the pendulum, cycles of evolution and revolution that the academics called "punctuated equilibrium." One could ride these swings, rather like the investor who senses the bear market and sells short, and leadership careers have been made on this ability. An organization decentralizes, releasing a flood of entrepreneurial energy. The name of the game is to recognize the ills that this can eventually bring – empire building, not invented here, slow adjustment to big strategic changes – and to argue for the opposite, re-centralization. When the pendulum does begin to swing, you will be recognized as a foresighted hero and promoted as the savior. But an acute sense of timing is needed – argue too early for the opposite and you will be ejected as a tiresome troublemaker; argue too late, and you have missed the boat.

Recently I attended a discussion with a Nobel prize-winning economist who was enlightening we mortal academics on how to make it in research. In the post-war era of government intervention in all quarters, his data led him to believe in the power of unregulated market forces. Result? Derision by the establishment, ejection by established universities, but stick with it . . . and one day the pendulum swings and you are acknowledged as a foresighted hero.

However, those who preach the virtues of unbridled capitalism should beware since the excesses seem to be swinging the pendulum the other way. One of the laws of duality is that if you take anything to an extreme, you create a pathology. It is the hero's trap that has led to many a decline.

In recent decades we have seen waves of business solutions, swinging the pendulum from soft "profit-through-people" to hard re-engineering, from bottom-line restructuring to "competing for the future." Today those pendulums are swinging so fast that you can get caught by the rebound while still in the same job. We get impatient with the transparently short-term careerist leader, the person who starts off a new strategy, begins to get visible short-term results, and then rides the acclaim to another site, leaving a successor to take the firm in a different direction. We are equally impatient with the J-curve promises of those leaders with grandiose but hollow visions because they cannot manage the today that is so different from their appealing tomorrow. The leaders we admire are the Jack Welch (GE) and the Percy Barnevik (ABB), who seem to be able to steer constructively to the long term via the short term.

Competition yachting might be a good training ground for leaders. The job of the skilled helmsperson is to manage a constant but shifting tension between the need to maintain a particular course and the changing winds and current.[3] Steered by a skilled person, the path of the boat toward its destination is a series of controlled curves according to wind and current. The unskilled helmsperson fights to maintain a course, overcorrecting when the boat is blown off route, failing to anticipate the storms and calms that lie ahead. The resulting path is a series of excessive zigzags that slow down progress to the destination.

Navigating between short-term imperatives and long-term goals, between functional excellence and interfunctional co-ordination, between low cost and high quality, is the skill of leadership. Some firms focus on a timely strategy but get fixated. For example, they align the firm around the development of functional excellence, leading to initial success. But when that success is threatened by opposing pressures (slow decision making due to lack of co-ordination), the leaders respond by reinforcing what led them to be successful in the first place (heightened pressure for functional excellence). This leads to a vicious circle of threat, reinforced efforts, and further threat, culminating in crisis. A savior is recruited whose strategy is teamwork . . . and the fixated cycle may begin again in the opposite direction.

In contrast, the leaders of other firms can anticipate the needed change in course, gently steering specialized functions toward greater teamwork before the problems of slow decision making show up. Alternating between one course and the other, they steer toward their aims of higher profits and better return on investments in a virtuous spiral of increasing capabilities in both functional excellence and integrated teamwork.[4]

The pattern of polarized fixation typifies the 20th century. Danny Miller calls it the "Icarus phenomenon," others call it "the failure of success."[5] Miller's analysis of the rise and fall of corporations such as ITT, TI, Litton, IBM, and A&P leads him to expect that outstanding firms will perfect what led them to be successful until they reach dangerous extremes, ultimately leading to trajectories of decline. He looks at the focussed craftsman, with a single-minded orientation on cost leadership (TI) or quality (Digital), the inventive pioneer (Apple), and the salesman with genius in marketing and image management

(IBM, P&G). Each of these corporations brilliantly executed an appropriate strategy, developing a distinctive competence that led to their initial success. But when the winds began to change and that success came under threat, their leaders intensified the focus on that capability rather than turning to develop complementary strengths. The cost leadership of the craftsman becomes miserly obsession that drives away any talent in marketing or design. Pioneers become escapists who retreat into their own game, and image replaces substance in the salesman. As the vicious circle accelerates, pride becomes obsession, focus becomes machine-like order with the suppression of any dissent, strategy becomes recipe – the polarization that portends impending crisis.

Opposing forces such as differentiation and integration, external and internal orientation, hierarchy and network, short term and long term, change and continuity can never be reconciled once and for all. They create tensions. As Richard Pascale rightly comments, there are many tensions in organizations that should never be resolved – the tension between cost control and quality, or between manufacturing efficiency and customer service, or local and global orientation.[6] I dislike the terms of "balance," "resolution," or "reconciliation of opposites" that are often used; they are too static, there is no energy in balance, and it is most uncomfortable to try to sit on the fulcrum.

Since the future is always in the present, we can see in some of today's examples the path that lies ahead. Let us look at the way in which some leaders try to harness the tensions of those opposites.

A WALK THROUGH THE WORLD OF PARADOX

L'Oréal is a company that recognizes the importance of duality and tension. It is the world's leading firm in the toughly competitive cosmetics industry, and the most consistently profitable corporation in France. The culture of l'Oréal is based on the foresighted values of the founding family last century, "Etre poête et paysan en même temps" – to be at the same time the creative poet and the conservative peasant who hoards the centimes. The belief that growth and profits will come if we can combine creativity with sound financial management manifests itself in practices of tension management. Reminiscent of King Arthur's Round Table, l'Oréal uses "confrontation rooms" where all parties can gather round the table to freely explore decisions on, for example, the launch of a new product.

L'Oréal recognizes that one of the most important tensions is between the short-term "bottom line" and long-term development. It is not easy. There is a natural tendency in decision making to privilege the short term since it is so immediate and concrete. One area where this hurts many companies is people development. Faced with an immediate profit squeeze, the budgetary valve on recruitment, training and team development is turned off. Consequently the major constraint in boom times seven years later is that there are no skilled people in the pipeline to exploit those opportunities. Similarly it is tempting for business unit managers to cling to their best people rather than releasing them to other units, even though the price may be that these people ultimately get bored at lack of opportunity and leave the corporation to seek challenges elsewhere.

There are no magic policies that will resolve such dilemmas. Since the short term typically drives out the long term, the role of the human resource function at l'Oréal is to act as the guardians of the strategic and long-term perspective, especially concerning decisions about the recruitment, promotion and development of people. But it does not give human resources the right of veto, by waving some policy blue book. It gives them the right to stop the music, to say, "Time out folks! Let's look at the long-term arguments before we decide." Sometimes the decision may favor the short term, sometimes the long term, and sometimes a creative solution favoring both may be found.

The practice of l'Oréal illustrates what is critical to harness the tension between opposites, namely the capacity for constructive debate. It is perhaps the most characteristic quality of GE's Jack Welch.

> "Welch's decision-making methods have not changed much since his days at (GE) Plastics. He would corral everyone he could find who knew something relevant about the subject at hand – whether chemists, production engineers, or finance types – and thoroughly debrief them. He wanted on-the-spot answers, not formal, written reports. Then he would join his subordinates in fierce, no-holds-barred debates about which decision to make. Welch calls this 'constructive conflict.' His theory is that if an idea can't survive a spirited argument, the marketplace surely will kill it."[7]

Stanford's Kathy Eisenhardt has studied firms in hypercompetitive environments such as microcomputers where strategic windows open and close quickly and where the consequence of a bad strategic decision is that you are finished. Her findings are well summarized by the title of a recent article: "How management teams can have a good fight."[8]

Contrast this with today's reality. Andrew Kakabadse at Cranfield Business School has surveyed thousands of European management teams, finding that nearly 40 percent of them have serious and undiscussed differences of view about strategy and vision hidden under the table. It is not the fact that there are differences – these are the potential source of creative decision making – it is that these are not worked through. In those sterile Monday morning management meetings, constructive debate is a surprisingly rare commodity.

But a capacity for constructive debate is not sufficient. Ken Olsen, the founder of Digital Equipment, also believed in constructive conflict. His theory on how to build an organization was to create a family in which debate and conflict resolution were the primary ways of deciding what to do, also ensuring the commitment to implement those decisions. But this depends on people's relationships and trust. Digital's success led it to grow at such a pace that soon many people did not know and trust each other. The healthy debate degenerated into slow and politicized decision making, leading Digital to miss market windows, and to poor implementation of decisions.[9]

One duality leads to another. Digital might have avoided its crisis if Olsen had structured the firm into smaller business units, facing up to another fundamental duality of organization that takes different forms – centralization/decentralization, differentiation/integration, global/local. This is where the researchers look to ABB, a big firm of 210 000 people moulded 12 years ago by Percy Barnevik out of the merger of Swiss and Swedish competitors.

Barnevik believes decentralization is vital for customer orientation and local entrepreneurship. He contrasts his formative experiences in his family's printing firm, where everyone knew how important it was to get that order out, with his later jobs in large corporations where the head office bureaucracy holding the reins had never seen a customer. That belief in decentralization was carried to an extreme at ABB, structured into no less than 5000 business units with profit and loss responsibility. However, Barnevik believes equally strongly in exploiting the advantages of the big company – using common research and leveraging common customers, exploiting the economies of scale in manufacturing and distribution channels, transferring know-how and people, and exploiting the financial clout and visibility in emerging countries. As he puts it: "We want to be global and local, big and small, radically decentralized with central reporting and control. If we can resolve those contradictions we can create real organizational advantage."[10]

Decentralized business unit managers are responsible for their results but are also expected to collaborate if they want a future at ABB. The corporate "glue," as I have called it,[11] comes from the way in which performance is measured, from councils and boards, and rigorous attention to leadership development.

As globalization accelerates, it is vital that the leaders in such organizations have international experience. Matrix is not a structure, it is a frame of mind[12] fostered by diverse formative challenges, and without this managers will inevitably take one-sided decisions. Dan Karp, number two at Kodak, gave a good example. Kodak's organization until the mid-eighties had been structured around countries, which had made sense when the challenge was one of expanding market share on film around the world. But photographic film was becoming the more complex imaging industry, with different segments (the movie industry, medical imaging, professional markets) and new electronic imaging technologies. To manage this, Kodak sensibly decided to reorganize around worldwide product markets. "And we blew it," said Karp. Kodak put their most capable leaders into these new product division roles. However, with one exception none had ever worked outside the United States, and some had never ventured beyond the headquarters in Rochester, New York. With the best of intentions and full gusto, these new business managers swung the pendulum. "We effectively neutered those country managers and the local expertise around the world that had taken us 50 years to nurture," said Karp. The more capable the country staff, the more likely they were to feel frustrated at the insensitive decisions coming from Rochester.

Later, Karp found himself as regional head of Europe with the task of rebalancing the pendulum. He told me that his number one challenge was grooming his successor. "There's never been a European heading up Europe, and my predecessors never spent more than two to three years here. I had to find a European. But to function in this role, that European would have to prove him or herself as a product manager in Rochester, so it would be four years before I could move on." Never put a local manager into a job heading up a lead country unless they have proved themselves in a product or business unit role. And never put a person into a headquarters staff role unless they have successfully run a local subsidiary. That's how the matrix tension gets set in the mind.

Mobility is the vehicle for developing the perspective needed to lead effectively in this world of paradox. But again it is a two-edged sword, as one duality leads to another. A generation of leaders was mismanaged under a perversion of this logic taken to the extreme, and they in turn mismanaged their own firms. In the seventies and eighties many leading companies believed that future top managers had to have experience in the mother company and international operations, in different strategic functions, in staff roles as well as line roles. You could work it out mathematically, as I heard the heads of management development for IBM and Exxon doing. "If you accept that a person will move into general management around age 40, then you have to identify potential early and move them every two years." What is the result? Leaders who are superb in their grasp of strategy, but who have never executed anything. Leaders who are scintillating in the art of superficial socializing but shallow in human resource management since they have never been long enough in a position for the consequences of their actions affecting employees to catch up with them.

> *Mobility is the vehicle for developing the perspective needed to lead effectively in this world of paradox.*

We are obsessed with change these days. If we take note of how long that deep transformational change takes, we ought to balance this with an equal concern for continuity. I heard Jack Welch in 1991 commenting to his people at GE: "We started this in 1982, nine years ago. And we are 30 percent of the way there. We've done the easy 30 percent." Every time we move a person into a new leadership role, they try to initiate change since there are no brownie points for continuing to implement what your predecessor started off.

The challenge today is not change but continuity, or rather continuity in change. It is an age-old problem. What Gaius Petronius learned in AD 66 remains true: "We trained hard . . . every time we began forming up into teams, we would be reorganized. I was to learn later in life that we tend to meet any new situation by reorganizing . . . and a wonderful method it can be for creating the illusion of progress while producing inefficiency and demoralization."

One of the features of firms that I admire is the constructive tension found in their value systems. Some common value system is certainly necessary to provide the glue for a complex organization. But all too often those value systems are trite clichés that do not energize anything.

Contrast these lists with the credo of l'Oréal, where the value system is to try to combine the qualities of the poet and the cautious peasant, the long-term focus on innovation with the short-term focus on profits. Look at Welch's value system that emerged from his years with GE Plastics:

- practice planful opportunism
- wallow in information until you find the simple solution
- test ideas through constructive conflict
- treat all subordinates as equals, but reward each one strictly according to merit.[13]

AP Møller is a family-owned corporation, by far Denmark's largest, most profitable and most admired. A Fortune 100 corporation in size, with the world's largest shipping container company at its core, it also has successful sectors in shipbuilding, supermarkets and industrial products. The 86-year-old Maersk McKinney Møller, a legendary figure in Denmark, is passing the reins on to his successor. The corporate glue at AP Møller is an unwritten code of values that emerged out of the experience of Mr Møller and his father, the founder, and it is inculcated into every aspiring manager who joins the firm. Most of these values express the tensions of dualities. Mr Møller strongly believes in hiring and developing people for the long term rather than according to short-term budgetary constraints. But this implies paying meticulous attention to hiring and development practices, and he personally still keeps an eye on them – otherwise such hiring would lead to a vicious circle. He strongly believes that one's word is one's bond, that a promise must always be delivered. However, managers learn the implication – before committing oneself, such decisions should be carefully debated and exposed to criticism. Managers are obviously accountable for their own businesses, but not at the expense of the whole. They are expected to uphold the heritage of the group and its Danish roots, but also to build strong independent organizations in Asia and abroad. The hierarchic power of leadership should never become excessive; it is vital to treat others below with respect, to be accessible, and never to kill dissent.

James C. Collins and Jerry I. Porras found these dualistic values in their study of corporations that are "built to last."[14] They studied enduring companies like Citibank, 3M, Sony and Hewlett-Packard, firms that are more than 50 years old and have survived changes in product technologies and chief executives; gold medal companies with premier reputations which have outperformed solid but bronze medal competitors. The distinguishing quality characterizing these firms was their dualistic cultures and value systems. They had some purpose that went beyond profit, but they pragmatically pursued profit goals. Clear vision and sense of direction went hand in hand with constant experimentation and superb execution of the everyday workload.

HOW TO THRIVE IN A WORLD OF PARADOX

What advice would one provide to the current or aspiring leader about how to survive, and indeed thrive, in a world of tension and paradox?

Your assets are your potential liabilities

The respect and authority of others has to be earned. A track record of successful accomplishment (together with the capacity to learn from failures) builds up the credibility that encourages a following. This in turn reinforces the self-confidence that is the hallmark of leadership. If you are not totally confident in your own visions, how can you expect others to believe in them?

And here lies the trap. That very self-confidence when combined with the authority of leadership can create a pendulum swing toward failure. Manfred Kets de Vries and Danny Miller have called this the neurotic or dark side of leadership.[15] Confidence can so easily become arrogance. When that success is challenged, the qualities that led to success are accentuated, and the stress tips the behavior toward the obsessive. The capacity of a François Mitterrand for detached analysis becomes isolation, the ability of a Clinton to argue oneself out of difficult corners becomes the grounds for potential impeachment.

Leadership demands dedicated, indeed single-minded, pursuit of a goal at the expense of others. The paradoxical act of leadership is to believe in oneself . . . and yet still to maintain that element of doubt so that one will not lose contact with reality. It means tuning into what Carl Jung called the shadow self. Success may foster the ruthless, masculine, driving side of the self, but true leadership development means recognizing and allowing the softer, caring, feminine side to express itself as well. Any human quality taken to the extreme becomes pathological. Decisiveness is a virtue. But if it is not balanced with a measure of reflection, it leads to impulsiveness that can herald disaster. This is summed up by the 11 paradoxes of leadership that hang on the wall of every Lego manager's office (*see* Table 5.1).

> *Success may foster the ruthless, masculine, driving side of the self, but true leadership development means recognizing and allowing the softer, caring, feminine side to express itself as well.*

Manfred Kets de Vries asked ABB's Percy Barnevik to talk about his strengths and weaknesses.[16] Most people would single out his fast-thinking, analytical mind combined with his stupendous overview of ABB and the details of its operations. Yet he picks this out as his biggest weakness. The problem in being quick-thinking and fast-reacting, combined with the authority that goes with his role, is that people are intimidated and do not speak their minds. Often people say something that he clearly believes to be stupid. He has to discipline himself, smile and nod his head so as not to kill the expression of facts and dissent that is vital for sound decision making.

Table 5.1 The 11 paradoxes of leadership that hang on the wall of every Lego manager's office

- to be able to build a close relationship with one's staff . . . *and to keep a suitable distance*
- to be able to lead . . . *and to hold oneself in the background*
- to trust one's staff . . . *and to keep an eye on what is happening*
- to be tolerant . . . *and to know how you want things to function*
- to keep the goals of one's own department in mind . . . *and at the same time to be loyal to the whole firm*
- to do a good job of planning your own time . . . *and to be flexible with your schedule*
- to freely express your own views . . . *and to be diplomatic*
- to be a visionary . . . *and to keep one's feet on the ground*
- to try to win consensus . . . *and to be able to cut through*
- to be dynamic . . . *and to be reflective*
- to be sure of yourself . . . *and to be humble*

Don't be afraid of contradictions in yourself

Studies of leaders show that they cope well with, indeed thrive on, their own contradictions. They learn over the course of life to express and develop their shadow selves. Often this expresses itself as an oxymoron – the practical visionariness of Bill Gates, the ruthless charm and the planned opportunism of Jack Welch, the quick carefulness of Percy Barnevik.

The visionary ability of Bill Gates is legend; his capacity to foresee where technology is heading and to make abrupt changes in direction when he is mistaken, as when he recognized having missed the importance of the Internet. But the executives and technicians who work at Microsoft also comment on his command of financial and technical detail. What strikes those who know Jack Welch are the same paradoxical qualities:

> "His personality integrates many seeming contradictions. Welch has firm convictions about everything from corporate management to matters of right and wrong, yet he loves to listen and readily changes his mind. He is searingly analytical and intuitive at once . . . Unabashedly emotional, he can be enormously engaging in person, yet this warm and empathetic fellow has made decisions that caused enormous pain. During his years as CEO, Welch has evolved from a demanding boss to a helpful coach, from a man who seems hard, to one who allows his softness to show. That is part of what enabled him, long after he had gotten GE's businesses into shape, to win over GE's alienated employees."[17]

A few years ago I met the founder of Garantia, a diversified Brazilian group built around an investment bank that, prior to the stock market crash, was one of Latin America's fastest growing companies. He told us he had learned at an early age what others never learn or learn too late. "I have a good nose for opportunities," he said. "And when you see an opportunity, what do you want to do? You want to dive in and exploit it. I learned early to resist that temptation, though it was sometimes a struggle against myself." He told us that what he had learned is to try to find the best person to take advantage of that opportunity so as to free himself to look for the next opportunity. But how do you deal with your frustration, how do you maintain your nose for opportunities when you are letting others exploit them, we asked? It's lonely being one of those entrepreneurs that I've hired, he told us. They have to be confident and yet confront their doubts. So his role has been to act as the sparring partner to his entrepreneurs – never taking decisions for them but helping them to work out their decisions – and thereby maintaining subtle but deep control over his expanding operations. That is channeling contradiction into progress.

Team up with others who are different from yourself

Do not jump to the wrong conclusion, however. The price of trying to resolve and channel all of one's inner contradictions would probably be loss of personality. As Anthony Jay once put it, nobody is perfect . . . but a team can be.

As we move into the 21st century, leadership is becoming less an issue of the heroic person and more a question of teamwork. I have been struck by the number of organizations where if one looks at the leadership structure one finds not one person as the leader but a duo, a trio, or a team at the top. Would Hewlett-Packard exist today without the complementary leadership qualities of two very different people, the engineer's engineer and the manager's manager? Then there is Mr Honda, a crazy genius. Those familiar with the Honda story know that it was his partnership with Fujisawa, the hardheaded pragmatist, that explained how Honda successfully went against the might of the Japanese establishment. Sir David Scholey, former chairman of Warburg, freely concedes that the magic of the days when Warburg revolutionized the European invest-ment banking establishment stemmed from the complementary leadership qualities of Warburg and Grünefeld. Accor is the world's largest hotel company, run until last year by two-headed management, the founders Dubrule and Pélisson. The former is a strategy/marketing expert, the latter comes from administration/finance. But they complement each other in temperament. As Pélisson commented:

> "The combination works because Dubrule and I don't see everything through the same set of spectacles. When we agree on something, I believe we have nine chances out of ten to be right. When we disagree, then we know we have to pro-ceed carefully and take our time . . . So having a partner gives a certain balance. When only one person has all the power, he's tempted to use it."[18]

When I scrape below the surface of some heroic success within a corpora-tion, I typically find not a hero or heroine but a sparring partner relationship between very different people. Led by the Intel trio, Intel institutionalized this in a principle called "two-in-the-box," staffing key leadership positions where possible with a complementary duo. The company has abandoned this formal practice because while it may be great when it works, sometimes the chemistry isn't there. And open hostility or a vacuum in a shared leadership structure can be disastrous.

Tune into those dualities

I suspect that most problems and challenges in management and organization are the expression of duality. To test this out, I developed a methodology called "tension analysis." We have undertaken two such assessments, one with a European biotechnology company and the other with a division of a major Scandinavian corporation.

With the help of top management, we identified a small diagonal slice of 20 people in each firm. We interviewed them, with one simple request: "Tell us about all the problems, difficulties and frustrations that you experience in your work." From these interviews we were able to tease out about 30 tension points arising from dualities. Some were easy to identify, such as the frustration of slow decision making in a consensus-oriented culture; in other words, the tension between speed versus commitment in decision making. Others emerged from probing. For example, a manager might complain about the frustrations of working with an unreasonable boss whose only concern is measurable results. On further investigation, reinforced by other interviews, an underlying duality concerning performance evaluation emerged – emphasis on quantitative results versus the qualitative way in which those results were achieved.

These dualities were put into a questionnaire sent to all managers in the firm. A typical tension point was: "What should guide new product development? Market needs or biological research?" Or: "Who should be responsible for quality management? Line management or the QM function?" Response rates exceeded 90 percent, confirming our belief that this is an effective way of capturing the challenges that people experience. About 85 percent of them said these dualities accurately highlighted most of the problems and frustrations they experience in their work.

We worked through the results with the management teams. For example, new product development emerged in the biotechnology firm as an organizational capability to be carefully nurtured, a hard-to-imitate intangible asset. People had understood that collaboration between marketing and research was necessary for successful product development, sometimes favoring the market and sometimes the lab. On the other hand, the quality management issue was a divisive tension point that demanded attention. While a majority felt that the staff function should be responsible for quality, a significant minority felt this would create more staff bureaucracy and that quality should be the responsibility of every manager. The tension was eventually constructively resolved by continuing with the QM staff, but giving them a self-destruct assignment: "Your task within five years is to make sure that every manager is so competent in quality assurance that your function is no longer needed."[19]

The point here is not that one needs researchers to understand the organizational tension points, constructive and non-constructive. One simply needs to listen to people with the perspective of duality in mind. In that way, one learns the helmsperson's craft of managing paradox rather than falling unwittingly into the pendulum traps.

Organize one way, manage the other way

You cannot avoid pendulums, but the key is to avoid the pendulum swinging too far. When you are introducing a decentralized structure, what has to be in the back of the leader's mind is the opposite: How can I prevent duplication, reinventing the wheel, and all the losses of economies of scale and scope to which decentralization can lead? In other words, organize one way but manage the other way. When organizing the firm around product lines, what may have to be managed are the required relationships in particular countries or regions.

When introducing change, the deeper challenge is how to ensure the continuity that this change will need. I heard of a French change agent who tackled this well. Deep culture change in his firm was needed though it was controversial, and he would be subject to mandatory retirement as chief executive four years after initiating the change – not long enough for it to take root. He carefully recruited a vanguard of 20 key lieutenants at different levels of responsibility, indoctrinated them through personalized coaching, and gave them challenges so they could prove their credibility in the firm. Five years after he left, 15 of those individuals were continuing what he had started from key positions in the corporation.

> *When introducing change, the deeper challenge is how to ensure the continuity that this change will need.*

Nurture constructive tension

Virtually all the leaders I admire are people who nurture constructive tension, the sparring partner quality that is at the heart of those leadership duos. They pay great attention to orchestrating this in their organizations, and the structure of reporting lines, internal boards and councils creates a debating platform. This capacity to elicit constructive debate is a quality of Jack Welch, Bill Clinton, Tony Blair, Nelson Mandela, Percy Barnevik, and the millions of effective leaders at different levels of responsibility around the globe.

Then there are those leaders I admire less. They are undeniably successful (for the time being) but they are not admired by their followers, they cut off dialog and debate, and foster, perhaps unintentionally, a yes-man culture around them. Their leadership is built on fragile foundations.

At the heart of leadership is the ability to set goals and direction. If there is one thing that is clear from a century of leadership research it is this: leaders have a clear and often obsessive sense of what they want to achieve. And yet it is extraordinarily difficult to create a vision and set simple goals for a complex organization in a shifting, turbulent environment, and to instill a simple sense of direction out of all that complexity. Jack Welch's sense of direction for GE was not created in a day; it evolved over many years. How do such leaders do it? Analysis plays a role that is important but exaggerated. There is growing evidence that the core of the process is constructive debate.

A study undertaken by the oil company Exxon more than a decade ago is a good illustration. Exxon was breaking up its centralized bureaucracy so as to push responsibility down to business units, and top management knew that this required heightened leadership ability in the middle of the organization, not just at the top. An internal research team identified a group of excellent leaders in terms of their reputations, track records of results, and their ability to manage people. They put them under the microscope to find the common denominator. After batteries of psychological tests and 360° interviews with people who had worked with them, they found nothing in common. The person responsible for the study told me: "We looked for a common leadership style. But for every consultative person, we found someone for whom the name Attila the Hun would have been too kind a description of their leadership style!"

They looked deeper and eventually they could find only one common and distinguishing pattern: the process of goal-setting that these people went through when they moved into a new job. The first "100 days" in the new job consisted of three stages. The first was one of going around to talk with subordinates, clients, suppliers, superiors, officials – "Let's get acquainted, and tell me how you see the problems and challenges." The dominant behavior on the part of the new leaders was active listening. What they were doing was building relationships and assessing people, as well as collecting information and undertaking the analysis. Toward the end of this stage, a sense of what were the challenges and what should be the goals was starting to develop.

Whereas many people turn then to developing the action plan, these leaders went through a second stage characterized by active debate and discussion of this analysis. The dominant tone was constructive argument (constructive in the sense of being guided by facts), exposing the analysis to critique and debate. This is the critical stage that well known leaders such as Welch practice so well. They look for critique and then debate it back and forth. What happens is that the analysis is being worked through, adapted and changed. The process is one of simulation; simulating through debate the likely implications and knock-on effects at a time when plans can still be changed – once one moves to implementation, the leader can no longer afford to listen, and communication necessarily becomes one way. Typically the result is one of simplification, working out the essentials and finding the images that convey them to others.

The only way to work knowledge through into understanding and then into commitment fast is through open two-way dialog – two-way so that people can argue.

What is also happening in parallel is the building of necessary commitment. Many people confuse knowledge, understanding and commitment. There is a big difference between knowledge ("I've heard the words, I've seen the figures, but I don't understand what they mean"), understanding ("Yes, at last I begin to understand, though I don't necessarily agree") and commitment ("Yes, I begin to feel that this is indeed the right direction"). The only way to work knowledge through into understanding and then into commitment fast is through open two-way dialog – two-way so that people can argue.

One interesting example was a story in the press about a reorganization in Shell Malaysia, where the CEO brought all key staff together for a final workshop before moving to implementation. In the closing moments, one key executive expressed dissent. He was fired the following day. When questioned about the fairness of the decision, the CEO explained that he had no problem if people voiced their dissent, quite the contrary. But that individual had voiced his dissent for the first time in the final stages, and that could not be tolerated. This rationale was fully accepted by the staff. Indeed, the person who has no role in a 21st century management team is the one who plays safe, the one who never voices his or her views, who shifts with the tide. And then one day in the thick of implementation problems they say in a frank moment: "You know, I was never sure that this was a good idea . . ." The management team is seen as divided, and the project is in trouble.

One day the debate must end, and this was the third stage for those Exxon leaders. This stage is the announcement of the objectives and action plans to the fanfare of orchestrated communication. However, there is nothing new for most people in the information. The message behind the fanfare is that the time for argument, dissent, and discussion is over, and that from now on the only thing that counts is action and achievement of those targets. There is rarely, if ever, perfect consensus in any organization, but the leader believes there is sufficient commitment to move to action – "shut up and get on with it!" This was the message forcefully and successfully conveyed by the Shell Malaysia CEO.

THE ULTIMATE PARADOX

Leadership involves harnessing the tension of opposites at three levels – within oneself, through teamwork, and in the organizational structure. And all three at the same time. The failure to cope with the shadow side of oneself will block leadership. The absence of constructive debate in teamwork will block leadership. And that debate needs to be structured properly in any complex organization.

But let me leave you with a final paradox. There is no doubt that leadership means being dedicated to a job and having passion for it, and for what one is trying to achieve. But what happens if that passion blinds the individual to other more personal aspects of life?

We investigated this with a study on the relationship between the professional and private lives of 14 600 executives.[20] We found that 46 percent of these executives were dissatisfied, feeling that their lifestyles were unbalanced. When we looked into this, we found two major explanations. The first was the wrong person in the wrong job. People did not do their work well, did not enjoy it, and/or did not feel proud of what they were doing. Tensions spilled over into private life, compromising psychological availability and the quality of family and leisure time. Many companies do not manage human resources well in the sense of getting the right person into the right place. Everyone suffers.

If we had not understood duality, then we might have been tempted to conclude that enjoying a job would guarantee a well-functioning private life. Not so. The other people who were dissatisfied were those we called "prisoners of their success" – people who did their jobs superbly and loved them, and were loved by their companies. Absorbed by their work, they typically felt their real dilemmas lay in the private life arena. I have no doubt many readers of this book will fall into this category.

It is necessary to navigate between these two extremes. But some individuals always steer close to the professional shore. At the age of 60 they are still passionately absorbed by their work and loved by their organizations – and in their third marriage. Home is simply a haven to recharge batteries. And what happens then?

We started collecting pension statistics on companies renowned for their quality of management, notably in human resources. What started this off was the statistics for a high technology corporation that must be among the most frequently cited for excellence. You do not get far there unless you are extremely good at what you do and show exceptional dedication. The divorce rate for staff in this firm, especially at senior levels, was higher than the national average. One day they retire . . . and their pension statistics say that the average life expectancy for senior executives is less than one year! Alas, we find this to be a typical pattern in superb companies. In the retirement vacuum depression sets in, and the weak link in the body gives way. It takes longer than many people expect to develop sound post-working careers – we estimate at least ten years.

On the other hand, many of us know people in their 80s who are more dynamic than 25-year-olds.

Remember. Anything positive taken to extremes can be risky if not downright dangerous. Don't become a prisoner of success.

6

THE VALUE-BASED EDU-LEADER

STUART R. LEVINE

A new century is about to begin. Leaders will have a great opportunity and responsibility to guide their organizations and associates through an era of unparalleled transition. What will it mean to be a great leader in the year 2000? Technology and access to information have forever altered the nature of our work processes, markets and the way we manage our lives. Unlike computers, which can be reprogramed, human beings are not wired for change. We are being challenged to prioritize, digest and distill information, creating unprecedented levels of stress and chaos. Effective communication will create break-throughs in products, services and human energy.

As we continue on our journey into the new millennium, we must recognize the new realities that will shape the future. Technology is a great tool. However, even Michael Dell, CEO of Dell Computer, knows that technology is a means to an end. His "unwillingness to get mired in technology for technology's sake" is what keeps his company ahead of the pack.[1] Leaders will respond to a new set of dynamics that will invigorate the human spirit.

The world and work environment have changed, and the impact on people is defining those skills that will be required and admired in the new millennium. The most admired individual will be defined as an "Edu-leader" – a person, driven by core values, who builds trusting relationships through effective communication. By the nature of these skills, they are focussed on moving people and organizations forward by teaching and increasing the competency of their employees. The following seven principals will define the elements of successful transition from the 20th to the 21st century.

FROM CAREER-DRIVEN TO CORE VALUE-DRIVEN

Civilization has seen leaders who are respected, burned out, stressed out, incompetent and thrown out. How are competent leaders handling the work load, stress, and intensely competitive pressure?

People are working "24 – 7," and being asked to do more with less. Simply stated, technology has changed our lives forever. CEOs are investing in new hardware technology and constant software upgrades, involving a significant commitment of capital. Yet they are struggling to achieve return on investment. Communication and learning are continuous and constant. The response to this relentless pressure will require wholesome behavioral responses and new leadership capabilities.

When asked what fundamental truths of management still apply, Bob Haas, Levi Strauss chairman and CEO, says: "There are two essential things. The first is the value of people, and the second is the importance of values."[2]

Great leaders will have the courage to be true to their own core values and will inspire others through actions. Jean-Pierre Russo, chairman and chief executive of Case Corp., explains that "to perform globally, values, leadership, and communication become strategic imperatives." He believes that those companies with strong cultures – a set of core values that are sacrosanct and non-negotiable – will be those that win globally.[3]

Core values serve as the foundation for an individual's being. They define who we are. By identifying these important components, we strengthen our self-confidence and gain the ability to lead successful lives. The fundamentals of ethics, spirituality, family and intellectual curiosity are examples of such strong beliefs and character. By identifying your beliefs and revisiting them, an individual will gain strength. This perspective will allow the person to realize their natural intuitive abilities, which will help recognize opportunities.

Leaders will know themselves. In the past, people could rely on organizations to chart their career paths. Going forward, individuals will bear a greater responsibility for their personal development. Peter Drucker explains the importance of learning to develop ourselves, finding out where we can make the greatest contribution to our organizations and communities. There is a need to stay mentally alert during a 50-year working life; knowing how and when to change the work we do. According to Drucker, very few people know how to take advantage of their personal strengths. He urges people to concentrate on improving the skills they have and taking assignments that are tailored to their individual way of performing. When they understand their unique advantages and core values, they can recognize opportunities that present themselves.[4]

Edward Travaglianti, chairman and CEO of European American Bank, a wholly-owned subsidiary of Dutch group ABN AMRO, took charge of it in 1990. The size of their business was $1.25 billion with earnings of $15 million. In

1998, earnings increased to $133 million. He attributes his organization's success to the alignment of values with the parent corporation.

> "Our vision is steeped in an acknowledgement that the most important resource we have is people. The Dutch have a culture and history founded on fundamentals and patience. It was easy to align with their mentality. On one of the earliest trips I took to Amsterdam, I was asked to outline my vision and strategy for EAB. Once I did, there was full support and encouragement. I can't tell you how important that was for me. ABN AMRO is an organization founded on the belief in core values. We mirror those core values here. The good business strategy is anchored by core values. One of the best ways to drive a successful company is by leading in a way that people respect and makes them feel appreciated. Do that with intelligence and all the right combinations of technology and cognitive power. That translates to the customer and the bottom line – very pleasantly too.
>
> "Surrounding yourself with people who are like-minded, entrusting people, and providing leadership, encourages others to further the vision. When I was 17, my brother Charles, who was 14 months older, was killed in a car crash. It was a very tragic thing. It really underscored the important things in life. It was a family situation where we all focussed on working together, just getting up the next day. It was a building block for my outlook on life, coupled with the philosophy of being able to work with and rely on other people.
>
> "I keep everybody focussed on the fact that technology is only a tool to help people work more productively, efficiently and intelligently. People are inspired by the knowledge that we ultimately deal in a people business. The customer is going to sense and feel the very palpable and real attitudes of the bank only through its people, not through the balance sheet and the income statement."[5]

For a global executive recruiting company like Korn Ferry International, a $360 million enterprise which conducts business in 42 countries and employs 3500 people, it is important that they all share similar values. They may have different cultural or ethnic histories, but their interests are the same. They are oriented toward serving their clients, and there is a common thread that cuts across the network, whether it is Asia, Latin America or Europe.

Michael A. Wellman, president of global specialty practices in Korn Ferry International, often looks to his wife to develop a self-regulating system of balance. "Having a partner can be very helpful. If we've been busy with family or with other things, one or both of us looks at the other and says: we need to reorganize or rebalance between the personal and the professional. I think two people who are in sync have a way of governing that, and keeping an eye out for each other. You can be too obsessive or too compulsive. People are just hurting themselves in the long run. I try to keep myself organized by establishing priorities. I organize my day to get the most out of it. I know when I need to take a break so that I'm not burning myself out or doing something that is ultimately going to affect my performance, maybe not at that moment but a day later, or a week later."[6]

Carly Fiorina, former president of Lucent's Global Service Provider business and now CEO at Hewlett-Packard, also talks about priorities and focus. "My advice is to focus 100 percent on doing your job better than anybody else. I've seen a lot of highflying people fall flat because they were so focussed on the next job, they didn't get the current job done."[7]

FROM CHAOS-DRIVEN TO PROCESS-DRIVEN

As we enter the new millennium, speed and quality are the new realities. Products and services are moving from being sold, to being bought. To be responsive, leaders have to encourage people to continually be in a state of creativity and flexibility, enabling them to make the right decisions. An individual's ability to continuously learn, adapt to changes, and respond in a positive way is the key to success.

Yet companies are moving so fast they are neglecting to focus on their internal environments. Ultimately they will explode with creativity or implode due to chaos, lack of effective internal communication, emotional disconnections, and frustration. When a business reaches critical mass, a commitment to constantly review all work processes is essential. To stay in business amidst competition and to develop meaningful, productive relationships over time takes a different kind of planning and leadership. To get results, professional standards should be established through expectations and a system of responsibility and accountability.

As evolution continues, the number of distractions will challenge the introduction of process. Continuous lack of dedication to a direction creates an imbalance in thinking. This has a huge impact on the decision-making process, as it depletes positive energy and weakens the self-confidence of the decision maker. "Not every piece of mail you get is something you have to deal with. Not everybody in the world has the right to assign you work by sending you an e-mail or a letter. It's OK to forget that stuff. It's an unworthy pressure," says Max DePree, Herman Miller chairman emeritus.[8]

Embracing a proper sequence will define personal and organizational effectiveness. When Dan Hanson became president of Land O'Lakes's fluid–dairy division he began to question why people weren't finding meaning in work. There was an energy missing. He began to address organizational and personal problems that affected the workplace. "When an organization grows at the expense of treating its employees as people, the people inevitably start to feel alienated."[9] He sought to convene groups to find out which processes worked, what was wrong and what was getting in the way of relationships. Processes provide opportunities for inclusion, peace of mind, and results.

FROM TECHNOLOGY-DRIVEN TO RELATIONSHIP-DRIVEN

Institutions are investing significant amounts of capital in hardware and software. These initiatives are creating expectations that may not be realized. Visualize a CEO looking at his or her computer screen to gather data in preparation for an important decision. The quality of the decision about to be made will relate directly to the integrity of the data. Who generated that data and do they understand the company's mission and believe in it? As we continue to invest in the upgrade of technology we must approach with the same sense of urgency the development of and investment in people. Individuals understand and form stronger relationships with leaders who commit to their growth. The new world in which we live requires greater communication between all components of business operations. What we envisioned in the last decade as soft skills – communication, working with others, developing relationships – have become the vital skills for success in the future.

Joe Corella, systems engineering manager at Microsoft Corporation, prepared for a meeting with a potential customer. Throughout the early discussions, he made a commitment to learn more about the needs of the manager and her company. He determined that other competitors had missed an opportunity by lapsing into a "sales pitch." His goal was to establish a relationship with the new customer by making eye contact and encouraging his team members to follow up immediately on questions and concerns that were expressed. He achieved his objective by focussing his team on relationship solutions rather than technical sales.[10]

Trust is developed when people are able to listen to each other. "The absence of the human moment, on an organizational scale, can wreak havoc. Co-workers slowly but surely lose their sense of cohesiveness. It starts with one person, but distrust, disrespect, and dissatisfaction on the job are like contagions." "An organization's culture turns unfriendly and unforgiving. Good people leave. Those who remain are unhappy."[11] Researchers at Carnegie Mellon University found noticeable levels of depression and loneliness in people who spend just a few hours each week on the Internet.[12] E-mail and voice mails are efficient, but face-to-face contact is still essential to true communication. The positive hormones produced by human contact promote trust and bonding.

Truth translates into trust. Honest communication in a respectful environment sets a tone of professionalism that lifts the entire team. Mike Wellman of Korn Ferry International tries to be "pretty careful about what I say and how I say it. I try to be thoughtful about the way in which the message is given."[13]

> *Truth translates into trust. Honest communication in a respectful environment sets a tone of professionalism that lifts the entire team.*

Effective leaders will harness information technology and use it as a vehicle to increase the amount of data shared with their internal constituents. They will strengthen relationships with key components and employees by expressing trust and respect through the provision of timely and meaningful information. The discipline required for effective communication translates to a rhythm that is predictable and easy for individuals to absorb.

To decide how the global service provider unit at Lucent should allocate research and development dollars, Carly Fiorina, the then president, would meet regularly with Arun Netravali, executive vice-president of research at Bell Labs, a division of Lucent. "During these dialogs, he educated me about the technology, and I educated him as to the real application of this technology, the so-what from a business point of view," said Carly.[14]

The establishment of a regular and consistent rhythm of communication will expose people to data that helps them perform their tasks more effectively. Surveys begin the process of communication by listening and then putting leaders in a position to respond. As this system evolves, it is critical to manage all expectations so that people realize the commitments were fulfilled. The enthusiasm for strengthening relationships occurs when people ask open-ended questions and listen attentively.

FROM INFORMATION GATHERING TO DISTILLING AND SHARING INFORMATION

It used to be that information was power. In the 21st century, the process of distilling and sharing information will become the definable asset. When information is shared, it becomes part of a company's knowledge base, and it can be used to create better products, services and organizations. In today's world where skills and knowledge are completely portable, an organization is valuable to an employee only in as much as they are able to communicate and share their ideas, learn, and feel appreciated for their contributions.

Bernard F. Reynolds, chairman and CEO of ASI Solutions Incorporated, made it clear when he said:

> "We are in the middle of a data blitz and the next wave will be to trim that down into digestible pieces that are actionable. Distilling lots of data that can be digested readily by the consumer is the key to communication. Collecting the data, understanding its implications in an economic sense and then taking action to change what would otherwise be an inevitable outcome, is probably the most important set of actions companies are taking now and can take in the future."[15]

On one of ASI's projects, they obtained data for a client that had business process implications. Their research discovered that the address a customer would ask for when they wanted to pay a bill was rather long and cumbersome. It took the customer service representative too long to convey the address and it took the same amount of time for the customer to read it back. They suggested a simpler address through the creation of a post office box. It seems like a small change, but when you took that period of time customers were on the phone, and you started driving that back against the number of calls and the number of reps, you wound up with substantial numbers in terms of cost. So a little business process improvement can be obtained by analyzing data carefully and making a commitment to take action on it.

The next level of discipline will require people to learn the skill of analyzing and prioritizing data. As more information becomes available, questions should be raised as to its relevance and potential to improve work processes. People want to know how things affect them and what's going to happen to them. Leaders will develop the discipline to deliver a consistent message to both internal and external customers regarding the company, its products, and its vision for the future. A uniform message has the potential to increase revenues through delicate crafting – ensuring that it is fully understandable and absorbing. Ease of delivery, confidence in the message as well as marketability, are all critical elements. Once everyone is on board delivering the same unified communication, an organization becomes significantly stronger, more focussed, and able to point in the same direction to produce the desired revenues and results.

Mike Wellman observes that the world around you understands whether you are secure by the information flow reaching them. Human beings are quick to detect the subtle elements of communication. They can tell right away if the communicator is honest. Real leadership involves knowing how to impart information in such a way that it is taken to be honest and straightforward.

FROM ME TO WE

As new generations continue to develop their technology skills, success will be defined by their ability to motivate other members of their team. New electronic channels with platforms will form the marketplace of the 21st century. The fulfillment of customer expectations will depend on the proper deployment and engagement of people to function effectively and as a team.

When alignment of people is created through an organization, it usually stems from a clear understanding of the organization's mission and objectives. The price for unfocussed efforts can be the loss of a career or a company. By definition, a mission statement establishes the purpose for being, and helps to assess how to properly deploy energies and resources. When mission and core values are married, they provide a template for all consequent business decisions and actions.

Bob Galvin, chairman of Motorola's executive committee, and Max DePree, both believe in humility. DePree explains: "We have to learn how to abandon ourselves to people who can do things we can't do. That requires humility and vulnerability." And, "Learning how to establish and nurture relationships" is key.[16] Galvin feels that people who are humble do not think any less of themselves, they just think more of other people.[17]

Edwin S. Marks, president of Carl Marks & Co. Inc., a New York investment firm providing private equity investment, money management and advisory services, said he learned through his education at West Point about leading and setting an example. There is an old saying that you can't push a piece of string. Therefore, an individual needs substance, grounded in values, to develop as a contributing member of the team. In his early days at Carl Marks, his father put him in menial positions where he observed employees being underused and gaps in communication. These observations helped prepare him to lead his organization.[18]

You cannot succeed through intellectual arrogance. The new criteria for assessing the strength of an organization will be in the area of quality results obtained through people. After 23 years as president of Hofstra University, Dr James M. Shuart explains that the college is "more like a federated group. You can look at them as gangs or as teams. As a leader, if you can provide the resources to encourage them to co-operate and to improve the organization, you are a winner. I fell in love with this kind of organization, this kind of people. I get a kick out of it. Others would be driven crazy. You'd have to keep them on the first floor, so when they go out the window they won't hurt themselves."[19]

A leader's job is to constantly challenge the bureaucracy that smothers individual enthusiasm and the desire to contribute to an organization. Leaders in the new millennium will create an environment that encourages the development of skills, learning and openness so that those on their team can participate in the deployment of financial and human resources.

Organizational change and moving a cultural baseline is a difficult challenge. It takes respect, intensity, and commitment to stay the course. Some days will be tougher than others, due to human errors and lapses. Great leaders will not be put off by others; they will have the courage to stand up and establish rules. Their goal will be to go to a higher ground, and they will constantly use their own actions as a model for others to follow, reflecting consistency and stability. When tough decisions are required, wise leaders are patient with themselves. Establishing a sense of urgency, yet being able to spend time with those who want to move forward and share a vision for the future, is important. They will not check the daily emotional temperature of their environment, as they are in it for the longer haul.

The creation of culture is the operating concept. The most significant factor is acknowledging that it is built one brick at a time. It would be wrong to view it as a big event; rather, it is lots of little events over time that reflect an environment of fairness and decency. These positive vibrations draw people closer and create a healthy atmosphere. Remember that everything starts at the top.

> Mike Wellman says: "As we began to grow and add more talent, we would try to reward those people who exhibited characteristics reflecting our culture. We've had some people who had to adapt, and they've learned that adaptation was actually better than had they kept on with the old traditional manner. It's more an evolution than a revolution. And we're still evolving.
>
> "You have to reinforce your systems with behaviors. Top management has to start living by the behaviors themselves. You cannot have one set of rules for your management and one set of rules for your team and get people on the same page. So we started putting different people into different positions of leadership who believed in teamwork, who believed in collaboration. Synergy runs better in this collection of individuals.
>
> "I try to help people stay in balance and to keep a perspective on what they are doing. Part of my job is to take a pulse of the teams in high performance and to be occasionally an outlet for them. Sometimes it's just being a good listener and giving them the opportunity to get it out. Occasionally I'll give advice saying, 'It's not worth it,' 'don't punch too hard,' 'take a breather,' 'maybe give it a day before you come back at it,' or 'put perspective on it.'"[20]

When Bob Haas became CEO of Levi Strauss in 1984, the business was in a terrible state. He admits to being scared and unsure of what to do. His solution was to reach out to his team members and say: "We're in this together. I don't have the answers. I'm not the heroic leader. We've got to figure this out. Come back to me with your own perception." They had the answers, as painful as they were, and the organization got back on track.[21]

FROM PRODUCT FOCUS TO PEOPLE FOCUS

Competition has increased from the narrow focus on products and services offered by companies, to the broader issue of competing to attract and retain the best talent available in the marketplace. Those companies that will win in the marketplace of tomorrow will successfully attract the best global talent. A company's ability to respond and add value to professional relationships will depend on attracting high-caliber employees and developing an integrative and supportive workforce. Adding to the continuous cycle of new products and technological advances, there are increased demands throughout the world for skilled technology workers. Turnover rates for technology jobs worldwide continue to increase.

The new paradigm for competition will not just be about selling your products and services into the marketplace, but how to compete to find and retain qualified employees. Employee turnover is a way to assess your management team.

Edwin S. Marks believes in basic, old-fashioned ideas that he expects will be even more valuable as we enter the next century. He continues the successful heritage of his organization that began in 1925 by advising investments in organizations that have sound management – including experience, hard work, a clear sense of direction, the ability to fend off distractions, timing, and meticulous analysis. He prides his organization on being a "company with a heart."[22] Always seeking people better than himself has been one of his keys to success.

He decided to join the Young Presidents Organization, volunteering for every dirty job, and became the group's education chairman. He visited Harvard 16 times, always learning, and meeting competent people. His activities exposed him to other people in business and ensured he would never view the world from an ivory tower. These initiatives developed in him two cornerstones for his success – the desire to surround himself with people who could do a better job than he could, and the determination to follow up on ideas.

Bernard Reynolds of ASI Solutions recognizes the importance of determining the characteristics of a culture.

> "You have to set up a system to let people grow internally. You also have to have a very strong human component in the management of your business. You have to make allowances that people have a life beyond work. You want 100 percent commitment at work, but I think that goes in two directions. You have to have a commitment to the people that work in the organization. They will have family issues that require them to come in late periodically or take time off. You need to have some way to provide for that, recognizing that it's not a bad thing. It's an appropriate thing and it's a human thing. To the extent that you can humanize work, you will create greater levels of productivity and loyalty."[23]

FROM LEADER TO EDU-LEADER

Leaders of the new millennium will be teachers and developers of knowledge workers. They will have the ability to see new opportunities and achieve a higher level of awareness by maintaining perspective gained through learning. If you have a higher understanding of the world, you have a responsibility to share your knowledge. The identification of hurdles and how people can get over them by discerning new patterns, learning new systems, and developing new strategies will separate linear managers from Edu-leaders.

Highly effective leaders known for their teaching include Larry Bossidy of AlliedSignal, Roger Enrico of PepsiCo, Andy Grove of Intel, and the late Roberto Goizueta of Coca-Cola. Larry Bossidy transformed AlliedSignal into the best performing company on the Dow Jones Industrial Average within five years of his arrival at the company in 1991, largely by becoming a dedicated teacher.

He didn't replace senior managers. He evaluated the company, and decided to teach senior leaders about strategy. Bossidy reached 15 000 employees, teaching them personally.[24]

Environments that develop intellectual curiosity will deliver additional value for their shareholders. Those who aspire to lead will understand that their effectiveness begins with their own development and ability to share knowledge in a soluble manner. Teaching will be particularly important in a volatile workforce. Building a bond between people and the organizations they serve reduces costly turnover, and additionally helps leaders to maintain their most valuable asset – their people. In a world where knowledge and skills are completely portable, people are attracted to organizations that afford them the greatest opportunity to grow, enhance their skill level, and contribute in a meaningful way.

> *Those who aspire to lead will understand that their effectiveness begins with their own development and ability to share knowledge in a soluble manner.*

When asked what he does to retain his 550 employees, Bernie Reynolds explains: "Our view is that people always want to improve and have their skills enhanced. That is both good for our business and for the people individually. While we may not have as many vertical opportunities for supervision, we have opportunities for cross-training to pick up a broader array of skills inside the firm. As people get cross-trained, their rates of compensation increase based on what skills they have acquired. That gives us the flexibility of assigning them elsewhere."

Leaders will dedicate themselves to teaching people through sharing their experiences. Their successes in business will inspire others and yield financial results. Leaders will constantly be observing how to learn from different experiences, how to make things better, and how to communicate this knowledge to others in terms they will understand.

Helene Fortunoff, secretary treasurer of Fortunoff Fine Jewelry, is an Edu-leader committed to improving her knowledge and then sharing it with her associates and industry colleagues.

"Basically I am a down-and-dirty common sense person. I give an honest answer. If I can't give an answer correctly, I don't say it. I tell the truth. I am obsessive about reading and that makes a very big difference. I can quote where things are coming from. An early memorable experience was when I participated in a meeting as the only woman in the room. I had read *South African Diamond News* from cover to cover on the plane, just digesting what was going on. Now very, very few people in the USA subscribe to that magazine. I subscribe to so many magazines from all over the world. I have them coming in from just about every country.

"When Anthony Oppenheimer was giving his overview, I saw that what he was saying really didn't click with what was happening in the magazine. So right away, I'm only in the meeting for 20 minutes, and they say 'any questions?' And I timidly raise my hand because I have to ask this question. He gives the answer, and I really was not convinced by it, so I repeat my question. And the man next to me said very quietly, 'Please stop asking the question' and of course I did. We go out to lunch and they have changed the seating, and Anthony Oppenheimer is sitting next to me. They basically said, you can ask any questions you want but be discreet about it. So he sat next to me for the rest of the conference, and this was an amazing learning experience. Perhaps I'm foolish, but I am not afraid to talk to people. I'm not afraid to ask questions. I'm not afraid to probe and learn. That makes a very big difference."[25]

The Italian government honored Helene for her contributions to the jewelry industry, which have involved 30 years of establishing standards through education. Her commitment to continuous learning enables her to share information, and to develop knowledge workers in her organization.

CONCLUSION

We have discussed the seven characteristics that make up the "Edu-leader." These value-based skills will help leaders to learn, adapt, and respond positively in the new millennium. Succeeding in the future will require a new set of behaviors to navigate in a changing work environment. Those individuals who identify their core values will lead more productive, fulfilled and creative lives. Becoming process-driven, relationship-driven, being able to share and distill information, and understanding and appreciating the value of working together under a clear mission – these are the characteristics of leadership in the 21st century. And so is treating people with respect and allowing them to grow.

In Edwin Marks' office is a notice that sums up his philosophy: What is Genius? it asks. Genius is simply the power to make a continuous effort. The line between failure and success is so fine that we scarcely know when we pass it. So fine that we are often on the line and do not know it. There is no failure except in no longer trying.

If you are patient yet passionate, demanding yet encouraging, honest and empathetic, the future will be yours.

7

MASTERY: THE CRITICAL ADVANTAGE

CAELA FARREN

Work and private life in the new millennium will continue to revolve around the 12 human needs that have been around since the beginning of recorded history. Professions and trades have evolved to satisfy these needs – family, health and well-being, work/career, economic, learning, home/shelter, social relationships, spirituality, community, leisure, mobility, and environment/ safety. Mastery – becoming an acknowledged expert in a specific area of action – will be the centerpiece, the foreground of business excellence in the 21st century.

Joan Evelyn Ames says: "Mastery is an unending process . . . Those who have achieved mastery may have complete command of the skills and even the art of their disciplines, but new and ever increasingly refined aspects of their work continue to appear. True masters thrive on continuous learning and growth; they are committed to the process itself."[1]

Future managers will be masters or experts in their trades or professions. They will have experienced so many variations of what works, what doesn't, and what can go wrong that they will rarely be surprised or baffled by the un-usual. They will know instinctively what to do, whom to call, where to look and how to handle any crisis or opportunity. Because of their deep expertise, they can spot breakdowns early on and lead their teams in assessing and solving new and tough challenges.

Managers/leaders will continue to change work settings (organizations, proj-ects, jobs, and even industries). This will be in the service of building mastery in their profession, experiencing so many different aspects of a profession (e.g. computer science, marketing, sales, finance, molecular biology, physics, TV production, etc.) that their instincts are fine-tuned. Fellow workers will also develop a keen sense that their on-going employability and marketability will be based on their level of mastery in a profession or trade.

As in the old days, people will start practicing their profession or trade at an earlier age through work/study apprenticeships. School (learning) and work will exist once more in close partnerships, co-determining the requirements and achievements of each. Mentor/apprentice relationships, as in the guilds of old, will be the primary way of building work credentials and developing leadership competencies. Choosing a profession or a trade will become one of the most important career decisions for future workers. Sorting through one's values, interests, and "loves" will be the critical backdrop for choosing and crafting mastery of a profession or trade. Once a person has mastered it, he or she will have the level of experience and respect that will allow powerful coaching and management. Management will be about coaching and developing others so they can succeed at ever more complex projects. Mastery of a profession or trade will become a prerequisite to becoming a manager.

WHY MASTERY WILL BE SO CRITICAL FOR MANAGERS

Pattern recognition

Complexity will continue to increase at every level of society in the 21st century – financial, technological, political, cultural, generational, and educational. People will have more choices, more information, and more access to various work opportunities than ever before. Breakthroughs in science, technology, communication, and education will literally put the world at our fingertips. People will need the mental maps, conceptual frameworks, subtle distinctions, and historical reference points that come only with mastery, in order to experience this rich world as patterned and predictable rather than purely chaotic or confusing. Without such frameworks, managers will freeze, turn away in cowardice, feel lost and confused, or simply lash out against the barrage of stimulation. Managers without the depth and breadth that comes from mastery of a profession or trade will lack the intellectual refinement and the confidence to see the difference between change and chaos. Without the calm and confidence that comes with mastery, leaders will feel overwhelmed, anxious and unable to make sense out of the apparent chaos.

Without the calm and confidence that comes with mastery, leaders will feel overwhelmed, anxious and unable to make sense out of the apparent chaos.

Those who have mastered a profession, trade or art form pick up the subtle distinctions, the patterns, the slight fluctuations in conditions that others with a superficial or general knowledge cannot possibly apprehend. Michael

Moschen, the most renowned juggler of our time, has spent two decades developing and redefining his craft. He claims anyone could learn to juggle by breaking down the complex patterns and manoeuvers into simple tasks. "Chaos occurs," he says, "when we can't perceive a pattern and therefore can't attach a handle to it." According to him, juggling is simply about tosses, throws and putting your hands under the object. But distilling his art down to the basics has taken over 20 years. He is consequently able to do manoeuvers that no other juggler can claim. He sees the patterns rather than the chaos in having anywhere from three to ten balls in the air at once.

Pattern recognition is at the heart of mastery. Wall Street traders, advertising executives, financial planners, sports announcers, photographers, market researchers, electrical engineers, or software developers see and respond to distinct patterns in their trades, industries, customers, and competitors. Years of experience swimming around in the profession, trade or industry yield enough practical experiences from which they develop their instincts, assessment criteria, initiatives, and innovations. The number of experiences, variation of experiences, results, successes and failures all figure into the mastery equation. Managers and leaders without these in-depth experiences are simply not equipped to lead in complex environments.

Instincts of a master

As the rate of change accelerates in the 21st century, business success will require the eye and ear of a master. Others with a superficial or general knowledge of a field or trade rarely detect such things as the sound of an engine starting to malfunction; numbers on a spreadsheet or mathematical model that don't look quite right; the look on a project manager's face that suggests confusion or discomfort; or the slight fluctuations in the market that would suggest making changes in a financial portfolio. These so-called instincts are simply a form of complex pattern recognition developed by the master. They come only from years of practice. And even if a person could detect such subtle shifts without the respect and trust that comes from a masterful track record he or she would likely be unable to implement the changes and so provide confidence and reassurance to others. Coaching others to see and hear what the master experiences can occur only from this experience base.

Wisdom is embodied in the master, literally, "in the body." Repeated practices develop habits of action and response that become almost automatic. When asked, "Why did you say this, how did you see that?" the master can step back and describe exactly what he or she saw, heard, sensed. Most of the time this savvy lives in the area of unconscious competence. They have done it so many times – listened to the hum, watched the faces, or read thousands of spreadsheets – that they can quickly see the patterns suggesting success or necessary modifications. They take action immediately, sometimes so quickly and with such confidence that the novice never notices the problem.

Confidence

Mastery builds confidence as well as competence. In fact, the confidence is the more important aspect of mastery. As conditions change, breakthroughs occur, companies merge, downsize, outsource, spin off, centralize, get smaller or merge into giant conglomerates, the experienced workers see this has only to do with form and not with function. People who have set out to master a niche, a territory, a discipline, are continuing on the mastery journey while the arbitrary terrains are regrouping around them. "The more things change, the more they stay the same" is more than just an old saying. People who are great at their profession or trade are always learning, questioning, tinkering, and taking the practice to a new level. These people don't have to worry about whether they are employable. They are desperately needed by organizations and industries to address the ever-changing needs they are drawn to serve. They become natural managers and coaches for those around them, both formally and informally.

COACHING AND MENTORING

Mastery requires time and practice in the field. People who are accomplished in a profession or trade have spent 10–17 years developing their expertise. We see this all the time in sports. We don't expect sports professionals to get the gold until they have practiced for years. Swimmers, golfers, soccer players, or tennis masters alike have been playing the sport for ages, working up through the range of competitions from beginner to master.

We expect sports figures to practice the sport. It would seem ridiculous to expect a person who had only book knowledge of tennis or soccer to play at the master level. We would laugh at the concert pianist who never practiced but simply took courses on music theory. And yet we don't laugh when a young person of similar age and experience studies engineering, finance, marketing or human resources and then expects to perform at the master level within one or two years of graduate school. We have, in these business instances, detached learning from doing, knowledge from practice.

How many jingles or draft ads must an advertising executive write before finding the perfect one for the client? Hundreds, maybe thousands. How many websites must a webmaster design and implement before she acquires the ability to both see and deliver the perfect range of visual, audio, and conceptual images to get the message across almost instantaneously? It's not going to be on the first try but through the age-old approach of trial and error. One excellent website can create a range of learning and experience that quickens the creation of the next and the next and the next. Repetition, exploration and creative breakthroughs are linked in the learning continuum. After throwing 10 000 shots from the free throw line, the accuracy and confidence of the basketball player increases. Combinations of hundreds of subtle physical and psychological moves combine for ever-increasing odds of making the shot. This process of practice, correction, fine-tuning, and observing is required for excellence in every business profession or trade.

No matter how many books one has read on marketing, how many case studies have been discussed, or how many marketing proposals reviewed, nothing can substitute for the practice of marketing. In fact, in some cases, having intellectual knowledge without practical experience can be extremely jarring to a young adult. Many have been given Masters Degrees without the years of practicing the craft to become a master. It is no wonder that we find arrogance covering confusion, quick fixes substituting for the basic practices. Such beginners lack the practiced eye and tuned ear that allow for the creativity,

> *Having intellectual knowledge without practical experience can be extremely jarring to a young adult.*

innovation, and grace of the master. Their instincts have not been honed and their knowledge has not been put to the test of time. It is no wonder that, when faced with difficult, complex and conflicting strategies, inexperienced people often crumble or change jobs or professions. What else can they do?

Practice with a mentor makes perfect

As the world of the 21st century becomes more and more complex, the options for learning continue to explode. Working with a mentor short-circuits the many false starts and dead ends experienced by the lone learner. Mentors will educate their apprentices on the tools of the trade. Only a master is able to distill the thousands of skills into the critical few practices that have to be mastered. One can obviously learn many of these through diligent reading, researching, and studying the masters of one's trade. However, the techniques and breakthroughs of the profession or trade continue to evolve. The master manager will be able to help the apprentice fashion the necessary experiences into a manageable learning path.

Finding a mentor is critical for both speeding up learning and discovering the unique gifts one has as a sales person, an accountant, a trader, a manager, an engineer, a software designer, marketeer, etc. Manager/mentors will help others master their profession or trade in record time. Mentoring managers will keep apprentices motivated and excited both about their progress and the distance they still have to run.

Working with multiple mentors

In crafting a mastery path, multiple mentors are needed along the way. Masterful managers will be able to help assess in their protégés current levels of mastery in each of the areas described below:

- *technical mentors* are experts in the profession or trade in which you want to excel, i.e. marketing, finance, tax law, materials management, sales, computer systems design, TV production, administration, computer graphics, etc.;
- *learning mentors* will assist in uncovering primary learning styles; crafting learning and work experiences to maximize mastery. In future, interviewees will be required to discuss their learning styles and requirements;
- *industry mentors* work at the boundaries, speculate about and address the trends and major problems in the industry; often, they are the recognized leaders in the industry;
- *organization mentors* know what counts in the organization; who counts; the do's and don'ts; key and secondary projects; and the rules of the road for succeeding;
- *customer advocates* know what counts with each customer – problems, opportunities, or breakthroughs; who you need to know; customer history; customer expectations; and your competitors' history with the customer;
- *project facilitators* help expedite work in the system; they explain shortcuts and the people to know; how to get beyond red tape; and discuss the differences between public policies and private practices;
- *modem mentors* can be from any organization; they could be recognized leaders in the profession who agree to coach, problem-solve, and chat with protégés on-line;
- *peer mentors* will be invaluable, coaching on computer systems, budgeting protocols and meeting practices, as well as products, services, and interdisciplinary practices;
- *cultural mentors* have expertise in other cultures, languages, or practices that need to be known and respected when working with people abroad;
- *resource providers* will, for example, short-circuit a search for information.

Those aspiring to mastery surround themselves with capable people who help them traverse the entire terrain of their profession or trade. Business mastery in the future will require an ever stronger and broader network of support.

Performers in science and sports have known about the importance of mentor/apprentice relationships for ages. Mentors work with them for long hours, coaching them on the basics, inventing exercises to work on specific weaknesses or talents, and recommending various changes in routines, competitions, and even living arrangements, in order to create champions. We see the same guidance and discipline in most of the arts, whether dance, music, or painting.

Crafting learning experiences and projects

Training rooms and training courses will begin to disappear as the central learning platform for those on a mastery journey. Instead, mentoring managers and their apprentices will craft learning projects, experiences, developmental assignments, or practices that will increase the protégés' competence and confidence. Work will become more and more organized around changing projects or customers. Jobs as we have known them will continue to decline. Employability and marketability will depend on the "fit" between an organization's short and long-term needs for certain levels of mastery in different professions. Core professions (critical to the mission and strategies of the organization) will be staffed from within, while secondary professions (support services) will either be contracted in or outsourced. Managers and leaders will become much more interested in attracting and retaining core professionals and will begin to craft novel work contracts in order to keep the best.

In the late nineties, most talented people who left organizations were doing so because they weren't challenged or happy. Leavers said they were losing their competence, not working on challenging projects, not working up to their capacity, or supervising others instead of developing a higher level of excellence in themselves. Many said they were working longer hours, with not much change in pay and no promises for the future. They were not continuing to learn or adding to their level of expertise. They were underwhelmed. Many left to start up the businesses of the new millennium.

Hallmarks of mastery

Have you ever met a great teacher who isn't looking for other ways, better ways, to engage her students? Have you ever known an outstanding salesperson who isn't searching for other ways to serve his clients, bringing new ideas to R&D or giving new suggestions to customer service? Masters are like radar scanners, always looking for whatever will make them more effective, their company stronger, or their work more cost-effective.

WORK ONLY IN VITAL ORGANIZATIONS

Not all organizations are the same. Not all will provide a powerful incubator for gaining mastery or developing management potential. Indicators of an organization that does are discussed in my recent book.[2] Study these carefully and look long and hard at organizations you might choose from for your apprenticeship and development as a manager. When you become a manager and leader, create an organization with the same characteristics. You will then attract and retain people who aspire to mastery. Six things vital to an organization are:

1 A sense of purpose
2 Leaders from core professions in the industry
3 A research and development culture
4 An emphasis on encouraging learning
5 Sharing wealth
6 Entrepreneurial mindset.

Sense of purpose

This is probably the single most important factor in building or choosing an organization to work in. You want to be sure that your personal mission, values, and interests are closely aligned and attuned to those of the organization. If not, your talents will suffer and you will feel your creative powers weaken. You want to either create or be part of a team totally dedicated to making a breakthrough, solving a problem, or creating something distinctive in your profession or trade. Learning is tough enough, even in the presence of masterful craftsmanship and mentors. Choose wisely.

This sense of common cause is what separates great organizations from the merely good ones. With nothing to energize or inspire them, people can become petty, self-serving, bored, lazy, or simply demoralized. Let your pride and passion be the arbitrator. Are you motivated by the purpose and mission of the organization?

Leaders from core professions

Belonging to an organization seen as the best by competitors, customers and workers helps you develop depth and breadth in your profession or trade. Be sure leaders in the organization have more than ten years' experience in their industry or core professions. Find out if they are talked about as industry leaders by people outside the organization. We have seen many examples of companies destroyed by executives with little or no familiarity with either their industry or core professions.

Don't start out where your talent isn't essential for the organization's mission. And surround yourself with people who are much better than you are, who can give you on-going feedback on your work.

Research and development culture

Effective leaders balance short-term achievement with long-term development. Yielding too easily to the pressures to make fast profits can jeopardize the future of any company. Those leaders who want to ensure their organization will be around for a long time commit time, money, and resources to research and development.

Look for or build an organization that shares and discusses its business plans and strategies with employees. Knowing the company's research plans helps you keep in touch with industry trends, new technologies, growth opportunities, and changes in competency and skill requirements. You can spot the need for your services in other parts of the organization and prepare to compete for valued assignments. Making such information available shows the organization is committed not only to its own growth but also to that of its staff.

Assess an organization's commitment to R&D. Do the leaders expect breakthroughs in products or services? How does the organization encourage and reward entrepreneurship? How many new patents, trademarks, products, or services are in the pipeline? How much time is devoted to browsing, speculating, chat-room "what if" sessions, and listening to customers? If you can't find the answers, look at other organizations.

An emphasis on encouraging learning

The hallmark of learning is not the number of courses taken or the number of degrees achieved; learning shows up in results – bringing in clients from other cultures, seeing a way to use a technical process from another company or industry, recognizing financial patterns that suggest the need for a new pricing or payment schedule. Learning is a highly individualized process. We each have our unique ways of learning – alone, with others, through experimenting, reading, preparing papers for conferences, researching, tinkering, shadowing the best, scanning the Internet, and doing courses.

Professions and crafts are evolving and changing, developing and taking expertise from related and unrelated disciplines. Recently a dentist who specializes in surgery used a specific photographic film used by orthodontists to detect an infection in a colleague of mine. My colleague's own dentist had pulled out six of his teeth in less than five months but never solved the problem. The dental surgeon, however, asked relevant questions, used the photographic tool from another discipline to discover the infection, and was able to save three more endangered teeth. Who was the master?

Organizations that foster learning do not necessarily provide training. They reward breakthroughs in thinking, problem solving, ideas for new products or services, or expansion of existing lines of service. They recognize and reward learning that serves the organization's mission and strategies, and applaud the inventions of their experts. They expect people to keep learning and add more value to the organization. But they don't want their excellent technical professionals to become managers and switch professions.

Performance discussions in future will be more about how people will contribute rather than about what they have already achieved. What will they do for customers next year? How will that help the organization's strategies? These are the sort of questions to expect in an organization that fosters learning. And if that organization is your own company, you need to ask yourself the same questions.

Sharing wealth

Company success and profitability require long-term commitment from key employees. As a manager you will want to build financial partnerships with them. But good salaries alone are no longer enough to hold on to the loyalty and emotional energy of these masters. They expect to share in the rewards the organization gets from their expertise. This can mean childcare, flexible hours, pension and profit-sharing plans, membership of professional associations, stock options, and royalties on products. Organizations should find out what motivates employees and set out to share the benefits of increased productivity and financial success. Workers, meanwhile, should look for companies that consider their well-being.

Entrepreneurial mindset

The best organizations concentrate on products and services that will be needed by large numbers of customers well into the future. They position themselves to provide products or services that take care of one or more of the 12 basic needs that we have already discussed. They have a trend-capturing mindset. Their people read the writing on the wall and see what's going to happen in housing, food, health care, leisure pursuits, financial security, and transportation. They work double time, handling current commitments while anticipating future needs.

Tomorrow's managers will create roles and structures that will ensure their people are always looking around for new opportunities. These roles will include:

- converters – those taking today's technology and converting it to tomorrow's needs
- scanners – people charged with finding new niches and customers
- expediters – those who can help others to bypass red tape and bureaucratic regulations
- browsers – employees who scan related industries, technologies, and professions for ideas their organization can use

- linkers – those who persuade individuals and related companies to join short-term partnerships
- energy conservers – people who look to plug drains in emotional, physical, or intellectual energy brought about by ineffective managers or poor work environments
- talent scouts – those who look for people with the potential to become masters.

CONCLUSION

- Mastery of a profession or trade will be vital for successful managers. Don't short-change yourself – learn the ropes, do the groundwork, and understand the history of your trade or profession. Think in decades, not in years.
- Find several mentors to coach you. Just as companies need a board of directors to steer them, so too will you.
- Who you have learned from will be just as important as what you have learned.
- Managers who have stuck with a profession or trade as it has evolved will be more marketable than those who move from job to job.
- The best managers will have a large following because of their expertise, not because of the authority that goes with their position.
- Managers will become much more dedicated to attracting and retaining experts and will become skilled in drafting contracts which will achieve this.
- Managers will "read" the future and help protégés prepare for it.
- Development discussions will be common in the 21st century, focussing on what contribution will be needed to allow both the organization and the individual to grow.

8

MINDSETS FOR MANAGERS

PAUL DAINTY AND MOREEN ANDERSON

Information technology is a key force driving the pace of change at work. Technology is changing the tools that people use and the problems they must solve. As a result, managerial work is becoming more complex, abstract and subject to continuous change.

In this chapter, we argue that as technology advances, so must our understanding of where it can help, and in fact, hinder managers' attempts to become more informed and productive. For our part, we need to recognise how our own mental approach influences how we frame, analyse and interpret problems. More important, we need to understand our overall mental approach or "mindset", when dealing with the changes that technology can bring – be these in the form of different problems to solve, new people to relate to or new work practices to adopt. Indeed, we predict that for many companies, the corporate battles of the millennium will be more about changing mindsets than keeping pace with technological advance.

BACKGROUND

For the most part, work is becoming more demanding of people's skills and abilities. McKinsey and Company estimate that by the year 2000 70 percent of jobs in Europe and 80 per cent of those in the USA will require primarily cerebral rather than manual skills. According to management philosopher Charles Handy, "the ability to acquire and apply knowledge and know-how is the new source of wealth."[1] In future, he believes, people's ultimate security will lie not in land and buildings but in their brains.

Many others also argue that society is in the middle of another major transformation, one that promises to create a very different world to the one we know today. The rise of global competition and the spread of information technology are changing substantially the nature of work, who does the work, and what the work involves.[2] Technology has not only transformed the speed at which information can be distributed and processed, it has forced organizations to streamline and upgrade their work processes and systems. To date, it has been focussed largely on making business operations more efficient. Increasingly, it will challenge industry leaders to rethink the strategic fundamentals on which their businesses are based.[3]

As the demand for leaders who can challenge and redefine the status quo increases, the capabilities associated with effective performance, particularly at senior levels, has come under scrutiny.[4] While industry expertise and functional knowledge will continue to be of critical importance, executives need to draw upon a broader range of capabilities if they are to succeed in highly competitive, changing environments. For example, at Microsoft, Bill Gates places a huge emphasis on hiring the "right" people into his organization. Of the 10 000 resumés received each month, only 2 percent of applicants are hired. But, he argues, he is not just looking for technical skills. "The ideal Microsoft candidate has technical expertise plus the capacity to quickly acquire new skills to keep pace with changing technology. Smart employees are creative and possess market knowledge, an entrepreneurial spirit, problem-solving skills, and the ability to work without needing detailed, constricting rules and procedures."

Thus, specific technical expertise and industry knowledge, while important, do not in themselves seem to provide a sufficiently broad basis for sustainable employment. Indeed, successful organizations are looking beyond specific, job-related skills (which are easily acquired) and more towards the attitudes, values, and overall mental approach of the individual. The extent to which individual values and attitudes and the culture of the organization are aligned seems to be a significant predictor of subsequent turnover and performance.[5] Others focus on "learn-how" rather than "know-how," arguing that organizations want people who can rise to the challenge of the emerging technologies, who can adapt and change their work patterns as a result.[6] To do this, we believe, managers need to become more aware of their own patterns of thinking and behaving and how these influence their everyday behavior.

INTELLIGENT USE OF TECHNOLOGY

If current trends continue, the workplace of the next millennium will be one in which there will be far greater quantities of data, distributed more widely than ever before. The rapid uptake of e-mail, voice mailboxes, cellular phones and pagers, not to mention Internet usage, shows we are keen to take advantage of products that will keep us in touch and informed.

Yet organizations still require the experience and intelligence of human beings to turn information into useful knowledge and make good decisions.[7] When we take a closer look at the issues generated by today's "pervasive, invasive information infrastructure"[8] and the impact technology is having on people's work lives, it would seem we are a long way from being able to use these new tools effectively. For example, in a survey which examined the impact of IT on a sample of 350 executives' working lives some 58 percent said that "technology had not made their lives better, just busier."[9] Over 55 percent of those surveyed viewed IT's ability to add value as being "vastly overrated," with a similar percentage saying IT "wasted as much time as it saves." Half the respondents claimed IT meant "serious information redundancy and overload for me."

To avoid these problems, managers will need to design and use information systems more intelligently. They also need to understand something about their own mental capabilities to sort through problems, analyze information, and make decisions. They need to know where technology can be of help and where it can, in fact, hamper their attempts to become more productive and well informed.

It is our prediction that many firms will face a disconnection among their employees between, on the one hand, the accelerated advancement of technology and, on the other hand, the more limited capacity of the individual to cope and adapt to these new challenges. Moreover, this disconnection will not be overcome by more and louder exhortations for people to become more capable of learning and adapting. Instead, it will be those organizations that understand the subtleties and limitations of human capacities, and how these can be developed and managed in relation to the new technologies, that will succeed. Those organizations which fail will be those that believe that simple communication messages will "do the trick," or that people "will adapt anyway."

To understand this argument it is necessary to explore briefly some of the mental strengths and limitations of individuals. In the sections that follow we look at how the individual's psychological make-up and overall mental approach influence perceptions, and how problems are analyzed and dealt with. By so doing we hope to show why faster delivery of more information is not, in itself, necessarily of benefit to managers in the new millennium.

MINDSET AFFECTS WHAT WE DO

People use a range of mental processes to sort through and analyze information. The mental approach or mindsets we adopt help shape the way in which we approach everyday problems, what we listen to and ignore, and what conclusions we reach. Mindsets are ways of viewing the world around us and are a product of our past experiences, assumptions, values, and beliefs. They are part of the perceptual filtering process that enables everyone to deal with the complexity of their environment. We filter information quite instinctively and this affects both what we notice and how this is interpreted.

> *The mental approach or mindsets we adopt help shape the way in which we approach everyday problems, what we listen to and ignore, and what conclusions we reach.*

Some refer to these interpretations as "foregrounds" and "backgrounds." Foregrounds tend to be at the forefront of our thinking and can cause individuals to overlook or ignore important background events. Thus, we have a propensity to see what we want to see. In interpreting data, our perceptual frameworks categorize and hide data, assign likelihoods, and also fill in missing links. Often this process serves us well. At other times it can make us vulnerable. For example, managers develop classifications to help them think about their competitive environments but in so doing have a tendency to focus on existing and known competitors and, as a result, may miss newer entrants to the market. This may well be the reason why executives at Encyclopedia Britannica when their sales plummeted in the early 1990's and the introduced CD-ROM-based encyclopedias.[10] Apparently, early on they viewed CD-ROM equivalents as being of an inferior intellectual quality and incorrectly assumed that parents would stick to their original product. In fact, parents were interested in ensuring their children had a computer and would acquire knowledge through the use of this, rather than a large, hardbound encyclopedia.

Other factors – even success – can affect what we notice. Success creates confidence, which can lead to the creation of buffers that insulate us from a range of events and exclude background stimuli from consideration. The success of Nasa, for instance, in overcoming insurmountable technological problems gave rise to confidence. It also gave rise to complacency – one of the contributing causes of the Challenger space shuttle disaster.

Such perceptual limitations will be as evident in the next millennium as they are now. They are part of our make-up and profoundly influence how we view the world and events around us. We need to observe these processes at work within ourselves and understand their limitations as well as their strengths. Where possible, we need to work at broadening our perceptions in order to cope more effectively with the changes that lie ahead. Those organizations that can create a culture that challenges unhelpful perceptual processes (stemming, say, from ignorance, prejudice or arrogance) will, in our view, be more able to absorb new information and respond intelligently to change.

Perception, values and beliefs

Broadening our mind, however, is much easier said than done. To understand why this is so, it is worth looking at influences on our perceptual processes. At the most fundamental level lie our values and beliefs. These also color what we see and how we interpret events. Given this, it is important we reflect on how our own values influence the decisions we make.

Values are the guidelines a person uses to make choices. Truth, honesty, integrity and wealth creation are values which influence our view of the world and our place within it. Early childhood experiences and upbringing help form these beliefs which can guide our actions throughout our adult life. Within organizations, basic beliefs affect what decisions are made, how people inter-act, and the kind of work practices that are pursued and developed. They form the glue that binds an organization's culture. That culture can work for the organization, or against it, with results that can dramatically affect the bottom line.[11]

Building an understanding of the values that are shared within an organi-zation will be as important in the 21st century as it is today. In fact, many feel that organizations and people should be returning to more fundamental values, rather than moving away from them. Increasingly, organizations are spending time working out and agreeing the values by which they want their organiza-tions to be managed. From these they have to develop guiding principles which determine how work should be carried out as well as what needs to be done.[12] This emphasis on the *how* rather than the *what* challenges people to think about their beliefs, how they relate to others, whether they value trust and fair treatment, and under what circumstances. In the world of managerial work, values are as much a part of the cultural infrastructure as the microchip is to information systems. The smart organization will try to ensure progress on both fronts.

Personality and creativity

In addition to one's values and beliefs, the overall personality of the individual will influence how information is gathered, interpreted, and acted upon. A pop-ular categorization in the management field is the Myers Briggs personality test. This is concerned with several aspects of personality, including an indi-vidual's preference for gathering information and how decisions are made. The test highlights how an individual can gather data through their senses in a fac-tual, data-driven way, or through intuitive processes. It also highlights the extent to which we make decisions either through logical, rational processes or based on feelings and principles.

An understanding of categorizations like this can assist in creating leaders within organizations who may cope better with future challenges. As part of an exercise designed to create a more flexible, adaptive organization, Royal/Dutch Shell organized for its top 100 managers to take this test.[13] The results were particularly revealing, showing that 86 percent of its top people were "thinkers", i.e. people who make decisions based on logic and objective analysis. At the very top of the organization, on the six-man management committee, 60 percent were on the opposite scale, i.e. "feelers" who had a predisposition towards making decisions based on values and subjective evaluation. Such tests are not the panacea, but we predict that individuals who attempt to better understand the differences in people's thinking patterns and how this may affect their problem-solving and decision-making styles will be more able to exploit the advances of the future.

This is particularly true in discussing creativity. An aspect of cognitive style, which is implicitly incorporated in the Myers Briggs personality test, is the division between right and left-brain thinking. For some years, this classification has been used to distinguish between two different clusters of cognitive activity. In a nutshell, the division is between an analytical capacity and an intuitive one. The left side of the brain is concerned with analytical processes and specializes in verbal and mathematical functions. The right side intuits information from a variety of inputs and is concerned with visual imagery, creative synthesis, intuition, fantasy, and associative processes.

Depending on which hemisphere of the brain is dominant, people differ in the way they process information. Historically, managers have been encouraged to use rational or left-brain thinking processes. The logical, analytical approach to problem solving is often seen as the correct one. Nowadays, right-brain activities are increasingly being promoted as the kind of thought processes needed, particularly at senior level. Henry Mintzberg has long been one of the most influential proponents of this idea, arguing that right-hemisphere activities should be used to think through strategic management problems.[14]

Indeed, creativity would seem to be one of the musts for the millennium. Increasingly, the most successful companies take innovation and creativity very seriously, which appears to help their business results quite significantly. In *Fortune*'s 1997 list of America's most admired companies, virtually all of those awarded high marks for innovation had had a significant impact on their industry and in the process, produced impressive increases in earnings and market capitalization.[15]

London Business School Professor Gary Hamel places a big emphasis on creativity, imagination, and any other right-brain process which helps managers think outside the box and break the rules. He argues that intense competition is the norm in many industries and, increasingly, the best way to compete is to totally rethink traditional industry boundaries and strategic gameplans. Organizations are being exhorted to compete on the basis of their core competencies which, in Hamel's view, is essentially a creative task. In his mind it involves "getting down to the very essence of who we are and what it is we're capable of." Those wishing to compete for the future must realize "it is shaped not by prophets but by heretics, seeing unconventionally into the past."[16]

But will the future really be characterized by the flow of such creative juices throughout organizations? We are not convinced. People build many different kinds of walls that can prevent them and others from scrutinizing their thought processes. In the managerial world, ego, not wanting to be seen to be wrong, the belief that managers must know what's going on, are all factors which have the potential to limit people's thinking – and prevent them from acting even when the evidence for change is overwhelming.

Organizations that are in the top league for creativity (i.e. Coca-Cola, Merck, and Microsoft) understand these limitations and actively cultivate organizational cultures that support people taking risks, and even failing, in order to help generate new ideas. Nor do they try to limit creativity to the R&D departments. Instead they argue that creativity should be demonstrated throughout the organization and in how everyone goes about their work. They also understand that it is not just about generating ideas, it is about making sure they get implemented. Organizations that can manage individual differences successfully and create climates where intellectual strengths can be exploited to the full may well be the ones which prosper in future.

Emotional intelligence

In looking at how people might react and cope with a different information and technological future, it is also important to emphasize that managerial thought processes are affected not only by cognitive style, values, and ego but also by an individual's emotional make-up. Responding to other people and situations that are different and challenging (and which may involve a degree of conflict, stress and setback) has, and always will have, emotional consequences. However, it is only relatively recently that emotion and the effect it can have on managerial decision making has come to the fore.

Developing what Goleman calls "emotional intelligence" will be critical if people are to cope with the pressures of the future.[17] He uses this term to describe the range of abilities which people use to manage their emotional selves and get the most out of their relationships with others. He identifies a range of emotional competences, such as the capacity to empathize, handle conflict, and use one's anger appropriately. According to him, emotional intelligence can not only help someone perform more effectively on the job, it can also contribute to one's physical well-being and sense of emotional stability. He believes that "a new competitive reality is putting emotional intelligence at a premium in the workplace." We predict that, in future, organizations which fail to recognize the impact of this reality and the need to develop emotional intelligence will produce a workforce that is only partially equipped to deal with the new economic and technological realities. We also believe that this failure to acknowledge emotional consequences will continue to be the norm rather than the exception.

TECHNOLOGY AND THE NEED TO INTERACT

Clearly, in looking at the future, the impact of information flows and technology on the individual cannot be seen in isolation. People work in a social context. In the new millennium this context is likely to be one where work is subject to continual change, to be more interconnected and team-based.[18] Although technology may provide different and faster ways of staying in touch, people will still need to work hard at how they interact and communicate, particularly at an interpersonal level. In the survey cited earlier (which examined the impact of technology on 350 executives' working lives), 54 percent argued that "IT had produced more misunderstandings than real-time human conversation." Over 50 percent of respondents said "IT had caused work relationships to deteriorate."

Technology does not replace the need for human interaction and we believe that many companies in the future will miss this point to their detriment. They could well focus on the technology-based advantages of communication and pay less attention to the inescapable need of human beings to continue to interact beyond mere information flow. In the early seventies Mintzberg highlighted the interaction processes of managers, observing that much of the information they are exposed to comes through social processes and interpersonal contact. There is every reason to believe this will continue. This is because managerial roles, at least, will continue to be characterized by fleeting interactions and brief contact with a range of people during the working day.

> *Technology does not replace the need for human interaction and we believe that many companies in the future will miss this point to their detriment.*

Despite advances in technology, the quality of the information managers receive will continue to vary enormously for a number of different reasons. Quite often, information comes from those people to whom managers have easy access and with whom they get on. The ease of acquisition is sometimes more important than the quality of information they receive. As a consequence, decision makers may use sources that provide lower quality information but are readily accessible.

Also, there is a general bias towards positive as against negative information. Information is more likely to be used by decision makers if it is supportive of outcomes already favoured, if it avoids conflict, and if it cannot be challenged.[19] Many staff members tell their managers what they want to hear, withholding a contradictory personal opinion or neglecting to report all the uncomfortable facts. Managers will often take positive feedback at face value, failing to consider that the information may not be completely valid.

Political processes may also affect the reliability of the information. It is unlikely that politics will not exist in the organization of the future. Decision making as a process of muddling through, with organizations set up and sustained by a dominant coalition of powerful stakeholders, will be as much a feature of the workplace in the new millennium as it is today. Those in power will still be prepared to pay high prices (and play hard games) for the information or ideas which make a difference.

A consequence of this is that organizations will have to continue to develop the ability of their staff to manage their jobs and work situations effectively. It is more likely, however, that they will be seduced by the grandiose claims of what technology can do and the constant barrage that the only soft organizational ability to worry about is leadership. We believe that many will miss the fundamental need to continue to develop the skills of effective time and resource management. If we have not learned to prioritize, what use is the latest hand-held organizer? We need to remind ourselves that technology cannot supplant the basics. We still need to think these through if we are to remain in charge of our own destinies.

DEVELOPING BREADTH AND FOCUS

As the new millennium approaches, managers face a very real danger of becoming *less* effective as a result of the volume of information available. To date, computers still do not deliver information that has the variety, currency and relevance managers need.[20] Instead information is usually dated, focussed on the internal workings of the organization, and in much greater volume than people want. Indeed, we argue, until the emphasis shifts from the technology and moves towards the creation of information and knowledge which is of value to the end user, this shortcoming is likely to continue.

In order to make use of increased sources of information, managers will need to cultivate an intellectual ability to combine the broad picture (breadth) together with an ability to focus on the critical issues.[21] Although the two qualities of breadth and focus look contradictory, several writers have highlighted the need for a similar combination. Senge has talked of the need to have both a broad scope and the capacity to focus one's actions through leverage.[22] Others have commented that, in addition to thinking about broader processes, senior managers think about how to deal with one or two overriding concerns, or very general goals.[23]

Managers must be able to expand their minds to try to take in as much of the data pertinent to a problem that is available. An awareness of the filtering processes, discussed earlier, may help with this. However, breadth is not just about how much data one can absorb. It is also concerned with constructive capacities: namely, the capacity for integration, abstraction, independent thought, and the use of broad and complex frames of reference.

In addition, managers and critical decision-makers need to bring focus to the problems they face. Ultimately, they must be capable of reducing complex situations to their essentials, identifying opportunities and proposing well-founded courses of action. Whether technology can help in this regard is a matter of some debate. Paul Saffo, a director of the Institute for the Future in California, believes that executives will need to be careful not to be seduced by the new tools that become available. Instead they need to become "machine wise," i.e. they need to know when and how to use these new tools but also when to switch off their computers and take their own counsel.[24]

Breadth is critical when one is trying to understand the environment, identify problems, seek alternatives, and find solutions. It is necessary when one needs to think outside one's current paradigm, see new possibilities, and identify linkages. While advances in technology may help us do this better, ultimately it is the manager who has to make these links. Similarly, focus is important when selecting alternatives, choosing solutions, and implementing them. But again, while computer technology may well be able to sort through and implement routine activities, ultimately the capacity to prioritize and implement will depend on the manager's drive and their decision-making capability.

MANAGERIAL MINDSETS

In this chapter we have argued that we need to understand both the cognitive processes we use and our own emotional capability and make-up. Both have an influence on our capacity to manage our managerial mindset. Those who are most successful at reducing the disconnection caused by technological change will be those who can combine and exploit their intellectual and emotional capacities in particular ways. A framework we have developed illustrates this (*see* Figure 8.1). It combines two aspects:

- an individual's capacity to have both breadth and focus
- the manager's emotional disposition, in particular, whether they tend to be positive or negative in outlook. These dimensions combine to produce different mindsets.

These mindsets are not permanent states and individuals may change from one mindset to another. The optimum approach is the flexible mindset – one

Fig. 8.1 Managerial Mindset

that successful workers in the new millennium will be increasingly called upon to adopt. (However, we would go even further and argue that individuals who can't shift out of the despondent or conservative mindsets may find themselves at a particular disadvantage.) The characteristics of each mindset are described below:

- the despondent mindset is where an individual has a negative attitude and narrow outlook. The attitude people adopt with this mindset tends to be (almost always) some variation of the theme: "That's the way things are" or "There's not much we can do." In future, no organization can afford to have people whose predominant mindset is both despondent and narrow in focus;

- the conservative mindset is where the individual may have breadth, see inter-linkages, and accommodate a wide range of information, but their emotional and attitudinal response is again to emphasize why things cannot be done by focussing on the hurdles that stand in their way. The person here is typically risk-averse. This mindset exemplifies the critic rather than the creator. Their preferred response of can't do rather than can do limits not only themselves but also their judgement of what others are capable of achieving. It is not a lack of analysis but a lack of confidence which is the major problem. If the next millennium does in fact turn out to be as dynamic as many predict, individuals with a conservative mindset may simply take too long to act and find that, instead, events simply pass them by;

- the bounded mindset displays confidence and a positive mental attitude, but takes a narrow focus. This mindset is best where there is a clear direction and the manager does not need to worry about doing further analysis or questioning the path that is being taken. Indeed, in some circumstances (particularly in extremely difficult times when change has to be driven through) it may be impossible to succeed without such a mindset. This mindset can also become a liability. Having confidence, but too narrow a focus at the wrong time, or at the wrong stage of the decision-making process, can lead to complacency or arrogance. In a survey of top-level executives, complacency and a low sense of urgency were cited as the second most important obstacles to making strategic change happen.[25] They described complacency as a kind of passive resistance which happens when things are going too well;

* the flexible mindset is one that combines a broad outlook with a positive mental attitude – often a critical asset during times of change. With this mindset, one is positive but also willing to accept new information, possibilities, and inter-relationships. Overall, the emphasis is on seeking alternative ways forward with the underlying assumption that somewhere, there is a solution. Those looking to succeed in tomorrow's organization would do well to consider this kind of mindset. Those who do will find they are more resilient mentally, more flexible, and creative in their responses. Indeed, we predict this kind of mindset will be key to developing new directions in many organizations.

CONCLUSION

In this chapter we have argued that complexity and constant change will characterize people's work environments and that to succeed individuals need to think more broadly about the capabilities and mindsets they bring to their jobs. The emergence of knowledge as a key economic resource and the importance of technology and information systems are forces that are here to stay. Increasingly, however, the demand will be for people with both the intellect and overall capability to adapt and change to this new reality. At all levels of an organization, a premium will be placed on those who can think more broadly but also bring focus to what they do.

The issues we have raised highlight the likelihood that fewer, rather than more, people will be able to fully exploit the technologies of the future and possibly cope well with the rapid changes that lie ahead. As stated at the outset, we predict that for many companies the corporate battles of the millennium will be more about changing mindsets than about changing technology.

II

21C

PROCESSES

It is time to call on managers to embrace collectively a new philosophy of management, one that enables managerial action as part of a positive role that can release the vast potential that remains trapped by a clawing adherence to the old model. In a powerful piece of writing Sumantra Ghoshal and Peter Moran of London Business School and Christopher A. Bartlett of Harvard Business School open the second part of the book. With eye-opening, detailed tours into corporations from the USA, Europe and Asia, they boldly suggest: "Throw out the old paradigm and start experimenting with new, more fertile possibilities. Otherwise the fatal gap between companies' economic power and their social legitimacy will continue to grow, stunting the growth potential of individuals, companies and society as a whole."

Renowned strategist C.K. Prahalad strongly believes we will have to re-examine concepts and tools that have dominated our thinking about managing – power, structure, hierarchy, control, co-ordination, ownership, and incentives – and that newer concepts and tools will emerge. He outlines the changing nature of the competitive landscape and how these forces will challenge the notions of "managing." He also discusses the emerging nature of managerial work and suggests that its transformation will demand basic organizational innovations. The changing role of managing suggests that we should pay special attention to the role of senior managers and the six critical elements on which they must concentrate in the 21st century.

Management processes in the new millennium will be much more behavioral in nature, focussing on the key human resource-driven issues: learning, team-based visions, driving human resource processes, incentives to enhance growth, holistic budgeting, and proactive controls. Peter Lorange, president of the International Institute of Management Development, discusses all these vital processes and confidently predicts that "ultra-rapid growth" will be the key to shaping management processes in the next century.

Management is of pivotal importance in modern society. Management education programs foster social competency and proficiency in intellectual analysis, and should be flexible to facilitate managers to be more effective in a complex changing world. J. Wil Foppen, dean of the Rotterdam School of Management, looks at knowledge leadership and management education. He strongly believes that both are making a considerable contribution to the strategic business aims of safeguarding organizational flexibility, adaptability, and creativity.

Business Week estimates that companies spend $15 billion annually on executive education and leadership development. How do organizations pick their leaders? What processes transform managers into leaders ready for strategic action? Robert M. Fulmer and Marshall Goldsmith show us the key trends and challenges in leadership development of the 21st century. They also outline their experiences with some of the world's best practitioners of leadership development – Arthur Andersen, General Electric, Hewlett-Packard, Johnson & Johnson, Shell International, and the World Bank.

How can we better understand and nurture leadership communities, people in diverse positions who collectively help the members of an enterprise shape their future? Eminent thinker Peter M. Senge and Sloan researcher Katrin H. Käufer argue that rather than making executives less important, understanding leadership communities brings the unique roles of executive leaders into much clearer relief, as it does the roles for other types of leaders, all of whom will ultimately depend upon each other in creating successful 21st century enterprises. In a unique style, Senge and Käufer present the beginnings of a theory in the concluding chapter of Part II and suggest that translating this theory into practice requires developing the capacity of people engaged in real change processes to think systemically.

9

VALUE CREATION: THE NEW MILLENNIUM MANAGEMENT MANIFESTO

SUMANTRA GHOSHAL, CHRISTOPHER A. BARTLETT AND PETER MORAN

In business circles, a story is often told of two hikers who wake up one night to find a tiger lurking near their tent. One of the hikers immediately reaches for his running shoes. "You cannot outrun a tiger," reminds his partner. "Yes," he responds, "but all I have to do is outrun you."

A good joke, perhaps, but bad strategy. Think again, and it will become clear that the hiker's survival prospects are poor in the long run. Given this strategy, in a world of tigers and hikers, tigers will prevail. Even if one hiker survives the first encounter by outrunning his partner, he will succumb in some subsequent encounter either to a faster partner or because he will have run out of partners and will have to go hiking alone. The source of his ultimate defeat would lie in precisely the same strategy that won him his earlier success: instead of doing something a tiger cannot, such as lighting a fire or going up a tree, he chose to play the tiger's game by running.

Managers of most companies think of other companies as their competitors and, indeed, they are. In some sense, however, all of them are also like our hikers; and the tiger, for these companies, is the market. Companies try to make high profits. The market marshals forces that bring prices down to the level of variable costs. Companies try to grow, to diversify, to globalize – to become big and powerful. The market's forces work to break them up, to make them small, and powerless. For each and every company, big or small, the ultimate competitor is not another company but the market. A company survives and prospers only when it can beat the market, and it loses its right to exist when this is no longer the case.

If all of this appears too abstract or theoretical, just remind yourself of all the advice you have recently been given: to create sharp, performance-based incentives for your managers, to outsource as much as you can, to create market-based transfer prices within the company, and so on. These are all efforts to bring the market's rules into your organization, to make it more like a market – the functional equivalent of running to save yourself from the tiger. You must do some of these things, of course, as a matter of adopting healthy habits. But adopt them as your core management philosophy, and you will be making the same mistake our hiker did. By making your company more and more like a market, you may succeed in the short run, but in the long run you will be devoured by the market. You will prune your portfolio, outsource, and prune again until there is nothing left to prune.

If mimicking the market is so bad, why is the advice to do it so pervasive? Why are companies so focussed on their competitors? What alternatives are there? We believe the answer to these questions lies in the assumptions about individuals and institutions that have led to this view of management held by many. It is time to replace these disabling assumptions with those that collectively call on managers to embrace a very different management philosophy. Grounded in an alternative set of assumptions about both individuals and institutions, this philosophy leads to some very different beliefs about the role of the company in society, about the relationship between employers and employees, and about the functions of management and its obligations as a profession. Overall, it posits a very different moral contract between the individual, the company, and society.

CREATING VALUE FOR SOCIETY

There is much truth in the saying that every living practitioner is prisoner to the ideas of a dead theorist. Immunized by their daily confrontation with the "real world," corporate managers typically exhibit a healthy distrust of theory that has, in general, served them well. Despite this ingrained circumspection, many managers nonetheless have become unwitting victims of ideas that have run out of explanatory power.

> *There is much truth in the saying that every living practitioner is prisoner to the ideas of a dead theorist.*

Much of modern management practice stems from theories rooted in the era that ranged from the trust-busting early decades of the 20th century to the post-Vietnam period of profound pessimism about people and institutions in general. The theories of corporate behavior that rose out of this period of distrust of companies have contributed to an amoral philosophy of management, premised on highly instrumental relationships between the company and society on the one hand, and between the company and its employee on the other. For example, it was the economists' mistrust of the motivations and actions of corporations that led to the nationalization movement in Europe and the regulatory environment in the USA. On both sides of the Atlantic, economists supported these broad movements with well-developed theories of how companies distorted the beauty of open markets and pure competition by erecting barriers and obstructing the free flows of resources. The battle lines between companies and markets soon became clear.

Companies as value appropriators

It did not take long before industrial organization economists, and the business strategists who followed them, saw the opportunity to turn these findings on their head. If social welfare can be served by preventing industries and individual companies from impeding and obstructing competition, then it stands to reason that one way companies can enhance their position is by maintaining – or, even better, raising – obstacles to competition.

Nowhere was the power and influence of this insight better articulated and developed than in Michael Porter's theory of competitive strategy.[1] Porter sees companies as positioned in the midst of a set of competing forces that pits them against all others. Thus, a company is seen as competing not just with its direct competitors, but with its suppliers, customers, and any potential competitor who threatens either to overcome the barriers to entry in the company's businesses or to find substitutes for the company's products or services. Porter leads us to conclude that management's core challenge is to enhance the company's power over its suppliers and customers and to find ways to keep existing and future competitors at bay, in order to protect the firm's strategic advantages and to benefit maximally from them.

The essence of this theory is simple: a company prospers most when it can capture as much as possible of the value that is embodied in its products and services. Its objective, then, is to focus on how best to seize whatever value is being realized in its midst. The problem is that there are others – customers, suppliers and competitors – who want to do the same. As the economists point out, if there is genuine, free competition, companies can make no profits above the market value of their resources. The purpose of strategy, therefore, is to prevent such open and free competition: to claim the largest share of the pie while preventing others from doing the same.

The difficulty in this view is that the interests of the company are incompatible with those of society. For society, the freer the competition among companies the better. But given the notion of competition as a battle of appropriation, the lesson for the individual firm is clear: restrict the competition to keep maximum value for yourself. To do their job (of enhancing corporate profits), managers must prevent free competition at the cost of social welfare. So the destruction of social welfare is not just a consequence of firm strategy, it is the fundamental objective of profit-seeking companies.

Yet this view of a company simply does not square with the reality of modern societies. The past 100 years have seen an uninterrupted and unprecedented improvement in the quality of human life, due, in a large measure, to the ability of companies to continuously improve their productivity and their talent for creating new products and services. As Nobel Laureate Herbert Simon has said, to call modern society a "market economy" is a misnomer; it is primarily an "organizational economy" in which most of the economic value is created not through economists' ideal of highly fragmented, pure competition in a completely free market, but within efficient, well-functioning organizations involving large numbers of people acting collectively, co-ordinated by the broader purpose of the total organization.[2]

Most companies do not usurp markets to appropriate value for themselves at the cost of social welfare. Rather, in healthy economies, many successful and prosperous corporations coexist with intensely competitive markets in a state of vigorous and creative tension with one another, each contributing to economic progress but in different ways. Companies create new value for society by continuously creating innovative products and services and by finding better ways to make and offer existing ones; markets, on the other hand, relentlessly force the same companies to surrender, over time, most of this value to others. In this symbiotic coexistence, companies and markets interact *jointly* to drive the process of creative destruction that Joseph Schumpeter, the Austrian economist, showed to be the engine that powers economic progress in capitalist societies.[3]

The problem with Porter's conceptualization, which has shaped the thinking of a whole generation of managers, lies not so much with its hard-nosed focus on value appropriation; this was in fact a significant step forward, particularly in Porter's dissection of the "value chain" and his articulation of how industry structure influences the firm's conduct, as well as its performance. Rather, it is when the value chain is taken as given that faulty analysis begins. After all, with no theory to guide us on how the economic pie grows, any consideration of "who gets what?" must necessarily become a zero-sum game; all that is left to be decided is how the pie is to be divided up. When the source of value is taken for granted and consequently ignored, profits can come only at a cost to someone – and this cost is all too often borne by society. In sharp contrast, Schumpeter's very different view of companies focusses on the dynamics of how the pie gets bigger in a positive-sum game in which there is more for all to share. In this view, instead of merely appropriating value, companies serve as society's main engine of discovery; they progress by continuously creating new value out of its existing endowment of resources.

Companies as value creators

The contrast between these two views of a company comes sharply into focus if we compare the management approaches of Norton and 3M, or of

Westinghouse and ABB. As we have described elsewhere,[4] managers at Norton and Westinghouse lived in the zero-sum, dog-eat-dog world of traditional strategic theory. When they found a company that had created an attractive product or a business, they bought it. When they found the market for a product to be too competitive for them to dictate terms to their buyers and suppliers, they sold those businesses. Their primary management focus was on value appropriation, not only vis-à-vis their customers and suppliers, but vis-à-vis their own employees.

> *Managers at Norton and Westinghouse lived in the zero-sum, dog-eat-dog world of traditional strategic theory.*

In 3M and ABB, in contrast, a very different management philosophy was at work. While Norton tried to develop increasingly sophisticated strategic resource allocation models, 3M's entire strategy was based on the value-creating logic of continuous innovation. The same power equipment business that Westinghouse abandoned as unattractive (i.e. not enough opportunity for value appropriation), ABB rejuvenated, in part by its investments in productivity and in new technologies to enhance products' functionality or their appropriateness for new markets.

As these companies created products or markets, society rewarded them with high margins as a share of the new value they created. However, over time the margins eroded. As competitors caught up, what the companies lost in profits, their customers, specifically, and society, more generally, received in the form of additional value. Rather than focussing their efforts on impeding or slowing the forces working to "hand on" this value to a widening circle of beneficiaries (which generally keeps the value itself from expanding), these companies concentrated on finding ever more sources of new value. By the time most of the initially high profit margin of any given innovation had been handed on to society through such market pressures, the companies had discovered new opportunities in the form of new products and applications to start the process all over again.

The difference between these companies is not just that 3M and ABB focussed on innovation and improvement while Norton and Westinghouse did not, but that this difference in focus stemmed from very different beliefs about what a company is. At Norton and Westinghouse, managers thought of their companies in market terms: they bought and sold businesses, created internal markets whenever they could, and dealt with their people with market rules. Through the power of sharp, market-like incentives, they got what they wanted. People began to behave as they would in a market – acting alone as independent agents with an atomistic concern only for their self-interest.

By thinking of their companies in market terms, Norton and Westinghouse became the victims of a market logic in which all they could do was strive to squeeze out more efficiencies in everything. Their strategy focussed entirely on productivity improvement and cost cutting. Their structures for controlling behavior rewarded autonomy, while their elaborate systems for monitoring performance were finely tuned to eliminate even the smallest pools of waste. Yet they could not create innovations; not because they explicitly did not want to do so, but because the logic of the market that they adopted internally is simply not very good at anything other than enhancing the efficiency of existing activities.[5] With the uncertainties inherent in any innovative effort, both in terms of the size of ultimate benefits and the distribution of those benefits, the very sharp sense of self-interest these firms engendered in their people made them unable to co-operate among themselves and to pool their resources and capabilities to create new combinations – particularly new combinations of knowledge and expertise – that most innovations require.

To create innovations and new value, a company typically is required to create a level of slack – sacrifice some efficiencies – by allocating resources to uses that do not yield the highest immediate returns. This is because there is a built-in conflict between trying to extract the greatest productivity out of existing activities and the willingness to make short-term sacrifices of efficiency to invest in innovations. Even path-breaking innovations often start their lives at a disadvantage over existing alternatives, and they reach their potential only over time. As Schumpeter said:

> "A system – any system, economic or other – that at every given point of time fully utilizes its possibilities to the best advantage may yet in the long run be inferior to a system that does so at no point of time, because the latter's failure to do so may be a condition for the level or speed of long-run performance."[6]

By thinking of their companies in market terms, Westinghouse and Norton became victims of the market straightjacket, unable to create the conditions required to enhance the "level or speed of long-run performance" because of their total focus on fully utilizing their resources and relationships to whatever advantage the market dictated to be best.

The degree to which a philosophy of "market fundamentalism" became ingrained at Westinghouse is, perhaps, best captured in CEO Robert Kirby's claim that he would fire his own mother if she didn't meet her numbers.

The problem is that when its people act alone, and only in their own interest, the company loses its very essence as an institution of modern society – the essence of what distinguishes it from a market and endows it with the ability to create value in

When its people act alone, and only in their own interest, the company loses its very essence as an institution of modern society – the essence of what distinguishes it from a market and endows it with the ability to create value in a way that markets cannot.

a way that markets cannot. In a market where behavior is relatively less encumbered, people are encouraged to carry out only and all those economic exchanges from which they clearly see some individual gain.[7] Because markets have no purpose or vision of their own, they can ruthlessly weed out inefficiencies by allocating resources among a broader set of alternatives and by adjusting quickly and reallocating continually to new alternatives as they emerge. Indeed, this is the essence of the market's strength. But when transacting in a market, people tend to avoid those transactions whose success depends on the actions of others, particularly if those others have more attractive alternatives and are encouraged to pursue them. This is true, paradoxically, even if all would have been better off had they not followed those alternatives.

For this reason, the "corrective" discipline of market forces is prone to what are referred to commonly as "co-ordination failures" and also, as Schumpeter showed, these failures are biased systematically to preclude innovations that require altogether new combinations of resources.[8] This is why markets alone are not very good at bringing about innovations and why organizations are needed. It suggests also the kinds of organization that are needed, i.e. not those with an ability to amplify or focus market forces but those that are able to do just the opposite – to mute and diffuse the market's forces. The "organizational advantage" of companies over markets is not one of enhancing allocative efficiency, although some organizations clearly do this. Rather, the organizational advantage of a company stems directly from its own inertial forces that enable it to institutionalize the rationale of some longer term purpose. This ability to institutionalize new behaviors (long before any market recognizes their value) gives companies the leverage needed to escape the straightjacket of current productivity that the market locks us into.[9]

Visions like ABB's purpose "to make economic growth and improved living standards a reality for all nations throughout the world;" values such as Kao Corporation's espoused belief that "we are, first of all, an educational institution;" and norms like 3M's acceptance that "products belong to divisions but technologies belong to the company" all emphasize the non-market-like nature of a company, encouraging people to work collectively to shared goals and values rather than more restrictively, within their narrow self-interests. They can share resources, including knowledge, without having to be certain of how precisely each of them will benefit personally – as long as they believe that the company overall will benefit, to their collective gain.[10] It is, ultimately, this philosophical distinction in their beliefs about what a company is that allows these organizations to create innovations through a spirit of collaboration among people that markets, and companies that think of themselves as markets, cannot engender.

In fact, companies like 3M, Kao and ABB offer their people a temporary respite from market forces by actually muting the market's sharp incentives and creating others more supportive of collaboration and sharing, thereby creating a (temporarily) protected environment in which individuals can combine to challenge market forces to generate new combinations of resources that create new value for society. Markets allocate existing resources efficiently; these companies make (temporary) inefficiencies possible, which in time create new outputs that themselves become resources for the market to allocate at a different level. This is precisely what 3M does by allowing people 15 percent "bootleg" time to pursue their own projects. While inevitably some such efforts lead to inefficiency and waste, it is ultimately this ability and willingness of companies to challenge *existing* markets that has created most of the important innovations that have changed human lives and created *future* markets. In other words, a company's ability to create new value for society is a product of a management philosophy of viewing the company not just as an economic entity – a substitute for a market – but also as a social institution which allows individuals to behave differently from how they would in a market.

Companies and society

Over the 20th century, corporations have earned an enormous amount of social legitimacy, which has been both a cause and a consequence of their collective success. Amid a general decline of other institutions – political parties, churches, the community, even the family unit – corporations have emerged as perhaps the most influential institution of modern society, not only creating and distributing a large part of its wealth but also providing a social context for most of its people, thereby acting as a source of individual satisfaction and social succor.

Yet in the closing decades of the century, corporations and their managers suffer from a profound social ambivalence. The evidence is everywhere – in President Bill Clinton's White House conference on corporate responsibility amid a growing climate of downsizing in the United States; in Prime Minister Tony Blair's reviews of the role of the corporation in the United Kingdom; in the deep suspicion of large companies in France, Korea and even Germany; and in the public furor over executive pay in countries where the astronomical wealth of entertainers, entrepreneurs, sports people, or even independent professionals raises relatively few eyebrows. In fact, corporate managers have been knocked from the pedestal in most countries; they are fast becoming one of the least trusted constituents of society.

There is a clear lesson from history: institutions decline when they lose their social legitimacy. This is what happened to the monarchy, to organized religion, and to the state.

Given the powerful and largely positive role companies have played in society, this perception is unfair. Yet it persists, and a few visible misdeeds of some companies and individuals to appropriate more for themselves serve to give this perception its ascendancy and to make it potentially one of the greatest risks corporations face today. There is a clear lesson from history: institutions decline when they lose their social legitimacy. This is what happened to the monarchy, to organized religion, and to the state. This is what will happen to companies unless managers accord the same priority to the collective task of rebuilding the credibility and legitimacy of their institutions as they do to the individual task of enhancing their company's economic performance.

Far from thinking of their companies as agents for destroying social welfare, most managers we have met believe their primary role is to create value. Their guilt lies in their unwillingness to confront explicitly the role their companies play in society or to articulate a moral philosophy for their own profession. Through this act of omission, they have left others – economists, political scientists, journalists, and so on – to define the normative order that shapes public perceptions about themselves and their institutions. Those perceptions, in turn, have seduced many managers into thinking about their companies in very narrow terms and, in the process, have made them unconscious victims of the value appropriation logic and weakened their ability to create new value for society.

This is why we believe that individuals like Percy Barnevik, chairman of ABB, Jack Welch, CEO of General Electric, and Yoshio Maruta, chairman of Kao Corporation, will earn their places in history – not because of the economic performance of their firms while they were in the saddle, because hundreds of managers achieve that routinely, but because they have wrested back the initiative to define a new corporate philosophy that explicitly articulates a view of companies as value-creating institutions of society. They have not reinvented the old and tired debate of the social responsibility of business, instead they have made value creation for all constituencies their fundamental business. And then they have reshaped the organization and management processes of their companies around this new philosophy, to give birth to a new corporate form that we have labeled elsewhere the "individualized corporation."[11]

This new moral contract of creating value for society is not only more satisfying for managers, it is also a more effective basis for protecting and expanding their companies. The problem of a strategy of value appropriation is that, ultimately, it is a self-defeating posture. It is like a strategy of holding back the tide; and like the tide, the ability of others to overcome a company's defenses cannot be held back for ever. With such a strategy, the company gets squeezed more and more into a corner, with every round of value appropriation consuming ever more effort, until finally there is no value left to appropriate. By thinking of themselves as a market, such companies ultimately succumb to the market – as happened in Norton's acquisition by St Gobain, and in Westinghouse's dismemberment under Michael Jordan. Hansen Trust followed a classic value appropriation strategy, as did ITT under Harold Geneen. In so doing, all these companies unwittingly hastened the process of creative destruction by choosing a game that markets can always play better. As market forces did their job, resources were wrested systematically from each of these companies and reallocated to those omnipresent others that inevitably become even more efficient. Ultimately, each of these companies fell victim to the same market logic that they had embraced so enthusiastically within themselves. In the process, value was destroyed for all their constituents, including their customers, their shareholders, and their employees.

In contrast, 3M and Kao continue to grow profitably, spawning new products and businesses, creating customer satisfaction, employee enthusiasm, and shareholder wealth, and ABB continues to expand and strengthen its leadership position in its businesses, at times by acquiring the spent-up parts of companies like Westinghouse, and rejuvenating them with the power of its very different philosophy.

CREATING VALUE FOR PEOPLE

Within the concept of a company as a value-appropriating economic entity, its relationship with its employees is also shaped by appropriative norms. Like all other constituencies, people become a source from which the company can extract value to achieve its economic objectives. At its worst, this appropriative philosophy leads to a ruthless exploitation of workers. But in countries with an infrastructure of employment laws and at least some form of external labor markets, more typically it translates into something more benign – an employment relationship based on employment security. In this contract, the company guarantees the employees' jobs in exchange for their willingness to execute diligently the tasks that are allocated to them, and to abide by the strategies, rules, and norms that management establishes for the company.

The traditional employment contract

It is counterintuitive to think of the offer of employment security as exploitive of people, for this is not how this arrangement emerged, nor how most employees and employers think about such a relationship. Yet, benign as it may appear, it is this relationship of security for loyalty that historically has enabled companies to extract the greatest possible value out of their employees.

Unlike machines, people cannot be owned. Yet, like machines, the way they become most valuable to a company is by becoming specialized to the company's businesses and activities. The more specific the employee's knowledge and skills are to a company's unique set of customers, technologies, equipments, and so on, the more productive they become and the more efficient the company becomes in all that it does. Without employment security, employees hesitate to invest their time and energy to acquire such specialized knowledge and skills that may be very useful to the company, but may have limited value outside of it. Without any assurance of a long-term association, companies lack the incentive to commit resources to help employees develop such company-specific expertise. Employment security provides a viable basis for both to make such investments.[12]

> *Unlike machines, people cannot be owned. Yet, like machines, the way they become most valuable to a company is by becoming specialized to the company's businesses and activities.*

While the company benefits from such specialization directly, in terms of efficiency and productivity, it also benefits indirectly because the more specialized an employee becomes to the unique requirements of the company, the less attractive they become to other potential employers. Not only does this make employees less mobile, it also reduces their market value and allows the company to pay less and demand loyalty.

Exploitive or not, this contract defined a viable relationship. Employees developed the special knowledge and expertise the employer's business needed, thereby enhancing the company's efficiency but also narrowing their skills and mobility. While companies absorbed the risks by granting jobs for life, employees promised loyalty and obedience, which allowed managers to create strategies and implement them efficiently and made employees as reliable and controllable as other assets the company owned.

Over the past decade this moral contract has broken down. Company after company – not only in the United States and Europe but also in Brazil, India, Japan, and Korea – has pursued efficiencies through downsizing and outsourcing strategies that have abandoned any established policies of providing secure employment. Initially used by some as a stop-gap measure to stem the flow of red ink to the bottom line, such downsizing and outsourcing strategies have since become a standard procedure, to be used repeatedly, even by the healthiest of companies.[13] The lingering threat that survivors of one outsourcing program will emerge only to be caught in the undertow of the next wave of cuts effectively has made this traditional contract not only non-viable but also non-credible both for employers and employees.

Much of the blame for the breakdown of this traditional psychological contract has been placed at the doorstep of greedy management. Certainly, the process of downsizing has gone too far in some companies; at times, it has been carried out inhumanely, and too often it has been motivated by extremely short-term considerations. Yet in the end, it is not management but the market that has made the traditional contract non-viable. In a stable world, the old contract could work. Competitive advantage, once developed, could be sustained for long periods of time, as companies like IBM, Caterpillar, Kodak, and Xerox have shown. In such a world, top-level managers could determine the company's strategy, specify what they wanted employees to do, and define the skills needed to do it. For their part, employees could develop those skills gradually through training and apprenticeships and use them productively in the service of the corporate strategy, often over their entire careers.

However, in a dynamic world, a source of competitive advantage in one period easily can become not just irrelevant but a source of competitive disadvantage in some future period. Core competencies become core rigidities.[14] Valuable knowledge and skills become outdated rapidly, often at a rate faster than many people's learning capacities. As markets do their job, industries shift, technologies change, prices erode, and competitors quickly render obsolete not only once profitable products but whole business systems. This is the kind of environment that more and more companies face today. Under such conditions, not only is the old contract unviable, any effort to pretend otherwise is immoral.

> *In a dynamic world, a source of competitive advantage in one period easily can become not just irrelevant but a source of competitive disadvantage in some future period.*

Consider the case of ABB. Historically, North America and Europe accounted for a vast majority of new power plant demand. Today the situation has changed, and by the year 2000, the Asian crisis notwithstanding, China's demand will greatly exceed that of the USA or the whole of Europe. While the company's resources are all in the north and the west – yesterday's markets – its opportunities are all in the south and the east. To manage performance and to create a viable future, the company has had to reduce employment in North America and Western Europe by 54 000 people, while building up an organization of 46 000 people in the Asia-Pacific region, almost from scratch. Mismatches like this are increasingly the reality for many companies and, with such fleet-footed markets, to guarantee employment is to commit competitive suicide.

Besides, in such an environment of intensifying competition and rapid change, the model of top management as the grand strategist, ensuring the company's competitiveness, is bankrupt. Knowledge, rather than capital, is now the key strategic resource and, unlike capital, knowledge cannot be accumulated at the top of the organization to be redistributed by management according to a grand strategy. Instead, it is the frontline employees closest to the actual day-to-day operations who must take responsibility for the company's competitive performance. As a result, if top managers can no longer assure the company's competitiveness, they cannot guarantee employment security either. Indeed, where such historic undertakings endure, they are fictions – immoral contracts that the company and its management cannot continue to fulfill over the long term.

There is another problem with the traditional company-employee relationship that has more to do with its impact on employee motivation and behavior. "Obedience for employment" contracts produce what Jack Welch has described as "a paternal, feudal, fuzzy kind of loyalty." They create a climate of dependence that is antithetical to the distributed ownership of performance responsibility that the new competitive environment demands. Also, in a changing social context, the law of masters and servants that underlies the old psychological contract is no longer acceptable to many people, particularly the young. They are not willing to forgo their creativity, initiative, and autonomy for the right to live in a gilded cage.

Unfortunately, as many major corporations have come to recognize, the alternative of a free-market, hire-and-fire regime is not a viable replacement for the traditional employment contract. The same forces of global competition and turbulent change that make employment guarantees unfeasible also enhance the need for levels of trust and teamwork that cannot be fostered in an affection-free environment of reciprocal opportunism and continuous spot contracting. Similarly, even the star bond trader often comes to recognize, by the fifth job change in as many years, that the workplace is not just an arena for economic exchange but also a source of social engagement. While they may maximize their economic returns by hiring themselves out continuously as commercial mercenaries, most people also yearn for the sense of fulfillment that comes from belonging to an organizational family.

The new moral contract

To resolve this tension, the new management philosophy needs to be grounded in a very different moral contract with people. In this contract, each employee takes responsibility for best-in-class performance of the part of the company to which he or she belongs, and commits to a continuous process of learning that is necessary to support such performance amid continuous change. In exchange, the company undertakes to ensure not the dependence of employment security but the freedom of each individual's employability.[15] Companies do this by providing all employees with the opportunity for continuous skill-updating so as to protect and enhance both their job flexibility within the company and their opportunities outside. At the same time they create an exciting and invigorating work environment that not only enables the employees to use their skills to enhance the company's competitive performance but motivates them to stay with the company even though they have the option to leave.

Jack Welch articulated this contract when he described the new employment relationship at GE:

"The new psychological contract . . . is that jobs at GE are the best in the world for people who are willing to compete. We have the best training and development resources, and an environment committed to providing opportunities for personal and professional growth."

This new moral contract (*see* Figure 9.1) is more than a new spin on a company's old human resource policies to legitimize lay-offs; it represents a fundamental change in management philosophy from seeing people as a corporate asset from which value can be appropriated, to seeing them as a responsibility and a resource to add value to. Its adoption implies a rejection of the paternalism and even arrogance that underlie lifetime employment contracts by recognizing that only the market can guarantee employment, and that market performance flows not from the omnipotent wisdom of top management but from the initiative, creativity, and skills of all employees. At the same time, however, it acknowledges that companies have a moral responsibility for the long-term security and well-being of the people they employ, and for helping them to become the best they can be in what they choose to do.

> *This new moral contract also demands a lot of employees. It requires that they have the courage and the confidence to abandon the stability of lifetime employment and to embrace the invigorating force of continuous learning and personal development.*

This new moral contract also demands a lot of employees. It requires that they have the courage and the confidence to abandon the stability of lifetime employment and to embrace the invigorating force of continuous learning and personal development. They must accept that the security that comes from performance in the market ultimately is both more durable and more satisfying than the security offered by paternalistic management.

Responsibility for performance comes with some even more uncomfortable demands. Those on the front lines are no longer able to wait for the top management to legitimize unpleasant, but necessary, decisions. If assets can be reduced, they have to take the initiative to do so; if expenses are out of line, it is their responsibility to cut them; and if the work can be done with fewer people, the decision to increase productivity or reduce headcount is theirs. Rationalization can no longer be a once-in-ten-years clean-up job, driven by a management-led, corporate-wide program, but must become an ongoing activity, as a part of the continuous improvement process, led by frontline employees.

No one has emphasized this hard edge of the new contract more sharply than Intel's Andy Grove:

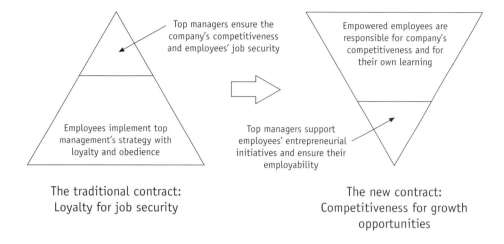

Fig. 9.1   The new moral contract – A role-responsibility reversal

"No matter where you work, you are not an employee. You are in a business with one employer – yourself – in competition with millions of similar businesses worldwide . . . Nobody owes you a career – you own it as a sole proprietor. And the key to survival is to learn to add more value every day."

At the same time, companies must strive to clarify how adopting such hard-edged expectations differs from mimicking the market. To become legitimized and institutionalized, these actions must be counterbalanced by a reciprocal commitment to add value to people. The need for significant investments in training and development is only a part of this commitment. These investments must be made to protect and enhance the employability of individuals as much as to increase the productivity and efficiency of the company; to support their broader, general education and not just to enhance their job-specific skills. As Anita Roddick of the Body Shop says: "You can train dogs; we educate people."

———

Few companies take their commitment to employees more seriously than Motorola. In a context of radical decentralization of resources and decisions to the divisional level, employee education is one activity that is managed by Motorola at the corporate level, through the large and well-funded Motorola University that has branches all over the world. Every employee, including the chief executive, has to undertake a minimum of 40 hours of formal coursework each year. Courses span a wide range of topics, from state-of-the-art coverage of new technologies to broad general management topics and issues, to allow Motorola employees around the world to update knowledge and skills in their chosen areas. It is this commitment to adding value to people that allowed Motorola to launch and implement its much-imitated "Six Sigma" total quality initiative. At the same time, the reputation of Motorola University has become a key source of the company's competitive advantage in recruiting and retaining the best graduates from leading schools in every country in which it operates.

More recently, Motorola has further upped the ante on its commitment to employability by launching the "Individual Dignity Entitlement" (IDE) program. This requires all supervisors to discuss, on a quarterly basis, six questions with everyone whose work they supervise:

1 Do you have a substantive, meaningful job that contributes to the success of Motorola?

2 Do you know the on-the-job behaviors and have the knowledge base to be successful?

3 Has the training been identified and been made available to continuously upgrade your skills?

4 Do you have a personal career plan, and is it exciting, achievable, and being acted upon?

5 Do you receive candid, positive or negative feedback at least every 30 days which is helpful in improving or achieving your personal career plan?

6 Is there appropriate sensitivity to your personal circumstances, gender, and/or cultural heritage so that such issues do not detract from your success?

A negative response from any employee to any one of these questions is treated as a quality failure, to be redressed in accordance with the principles of total quality management. Yet even in a company like Motorola, which has invested more in its people than most companies and has long been an adherent of employability, some units reported failures in excess of 70 percent the first time IDE was implemented.

In 1995, the company began addressing systematically the negatives by identifying and then eliminating their root causes. This is the hard edge of the new moral contract on the management side – the commitment to help people become the best they can be – that counterbalances the new demands on people that the "employability for competitiveness" contract creates.

––––––––

What the new contract is not

While we have described at some length what a moral contract based on employability is, it is important at this point to emphasize what it is not. First, it is not a catchy slogan to free management from a sense of responsibility to protect the jobs of their people. At Intel, Andy Grove could make the kind of demands he did on people because his own past actions had established, beyond any doubt, the extent to which he was willing to go to protect the interests of his employees. During the memory products bloodbath in the early eighties, when every other semiconductor company in the USA immediately laid off large numbers of people, Grove adopted the 90 percent rule, with everyone, from the chairman downward, accepting a 10 percent pay cut, to avoid lay-offs. To ride out the bad period without having to lose people he had nurtured over the years, Grove sold 20 percent of the company to IBM, for $250 million in cash. Then he implemented the 125 percent rule, asking everyone to work an extra ten hours a week with no pay increase, again to avoid cutbacks. It was only after all these efforts were proven to be insufficient that he finally closed some operations with the attending loss of jobs. It is this kind of proven commitment to people that makes a contract based on employability credible, and its hard-edged demands on people acceptable.

Second, it is not an altruistic contract to help educate and develop people at company cost, so they can then find better jobs elsewhere. In fact, this new relationship actually enhances a company's chances of retaining its best people. In a contract based on employment security, those who lost their mobility through overspecialization or skill obsolescence stayed with the company because, at least in part, they had no alternative. But the very best people often left, frustrated by the constraints and controls that were the other side of that coin. In contrast, the promise of employability itself is a great motivator for people to remain with a company because they know that even if they can cash in their current employability at a premium, they run the risk of falling

> *The same broad and advanced skills that make people employable outside the company make them more adaptable to different jobs and needs within the company.*

victim to the next round of skill obsolescence in a company that does not have the same commitment to adding value to people. In addition, the same broad and advanced skills that make people employable outside the company make them more adaptable to different jobs and needs within the company, thereby making it easier for the company to use their expertise more flexibly and in higher value jobs.

Third, the contract based on employability is not some program that can be installed. It is a very different philosophy that requires management to work hard, on an ongoing basis, to create an exciting and invigorating work environment and a context of enormous pride and satisfaction that would bond their people to the company even more tightly than any bond of dependency that employment security could create. The combination of a moral contract based on employability and a management commitment to empowerment leads, as a consequence, to a durable long-term and mutually satisfying relationship between the individual and the organization that the traditional employment contract abandoned. By building the new company-employee relationship on a platform of mutual value-adding and continuous choice, rather than on a self-degrading acceptance of one-way dependence, the new contract is not just functional, it is also moral.

In the ultimate analysis, companies – and indeed, all forms of organizations – exist and thrive because they make possible what otherwise would be impossible. And accomplishing what is possible requires a measure of faith among all employees that benefits ultimately will come their way if their company prospers. What this faith does, in turn, is allow individuals to stop looking for immediate personal advantage in everything they do within their organization and co-operate with one another – share ideas, exchange resources, combine knowledge – in a way that they cannot achieve by acting as individual agents in a market. Out of that trust and co-operation come innovations and improvements that a market cannot create, leading not only to the success of the company but also to progress the society.

A market is driven by spot transactions, a healthy company is driven by durable relationships. A market has no purpose or direction of its own; it reflects only the collective outcome of a relentless pursuit of individual gain. A company prospers by creating a broader sense of purpose which allows individuals to align their interests and engage in collective action. Because of the direct alignment with each individual's self-interest, markets are a powerful force for eliminating waste and improving productivity. But for exactly the same reason, they are also a force for atomization. While companies must embrace the discipline of market forces, it is a fatal mistake to manage a company by market rules. A company is not a portfolio of products and businesses. It is not a portfolio of resources and competencies. It is a shared social context that shapes the behaviors of people, stimulating initiative, trust, forbearance, loyalty, and sacrifice, to make them act differently within the organization than they do outside.

BUILDING SHARED DESTINY RELATIONSHIPS

Is this notion of the modern corporation focussed on creating value externally and internally what the British call "cloud cuckoo land?" Is it all wishful thinking of wet-behind-the-ears softies who do not know how hard and unforgiving the world of business really is; or worse, of ivory tower academics who preach what they cannot do?

The business world is full of examples of companies that earn healthy profits year after year by focussing continuously on the task of creating value for society rather than on expropriating as much value as they can from it.

The business world is full of examples of companies that earn healthy profits year after year by focussing continuously on the task of creating value for society rather than on expropriating as much value as they can from it. Canon made its own highly successful technology obsolete by inventing and then promoting aggressively the bubblejet on the grounds that its functionality-to-cost ratio yielded higher value to customers; Intel fueled the information revolution by relentlessly following "More's law," creating the next generation of chips that allowed its customers to do new things, while at the same time wiping out its earlier generation of products; and Kao decided to enter the cosmetics industry and use its advanced technology to create the high-functionality Sofina range to compete with overpriced mediocre products in expensive jars. In each of these companies, value creation was both the stated objective and the proven outcome.

Without a moral contract based on adding value to people, McKinsey and Andersen Consulting could not be in business. Recruiting the very best talent is the number one success factor in the consulting industry. Yet these companies can give partnership to only one in seven of all they hire. The rest must leave the company. The promise of employability, and proven ability to deliver on that promise, is the only reason that fresh graduates all over the world still seek to join them.

But these are examples of companies that have practiced the philosophy of value creation for a long time, often from their inception. Can others, steeped in the more traditional approach, adopt this philosophy? Yes, they can.

———

Unipart, a struggling auto parts manufacturer, is a good example of a company that transformed itself under this powerful management philosophy. At its birth out of the 1987 dismemberment of the chronically sick, government-owned British Leyland, Unipart suffered a two-to-one handicap vis-à-vis Japanese auto parts companies in terms of its costs and an astonishing 100-to-one gap in quality, according to a UK Department of Trade and Industry study. It inherited an extremely confrontational work climate, the product of a heavily unionized workforce crossed with a traditional and autocratic management. Furthermore, the company's adversarial relationships extended to its suppliers and its customers, principal among them being Rover, the UK car company that had been its sister unit within British Leyland.

A decade later, the story had changed completely. Turnover had shot up to over £1 billion ($1.6 billion), profits had quadrupled to £32 million, and a Department of Trade and Industry study had declared that Unipart was the only UK-based company in its business to meet world-class standards on quality.

Behind the company's transformation was one man, Unipart CEO John Neill, and his absolute commitment to what he called "shared destiny relationships." The philosophy was not an ex-post rationalization of success, but was stated clearly and firmly by Neill in 1987 as the fundamental principle on which the company would function:

"We have made a mess of our industry. The short-term power-based relationships have failed us. Many western companies still believe that it is a superior way to secure competitive advantage. I think they are absolutely wrong . . . We must create shared destiny relationships with all our stakeholders: customers, employees, suppliers, governments and the communities in which we operate. It is not altruism, it is commercial self-interest."

While acknowledging the interdependence between a company and all its key stakeholders, Neill's notion of shared destiny relationships is very different from "being and doing good to all" that the stakeholder concept is often portrayed as. With suppliers, his "ten(d) to zero" program emphasized the need to work together to radically improve performance across ten criteria ranging from transaction costs and lead times to defect rates and delivery errors – and to ultimately reduce each to as close to zero as possible. Similarly, within the organization, programs like "our contribution counts" emphasized the hard two-way dependence inherent in the concept of shared destiny, and the need for continuous performance improvement to make that destiny mutually attractive.

———

John Neill's vision for Unipart was born not out of the economist's narrowly defined model for achieving profitability through the zero-sum game of extracting value from others. Rather, it was based on an expansive positive-sum value creation perspective that we found much more typical of successful managers in the companies we have studied. Like Neill, these executives have enormous faith in what they can create by engaging, energizing and empowering their constituencies to work together for mutual benefit. The result of the collective actions of these executives is something rather more than they thought: the emergence of a more realistic and assertive philosophy of the role of the corporation as both a powerful economic entity and an important social institution, using its economic resources to add value to society generally and to people's lives individually. These executives are the standard-bearers for a new manifesto of companies and managers as value creators. They are role models demonstrating the spirit, passion and moral commitment of which management is capable, and which the dominant doctrine has all but destroyed.

Ideas matter. In a practical discipline like management, their normative influence can make them uniquely beneficial or uniquely dangerous. Bad theory and a philosophical vacuum has caused managers to subvert their own practice, trapping them in a vicious circle. But there is a choice. When the solution to a recurring problem is always "Try harder," there is usually something wrong with the terms, not the execution. So it is time for both managers and management academics to throw out the old paradigm and to start experimenting with new, more fertile possibilities. Otherwise the fatal gap between companies' economic power and their social legitimacy will continue to widen, stunting the growth potential of individuals, companies, and society as a whole.

10

EMERGING WORK OF MANAGERS

C.K. PRAHALAD

In the new millennium, the methods and skills needed to manage large and small organizations will be different from those needed to be successful during the past three decades. This transformation will challenge our notion about the meaning of "managing" itself. Concepts and tools that dominated our thinking about managing – power, structure, hierarchy, control, co-ordination, ownership, and incentives – will have to be re-examined. Newer concepts and tools will emerge. In this chapter, I will outline the changing nature of the competitive landscape and how these forces will challenge our notions of managing. I will then discuss the emerging nature of managerial work. Finally, I will suggest that this transformation of managerial work will demand basic organizational innovations.

CHANGING COMPETITIVE LANDSCAPE

The discontinuous changes in the competitive landscape are numerous and it is my intention to identify just a few critical ones here. Most observers of management will agree that deregulation of industries (e.g. power, telecom, healthcare, and water), globalization, and the growing importance of emerging markets (e.g. China, India, Brazil) will have a significant effect on management. Further, the ongoing impact of convergence of technologies (e.g. fusion of food and pharmaceutical knowledge, communication, computing and consumer electronics), and the blurring of industry boundaries as in the case of retailing and financial services, will dramatically alter the competitive landscape. The role of the Internet in shaping industries, both old and new, is still hotly debated. These forces will affect both large, well-established multinationals (e.g. IBM, Philips, ABB, or Ford) and newer firms (e.g. Dell, Compaq, Yahoo!, and AOL). However, the impact on the two clusters of firms or their capacities to adapt will not be the same. Incumbent firms with long traditions have to "forget" old ways of doing business as well as learn the "new."

During the past decade, the impact of these discontinuities has been discussed by managers and scholars, mostly one discontinuity at a time. What is not widely debated are the patterns of influence that these trends collectively will have on managerial work. I propose to identify four key themes arising from these discontinuities:

- managing cultural and intellectual diversity
- managing market volatility
- managing the impact of the Internet
- managing new and emerging customer segments.

Managing cultural and intellectual diversity

Managers will be forced to deal with cultural and intellectual diversity on an unprecedented scale. For example, it is conceivable that China and India collectively could represent 30–50 percent of the total global market for telecom gear, television sets, and power plants. This implies that firms must reconfigure their resources to correspond with the reality of these markets. For example, Boeing is increasing the amount of components and subassemblies sourced from Asia to reflect the market opportunities. The managerial composition of these firms will also change. It is conceivable that by the year 2010, 30–40 percent of the leadership teams of large western multinational firms will be Asian. Understanding cultural diversity will be a challenge for both western and Asian managers. Further, the convergence of technologies such as chemicals and electronics (e.g. digital photography at Kodak) will force the development of intellectual diversity within organizations.

Managing market volatility

Managers will have to deal with volatility in markets around the world. With increasing costs of R&D and product development, and decreasing product life cycles, managers will be forced to reduce risk by subcontracting, depending on partners, and recognizing the need for scaling up and down quickly.

Managing the impact of the Internet

Increasingly, the Internet may be changing the role of the consumer. The power is shifting to the consumer from the manufacturer and the distributor/dealer. This implies that managers have to be sensitive to personalization of products and services. The move from segmentation to personalization has major implications.

Managing new and emerging customer segments

Consider the global market as a pyramid of consumers based on economic strength. The new and emerging opportunity in countries such as China, India, and Brazil is in the lower income segments – the tier # 2, 3 and 4. Serving these markets will dramatically influence the management process in multi-nationals.[1]

We will take these four major themes and examine their implications, one at a time, before we synthesize the implications to managing as we know it.

THE IMPACT OF DIVERSITY

Accepting and managing diversity is a managerial challenge. However, the preoccupation in most firms is in dealing with diversity in age, race, and gender. Firms based in the USA have been active in coping with race and gender issues for well over a decade. Cultural diversity is a relatively newer issue. As multinational firms increase their investments in emerging markets, sensitivity to culture has gained prominence. Business practices and the social assumptions behind business in Asia, for example, were promoted as the Asian way. The institutional infrastructure, political systems and intellectual heritage of these countries are also different from the West. The role of the extended family in business, and the importance placed on loyalty rather than on merit and performance, adds a further dimension to the diversity of approaches. Multinational firms involved in joint venture and collaborative arrangements of all kinds have to learn to understand these differences. Even when multinationals operate their own subsidiaries, dealing with the differences in approaches becomes critical in building a common bond between managers around the world.

Managers need to separate country *culture* from *business practices*. Until the crisis in Asia, Asian business practices based on nepotism and crony capitalism were seen as the Asian way and different from western business practices. US-based multinationals would be in violation of the law if they engaged in those practices. The clash of cultures is quite obvious. What should a western multinational do? I believe that managers in multinational firms

143

have to focus on their managerial culture and value systems as distinct from the prevailing business practices and country and ethnic cultures in markets in which they operate. While recognizing cultural diversity, managers must separate the business practices component from country and ethnic beliefs. Increasingly, to link markets around the world in terms of product flows, shared development tasks, and transfer of knowledge, managers must focus on a shared managerial culture. The value system of sharing, working together in teams, respecting differences, and identifying with common goals means that socialization of all associates into a common managerial culture is emerging as a critical element of competitive capability of large firms. Value systems, clearly articulated, and rigorously enforced is an element of managing.

Convergence of technologies and markets creates a new form of diversity – intellectual diversity. Consider for example personal care product firms such as Revlon, L'Oreal, Unilever, Shishiedo, and Procter & Gamble moving up the value chain in their businesses. With ageing population, skin creams may incorporate an anti-ageing ingredient (e.g. retinol) and shampoos may incorporate a hair growth hormone (e.g. rogaine). Personal care products certainly take on the sophistication, the knowledge base, and the need for clinical trials that were the primary focus of the pharmaceutical industry. P&G recently announced an "anti-rash diaper." This clinical claim (a first in the diaper business) could not be made without field trials and FDA approval. Similarly, food companies are moving up the chain to incorporate health claims, many of which need substantiation and approvals from the FDA. Traditional commodity processors of food such as Cargill have to be sensitive and knowledgeable about the new genetically manipulated seeds. Today it is possible to genetically influence output characteristics of the soy bean – to increase protein content or allow it to carry a higher percentage of oil. Processing requirements of these seeds are different from processing traditional soy beans.

A similar problem exists when consumer electronics firms such as Sony or Philips have to learn to cope with the demands of computing, software, and communications. Firms like Kodak and Fuji have to seamlessly integrate chemical and electronics technologies to create Photo CD and now a digital camera.

Examples of such convergence are everywhere. But what does this mean in terms of managing? How do we incorporate knowledge and disciplines of the pharmaceutical industry into the fashion industry? How do we cope with the pace and rhythm of different technologies – a well-known commodity-processing technology prone to few changes, to complex and fast-changing genetic technology?

The fusion of multiple intellectual heritages cannot be accomplished if the top management does not clearly articulate a vision of where the industry and the organization are headed. It is imperative that all associates in a food processing firm, for example, understand the critical need for biotechnology knowledge. Also, all managers must recognize that the acquisition of this knowledge requires a combination of hiring people into the organization who are dissimilar in terms of their backgrounds. Further, knowledge acquisition may call for collaborative arrangements with newer and smaller firms. Learning suggests that the new employees learn about the company and food processing and the incumbents learn about biotechnology. Learning requires effort on both sides. It cannot be accomplished without creating specific projects which act as carriers of new learning. Action bias is critical for learning to harmonize multiple technologies. Managing intellectual diversity requires a clear point of view about industry and firm direction as well as an ability to create specific projects that provide a platform for such learning. Strategic direction as well as strategy deployment (breaking strategic direction into bite-size pieces for small groups to act upon) capability will become an integral part of managing.

> *Learning requires effort on both sides. It cannot be accomplished without creating specific projects which act as carriers of new learning.*

MANAGING VOLATILITY

If there is a single lesson in managing that we have learned during the past decade, it is that volatility is pervasive. Nobody predicted the depth of the Asian crisis. There are no guarantees of success. It is common in high-volume electronics businesses, such as hand held devices, that products can become a great success in a very short time (e.g. Playstation from Sony). This calls for dramatic scaling up of capacity involving suppliers, logistics, manufacturing, and marketing. The entire chain has to work in unison. The reverse is also true. Scaling down, when demand falls precipitously for a product, is also critical. The geographical distribution of the total design to delivery task further complicates the problem. For example, in the laptop business it is quite common to have the design work done in the USA, components sourced from Japan, South Korea and the United States, and assembled in Taiwan, China, or Malaysia and introduced in global markets. The entire design-to-delivery cycle may be 12–18 months. All suppliers and participants in the total chain may be independent legal entities. Finally, the demand may be seasonal, centered around Christmas.

Managing global logistics becomes a critical source of competitive differentiation. This calls for an information infrastructure – the operating systems, application software, databases and analytics – of a very high quality. Furthermore, firms have to learn to manage and influence others in the supply chain – designers to component producers to assemblers and value-added resellers – without ownership. Influence without ownership is a critical capability. Finally, each launch, each product, has to be managed to exacting schedules and cost targets. Project management skills become critical. Global logistics, operational flexibility, excellence, and speed of reaction become the real hedges against volatility.

THE ROLE OF THE INTERNET

The Internet is profoundly changing the way business is conducted. Whether it is an established industry like toys, financial services, insurance, travel, advertising or newspapers, the impact of the Internet as an alternative channel to provide enhanced functionality at lower costs is apparent. Three themes emerge. First, power is shifting to the consumer for the first time. Consumers have the information and are willing to use it to negotiate, electronically, with big firms. The size of General Motors or GE does not scare the individual consumer in North Dakota, who has choices and is willing to exercise them. Second, customers want their products personalized. They want to be effectively involved in designing a service/product for them. They are unwilling to accept mass-produced, indistinguishable products. Third, consumers are eager to extract the value that is created by reducing the role of intermediaries, such as dealers and distributors.

Again, this discontinuity forces managers to come to terms with the importance of logistics. For example, accepting an order for a book on Amazon.com is easier than delivering it cost-effectively within two days. The role of the information infrastructure needed to dialog with customers on a real-time basis is obvious. Databases of products, customers and competitors are critical for rapid response. Pricing, for example, will depend on how much customers are willing to accept cross-selling from a large firm. As a consumer, should I accept one bundled price for my normal banking, mortgage, auto loan, and insurance from CitiGroup or should I deal with multiple vendors? Consumers will determine pricing levels that are acceptable to them. Firms cannot respond to these pressures without a very sophisticated information and logistics infrastructure.

THE EMERGING MARKETS

The big emerging markets such as China, India, and Brazil provide a significant opportunity for multinational corporations. There are between 600 and 1000 million potential consumers. However, they have little disposable income. Per capita gross domestic product measured in purchasing power parity terms may be around $2000. Managers in western firms have typically ignored this market and, therefore, a major opportunity. This market demands a fundamentally different type of capability. Firms ought to be able to rethink the price performance relationships of their products and services. For example, how can we provide a car for less than US$5000, a checking account with less than US$25, or a bar of ice cream for less than five cents? Managers from the West must basically think out of the box to create such capability. Further, sustainability of development requires that we understand that western products and services which demand a high level of usage of, say, water, detergents, and packaging would be untenable in emerging markets. Rethinking resource use may be a critical element. Finally, localization of products can be a major advantage. Even Coke, once considered the ultimate example of a universal product, is changing and using local brands in India.

Emerging markets provide a major opportunity but also pose a considerable challenge to multinationals. Penetrating the tier # 2 and # 3 markets needs a careful assessment of product development processes, overhead structure, sustainable development, and capital efficiency. We can summarize the implications of these forces as in Table 10.1.

> *Emerging markets provide a major opportunity but also pose a considerable challenge to multinationals.*

Table 10.1 Emerging managerial demands

Discontinuities	Critical issues	Managerial demands
Globalization	Cultural diversity	Managerial culture, values and behaviors
Convergence deregulation	Intellectual diversity	Shared competitive agenda Strategy deployment
	Volatility	Influence without ownership Information infrastructure Response/reaction time
The Internet	Balance of power: Shift to consumer	Educating, co-opting and competing with consumers Information infrastructure New business models – innovation
Emerging tier #2 and #3 markets	New levels of localization Price performance New product philosophy	Shared competitive agenda Managerial culture Strategy deployment Business innovation

We can add to the list of discontinuities and the critical managerial demands that each one of them generates. The purpose here is not to be exhaustive but indicative of the type of analysis that will lead us to thinking about the work of managing in the future.

THE WORK OF MANAGING

The change in the work of managing is obvious. Issues of formal structure and hierarchy, authority and power, industry experience and seniority, and control and co-ordination are all open to challenge. Let us examine a few of these traditional notions in the context of the new demands placed on managers.

Convergence of technologies and changing industry boundaries, for example, challenge the value of industry experience and seniority. Traditional industry experience in, say, food processing is of little value when confronted with new knowledge, such as biotechnology or gene therapy. Traditional banking experience is of little value when confronted with the Internet and virtual reality. Managers have to recognize that their accumulated experience will be devalued and the retention of value for their knowledge is incumbent on their recognizing the importance of intellectual diversity. Operationally this means that senior managers have to learn from associates who are much younger and with backgrounds different from theirs. Accessing, retaining, and integrating this new talent with the "body politic" of the organization is critical. Seniority, authority, and power have to give way to talent management. Administrative authority is of very little value in this situation.

Cultural diversity imposes a major constraint on reliance on authority, power, co-ordination, and control to influence how business is conducted around the world within a firm. Associates have to accept a shared set of norms of behavior to collaborate across borders. The authority to influence others becomes not the weight of administrative machinery but shared and enforced values and behaviors. No set of procedures, however detailed, is a substitute for predictable reactions to new and emerging business situations around the world. In fact, a procedural explosion to control managerial behavior and judgement is a futile approach. Socialization and value deployment is more likely to win.

Volatility requires us to examine the meaning of ownership and control. Traditionally, influence is related to ownership. In the global marketplace, sourcing of components and subassemblies from specialist manufacturers, joint venture partners, and other collaborators suggests that managers ought to learn to influence behavior without ownership. Learning to share a common competitive agenda, sharing information once considered confidential, allowing investments to be made in good faith, and reducing total costs through system-wide efficiencies require a commitment to build a powerful information infrastructure. This suggests that the analytics of managing must be explicit, and transparent. Information must become a corporate resource and not remain a source of private power. The analytical sophistication of managers, and as a consequence to value talent over age, becomes an imperative.

Whether it is in managing global supply chains, or in developing products, or in responding to consumers on the Internet, response time and reaction time become critical. Long internal chains of command and dependence on multiple authorizations as forms of control are dysfunctional. Control can be exercised only through training and empowering associates at all levels within the firm, and pushing decisions to the lowest levels. Control is also a function of the information infrastructure support to which associates have access.

Local innovations as well as global innovations are critical when approaching emerging markets. The notion of corporate center (or world headquarters) as the source of wisdom and knowledge is dated. Corporate role becomes one of facilitating information and knowledge exchange, imposing standards of behaviors, and ensuring resource leverage around the corporation. Control over allocation of resources must yield to concern for accumulating and leveraging resources.

THE CHANGING FACE OF MANAGING

The changing role of managing suggests that we should pay special attention to the role of senior managers. I believe they will have to concentrate on six critical elements:

1 the importance of a *shared competitive agenda*. Managers must encourage in the organization a sense of direction and an approach to shaping the future. In an era of discontinuous change, running a firm without a shared agenda is like taking a ship out to sea without a compass;

2 creating a clear charter of *values and behaviors* and enforcing them without exception. Values bind the organization, promote teamwork and facilitate transfer of knowledge;

3 focussing on *influence without ownership*. This assumes that as managers we have to accept that we compete as a "family of firms." The influence can be derived only from a shared agenda, trust, and a sound information infrastructure. Managing relationships rather than transactions becomes critical;

4 *competing for talent* and building the skill mix of the organization vital for retaining sources of competitive advantage. Training, empowerment, teamwork, performance orientation, transparency, and accountability are critical dimensions of a high-performance organization of the future;

5 *speed of reaction* in the organization, which requires decision making at the lowest levels. This means that all associates are aware of the overall direction, their role in the broad picture, and possess the competence to make informed choices. Hierarchy must yield to speed. Authority must yield to competence;

6 *leveraging corporate resources*, which requires that resources are constantly combined and recombined to address emerging opportunities. Rigid administrative boundaries and charters are dysfunctional. Seamless combination is a requirement.

The emerging dimensions of managerial work are clear. The soft issues such as values and behaviors, often dismissed as unimportant, are critical. Intellectual leadership is as important as administrative or charismatic leadership. Information infrastructure and analytical sophistication can be a source of great competitive vitality. Talent acquisition, retention, and motivation may be more important than managing financial resources. Sensitivity to cultural diversity around the world and at the same time commitment to a managerial culture is a must.

I believe the language, concepts, and tools of managing are undergoing major change. We all can look forward to an exciting ride.

11

ULTRA-RAPID MANAGEMENT PROCESSES

PETER LORANGE

Ultra-rapid growth will be key to shaping management processes in the next century. It will drive much of the value-creation effort in high-performance companies. One major implication of this is that there will be dramatic added emphasis on finding new business opportunities. How to accelerate the utilization of such opportunities will also become central, not in the least due to the fact that traditional product life cycles will be increasingly shorter, calling for a much more accelerated recovery of investment. The classical business position, where one's strategy is based on an established market share, and a consequent stable generation of funds will be the exception rather than the rule. Rather, the issue will be one of finding new opportunities and expanding them ultra-fast, so as to enjoy a typically short period when one is the sole supplier of a particular product or service on a worldwide basis. When competition comes in, it is time to move on, sooner rather than later, to other pioneering projects. More than ever, it will be a liability to be extensively "bogged down" in more mature business positions, with the most critical strategic resource for the firm, human know-how, tied up working on business-as-usual activities. It will be found that this key resource is better redeployed on new, pioneering, and rapid expansion business activities, to ensure that executives learn and the firm more effectively replenishes itself when it comes to human capital.

We will first discuss briefly what might be seen as an emerging planning process paradigm for ultra-rapid growth. We shall then look at aspects of the all-important learning process, as well as dramatically reshaped strategic human resource processes, which can be expected to take over from classic human resource management processes. Budgeting and control, on the other hand, will perhaps not change quite so much, though it will definitely take on a very different connotation from what is common today.

AN EMERGING STRATEGIC PROCESS PARADIGM

Emphasis will be put on seeing business opportunities that are entirely new, serving the final and/or intermediary customer in radically new ways. Equally vital will be the mobilization of the firm's most critical strategic resource, its people, to go after such opportunities. As a strategic advantage is typically short-lived, it is therefore of the utmost importance to be able to generate as many viable new business ideas as possible; this is what we mean by *pioneering*. Testing of these ideas must follow quickly, so that the most promising can be developed and marketed. These *rapid expansion* efforts must take place ultra-fast, so as to quickly establish a strong and exclusive global monopoly position, to be able to recover one's investment and more. To gain a strategic advantage through rapid expansion of pioneering business, it will be essential to form dedicated teams of people.

Strategy is thus no longer an issue of defending established status quo positions in order to maintain a competitive advantage. Rather, it will be increasingly important to utilize one's strategic human resources to develop *new* strategies to establish exclusive new positions. The focal points will thus be on pioneering, focussed experimentation, and rapid expansion, rather than on defending established market shares.

As we see, and not surprisingly, *people* in the organization will be the key strategic resource, even more so than today. Critical management processes will thus be those that have to do with people, and which will have a major impact on their behavior. Particularly, how can appropriately designed management processes help people to see new business opportunities? Furthermore, how can we stimulate the mobilization of people to go after such opportunities? Some of these behavioral processes will be more or less new. Others will imply a thorough modification of their existing focus, to become more creativity-driven. Several new management processes will therefore take on prominence, and others will be greatly modified, as we shall see now.

SPECIFIC MANAGEMENT PROCESS PREDICTIONS

Learning processes

When considering a new pioneering business opportunity, it will be particularly important to keep a holistic viewpoint, so that one can learn *fast* in order to judge whether we have a worthwhile business or not. Consider how fast a child learns a new language, for example. Perhaps we can find inspiration from the assimilation of knowledge that takes place in the child when it comes to moving fast along the learning curve in business contextual settings. As we know, the child learns by forming a holistic picture of a particular phenomenon and, as his or her experience and maturity increases, reformulates the holistic picture, adding more detailed accuracy. He/she keeps repeating this, usually at a relatively fast pace, until a reasonably full understanding has been established. We owe much of our understanding of how children learn to Piaget.[1]

This holistic approach, gradually accumulating knowledge through reshaping the holistic picture, seems to work faster than the typical Cartesian way of learning, where one establishes an understanding of each part of a phenomenon and then puts it together again. Traditionally, when something does not work, one would analyze the part(s) affected, undertake corrective actions on the part(s), and then come up with a revised aggregate approach – just the way we analyze budget deviations and take ameliorating actions.[2] The organization of the next century will, however, not be concerned with the analysis of why parts do not work, but rather will focus on how to more rapidly develop a clearer holistic picture of a particular workable business opportunity.

In line with this, we also need to learn to scale up faster. Here we can draw on important insights from Harold Lewitt, who claims that failures in attempts to implement should not be interpreted as anything other than inspiration to pursue a slightly modified path.[3] Scaling up and rapid implementation thus means finding the most useful path to walk through the wood. Learning by emphasizing the positive, and not by getting bogged down by failures, is therefore critical. Speed can be gained by realizing that temporary setbacks are in fact stimuli to seek a slightly different path.

We believe that fast-learning processes will become exceedingly prominent as part of management practices of the future. They will be based on the above positive and holistic approaches to learning.

Human resource management processes

We will see many changes in the behavioral side of human resource processes, contradicting the old dictum that people can be allocated to various jobs and that the organization consists of a relatively stable, typically hierarchical structure of people in specific job assignments. Rather, executives will now largely be allowed to organize themselves in teams, which they feel they can join to make the best contributions. These teams will typically be formed in such a way that they possess the eclectic capabilities to identify interesting new business opportunities. The formation of teams therefore will be focussed on realigning people to work together to find opportunities and learn how to exploit them. The human strategic resource process is thus attempting to guide people to find their productive places in such teams.

Typically, one would expect these teams to be highly virtual in nature. It would be taken for granted that people want to live where they find it most stimulating and comfortable, and that they consequently will interact through virtual networks. As noted, to enhance creativity the virtual teams will be highly eclectic and balanced in gender. The members of the organization will need to be aware of *who* knows *what* – in other words, where various types of talents can be found in the organization, and who belongs to what team. Strategic human resource processes will therefore be drawn up so as to support this proactive, mostly self-organized, pioneer-driven virtual team process.

The executive development process

One can justifiably ask what it would take to prepare the organization's members to be able to work better in such teams. We must assume that the members of the organization will be both mature enough and non-political enough to make this happen. But it is not likely to happen automatically, hence the key role of executive development.

Executive development becomes increasingly important in that it needs to provide the organization with vital development processes, both to establish a mature culture in general, and to make sure that the relevant human resource capabilities are in place, especially in two areas. First, cross-cultural teams will be crucial. The organization must receive support to make the development of their teamworking capabilities a reality. This implies enhanced communication and listening, both capabilities that entail development of individuals to act more maturely, so they take *and* give in a better way. Cross-cultural team capabilities must lead to an understanding of how to operate effectively as individuals in totally non-hierarchical, typically virtual networks. We can expect this to become increasingly critical.

Second, the ability to be visionary must be strengthened. As we have said, the majority of the organization must be keenly concerned with the question of attempting to see opportunities not obvious to everyone else. This process cannot be handed over to a few internal entrepreneurs who would then be expected to be the drivers. Rather, it is important that emergent visions be based on the broad, composite capabilities of teams. This visioning for pioneering and ultra-rapidly expanding success must be concrete, in the form of specific stories about what one wants to do. Abstract

> *It is important that emergent visions be based on the broad, composite capabilities of teams.*

statements, or wish-lists, will typically never materialize. Nor will extrapolations. It is therefore critical that the teams be cognizant of the danger of entrapments in the status quo – the executive development process of the future must focus on this through positive visioning.

Incentives

Incentive processes represent another area where we are likely to see great change. We should remember that incentive tends to have a clear impact on behavior, and this will continue to be the case. However, the types of incentives will change, focussing on new behavioral directions. First, when it comes to the business level, the issue will be one of providing incentives for the teams that create the pioneer opportunities as well as the subsequent ultra-rapid growth initiatives. The incentives are therefore likely to focus squarely on how to achieve growth. Certainly, ample incentives will have to be provided for coming up with excellent business ideas and good pioneering prospects. Incentives will also have to be provided for effective implementation for ultra-rapid growth. It is interesting that the thrust of business-level incentives will be on the creation of opportunities rather than on bottom-line profits for the existing established businesses. Consequently, milestone measurements for tracking growth will be essential. Classic, bottom-line profit measurements will be less so. The incentives are also likely to be largely team-based, acknowledging the critical importance of eclectic teams to produce ideas of sufficient quality for good pioneering and ultra-rapid growth. This too is in stark contrast with the typically individual incentives that tend to dominate at present.

Incentives at the top corporate executive level will also be expected to shift dramatically. Keeping in mind that the critical resource for the modern firm is human capital, it will be particularly important that top management incentives be directly linked to the maintenance and further development of the firm's human capital base. These incentives will be in contrast to what one tends to find today, with heavy emphasis on the bottom-line results. Specific rewards will primarily be given in the form of stock options, in order to ensure a more long-term perspective for the employees of the firm. One would want to avoid heavy bonus payments of cash, given that such funds will be necessary to support growth. The working capital should be kept in the firm to support the value-creation activities spearheaded by the good ideas of the teams.

So far we have discussed how management processes will be dominated by the behavioral aspects of strategic human resource management, with great emphasis on incentives and learning, with cross-cultural, pro-active teams as the foundation. Our message is that the bulk of the management processes for the next century will be focussed on one's key people as the key strategic resource. How to have the desired entrepreneurial impact on their behavior will be paramount. However, what about the more classical management processes, such as budgeting and control? We believe that budgeting and control will perhaps be as important as before, but the focus will change dramatically. Let's consider the nature of these probable changes.

The budgeting process

Two aspects of the classic budgeting process that surely will be expected to change are its content and a shift in the top-down/bottom-up, interactive and iterative dimension regarding how members of the organization become involved in dialog to develop a budget.

Regarding the content, it is clear that budgets will be focussed much more on the pioneer and rapid expansion projects. A main concern in this budgeting process will thus be whether we have the key people in the right place. Also, milestones for achieving specific growth targets will be critical. Finally, it will be important whether the key people can learn appropriately from their specific project assignments so that the human capital can be expected to sufficiently renew itself. The budget may have to be modified until management feels satisfied that it has an affirmative answer to the above three questions. The issue of the financial funds will also be critical, but will probably be subordinate to the issue of whether the right people are in the right place, learning the right things, and reaching the right milestones. If that is the case, the financial performance can largely be expected to follow as a consequence. Financial targets and bottom-line results will thus be secondary derivatives, not the starting points for the budgeting process.

Now to the interactive and iterative dialog that goes on within the organization to actually reach budget agreements. Here, a dialog between the project teams and senior managers will be more critical than ever. First, who are these senior managers? It should be pointed out that these will have been chosen primarily on their long-term experience with team processes, and on their insights from pioneering and developing ultra-rapid expansion initiatives. They will not have been chosen on the old criterion of managing established, mature business units for short-term success. Senior management thus has the experience to be able to effectively involve in dialog with the project teams at various stages of the formation of the strategic directions. It is important to note that:

- the embryonic team efforts, to establish whether we have a business idea or not, and whether we have a pioneering initiative or not, will be key in the budgeting process. Part of this embryonic effort will focus on the realignment of team compositions themselves, to ensure that team members adapt their actions to the emerging new business directions;
- the dialog on testing the business model, i.e. whether we indeed have a viable business idea or not, and, if so, the catalytic encouragement from the top to go full speed ahead, must be captured in the budget, again often with a somewhat different project team at play than was initially envisioned;
- the scaling up in an ultra-rapid-expansion fashion, with a focus on discussion on how to find the right path forward, must be part of the budget.

Again, this might also involve the delineation of a somewhat different human resource team than initially envisioned.

Top management's role in all of this is thus to provide an experience-based viewpoint, interactive and catalytic, where the issue is to lend support to the pioneering/rapid expansion business initiative process. This support is partly to give relevant input to the strategic choices at hand, and partly to provide input on what might be optional human resource staffing and team composition at each stage. It is thus not a task of command and control in the classic sense.

The control process

The control process will also change dramatically; perhaps the name "control" will no longer exist, given the behaviorally dysfunctional overtones that tend to come with it. We shall, however, still use it here as a convenient term of reference, and remember that the content behind the phenomenon will be dramatically different.

Again, just as we saw for budgeting, control in the future will take place through a dialog between senior management and the members of the pioneer/rapid expansion business teams. This control will be based principally on sharing experiences regarding how to interpret actual progress relative to plan, particularly when it comes to the milestones. Pragmatic judgements must come to bear regarding whether to proceed with a pioneering experiment and, if so, seeing how one should expand. This leads to two new and critical control process issues for the firm of the next century.

First, we will have the issue of a "go/no go" control challenge when it comes to the re-assessment of pioneering business initiatives.[4] Do we really have a business or not? Do we need to continue the experimentation for further verification, or are we ready to go full blast? Is this business idea too far-fetched to really merit a scaling up? The control process will thus focus on achieving an optimal activity level, whether to commit human resources (energy and time) on a larger scale for rapid expansion, to continue with the status quo, or even to drop the initiative altogether.

Second, the rapid expansion control scenario may typically represent a particularly important issue in itself. Is the business in the critical rapid expansion phase, developing the way we had expected? Alternatively, do we need to let corrective, mini-contingencies come into play, so that a slightly revised rapid expansion path can be drawn? In a more extreme case, does the entire path for expansion need to be shifted, by abandoning our growth scenario and changing over to an entirely new one? Interestingly, we are not talking here about incremental control in a classic sense by typically focussing on rather minor deviations, fixing these and then putting them together into slightly modified controllable budgets. We are talking instead about scenario control, or contingency control, where the issue is to what extent the critical underlying assumptions still hold or not.

IMPLICATIONS FOR FUTURE LEADERS

The management processes for the next century will be, as noted, much more behavioral in nature. They will be squarely focussed on a number of human resource-driven issues, the key ones of which we have already discussed: learning, team-based visions, driving human resource processes, incentives to enhance growth, holistic budgeting, and proactive controls. In an even more summary fashion, our prediction can be boiled down into three major themes:

- first, the challenge of developing management processes which will enhance aggressive pioneering of new business, as well as ultra-rapid expansion of the most promising ones, so as to enhance ultra-rapid internally-generated growth;

- second, to strengthen the focus on the appropriate human resource capabilities for ultra-rapid growth, both in terms of having the right people in the right place to spot business opportunities, and to follow through with organizational mobilization. This implies the need to regenerate human resources through the activity patterns of the firm, so that the premier strategic resource, the competencies of one's people, is enhanced, with relevant learning being the paramount dimension;

- third, the issue of budgets and controls will take on totally different meanings, with the emphasis being on proactive understanding of whether we have a business idea, keeping our human resources and capabilities in mind and, if so, how to scale it up based on involving the right people. This implies maintaining a holistic viewpoint and a close, catalytic dialog between top management and each project team.

SOME IMPLEMENTATION ISSUES

What are the major challenges associated with implementing the predictions given in this chapter? It should be kept in mind that, obviously, the predictions will be implemented over a relatively long period of time. We believe that there will be, above all, five interrelated implementation challenges that should be kept in focus to encourage an overall speedy evolution:

- we should start now to emphasize the positive thinking of our people, including the encouragement to be given to people to work in creative teams;

- we should start to emphasize the importance of allowing the right person to operate in the right place in the firm, focussing on self-organizing, and with the perspective being to achieve more rapid growth;

- organizational kingdoms, pyramidal levels in the organization, and bureaucracy will need to be broken down in order to let the flatter, network-driven organization emerge. This task should start now, with particular emphasis on modifying existing management processes to decrease support to such traditional practices;

- in line with this, we should start now to encourage people to work in flat organizations, to organize themselves in teams, to get used to wearing multiple hats, and to become more sensitive to organizational ambiguities. Organizational members must develop a realization of the dictum that their true responsibility will be larger than their formal authority. They must stand up to this test of maturity as soon as possible;

- last but not least, the organization should start now to practice more holistic thinking and pro-active management. When it comes to budget reviews, for instance, the issue will be to rethink the understanding of deviations as symptoms of broader changes affecting the organization rather than seeing these being just isolated incremental issues to be fixed. Similarly, temporary setbacks must be seen in a larger context, not as defeats, but as stimuli to further efforts in order to find new options to pursue. A defeatist attitude will not carry the organization forward.

All in all, we have pointed out what we see as important expected process changes to come, in order to ensure the proper workings of the successful firm of the future. This could be taken as a rather dramatic prediction. Or perhaps we are talking about allowing the common sense of good management practices to lead the evolution, so that our prediction does not have to be so dramatic after all. Only time will tell.

12

KNOWLEDGE LEADERSHIP

J. WIL FOPPEN

The relationship between management practice and management education is anything but equal. Opinions differ as to the degree in which management education contributes to the creation of effective managers. A lot of literature has been published which presents management trainers with techniques for improving management education. This same literature insists that a new period has already begun for management, bringing with it new and different demands.

There are two fundamentally divergent reactions to a period yet again termed new.[1] Many are of the opinion that what managers most need to improve their work and enhance their careers are new techniques and skills. Some examples of this are a striving for flexible firms with techniques such as total quality management, replacement of regulation-run bureaucratic structures by value-driven business cultures, the creation of virtual organizations, and the use of IT in order to re-engineer work processes. In addition to this, managers need to employ different modes of thought, ones which may range from the development of more managerial creativity to thriving on chaos. Management may have become more difficult, but there are always lots of new and different ways of dealing with it.

The other reaction which, though not shared by many as yet, is becoming increasingly popular among those involved, is more general and holds the view that due to uncontrollable turbulence, irrationality, and ambiguity, management is no longer viable. This position inevitably raises the question of whether management hasn't always been illusory.

Management is of pivotal importance for modern society. It is for this reason that, no matter what, thinking about management, certainly at university level, is of (great) relevance to management practice. So apart from the question of whether management's claim that it is indispensable is really valid or not, the fact that practically everyone believes it is is what counts. Besides, man's deep probings into nature and different forms of society have created a great number of problems, which in themselves have led to a far greater need for management and also because of the way in which they have been dealt with. All this once again underlines what has by now become the social importance of management and of course its reproduction via management education. At the same time, this stresses the importance of maintaining a critical approach to both.[2]

MANAGEMENT AND EDUCATION

On the whole there are two broad views on management education. The first is that the contents and methods should be changed radically in order to help managers be more effective within a complex and swiftly changing world. The second view holds that management is not important and consequently we should give up the idea of being able to equip managers with any kind of expertise.

At least several conditions need to be met for a learning process or other activity to call itself "education" or to be considered educational. Education implies first and foremost the transmission of something of value to which one has committed oneself. One is expected to have learned something of value. Education presupposes learning – the learning of valuable knowledge. Second, education should be about desired knowledge and insight in combination with a sufficient perspective of knowledge. Education is not a question of purely gathering facts or information for its own sake. It has primarily to do with a conceptual plan whose principles one can understand and explain whereby the perspective of knowledge will indicate that one is capable of placing the acquired knowledge, whether specific or specialized, into a broader frame-work.[3] In either case, education and learning always mean that the learner changes, and not purely as regards behavior. A change in behavior alone would sooner indicate a process of training.

Last but not least, ideally speaking, from the point of view of the learning individual, the process of education must revolve around a willingness to learn from a basis of complete freedom of thought and action. This is not to say that the above means that a training program can never be educative, nor that education has nothing to do with knowledge or skill. In a fairly large number of cases a certain skill is precisely what is required (being able to do calculations or conduct experiments, for instance) to be able to even acquire knowledge and insight in the first place. As R. Dearden maintains:

"The point of learning under the aspect of vocational training is to secure an operative efficiency; the person will be able to operate the word processor, give first aid, administer the injection, or run the shop. The point of learning under the aspect of education is to secure breadth and depth of understanding, a degree of critical reflectiveness, and corresponding autonomy of judgement.

Are the two compatible? There would seem to be no *a priori* reason why they should not be. A process of training could be liberally conceived in such a way as to explore relevant aspects of understanding, and in a way which satisfies the internal standards of truth and adequacy. Training for the liberal professions is often like this."[4]

It will be clear that management education will include not only aspects of vocational training but also of education, especially elements of "liberal education." From this it follows that a management education program which takes itself seriously will be keen to foster social competency and proficiency in intellectual analysis. In addition, attention will be paid to interpersonal skills such as decision making in uncertain situations, becoming familiar with budgeting, business enterprise, and so forth.[5] Moreover, it would be of great value to have extensive knowledge of organizations and, above all, to be able to analyze them.[6]

CAN MANAGERS BE EDUCATED?

Participants in every career-oriented training program may safely assume that their performance level is likely to undergo improvement. Management education, indirectly emulating what happens elsewhere in training courses for established professions, follows their example by supplying knowledge and skills in several functional areas.

It goes without saying that no management training program can replace experience. What can be done is to acquire the competence to make maximum use of one's experiences, whereby the aforementioned knowledge of perspective and the development of reflective and critical faculties would be helpful. Open and objective discussions would also contribute greatly to this. It is no doubt obvious that, once again, this approach portrays features of "liberal education."

A second link between education and managers' achievements lies in an improved ability to deal with change. After all, if in order to implement change one were to be solely dependent on managing culture, things would move too slowly.[7] Education and teaching would be more effective. A well-educated manager will be less inclined to be easily shocked by what is new and would be stimulated to view change as something constant.

The paradox is that on the one hand management education aims at making management more effective, but on the other it can, perhaps by definition, give no exact description of how to achieve this objective. "The paradox is that it is only by concern of broader goals, only by taking our eye off the ball, that education will prove to be useful. What seems to be required is some sleight of hand, some deception whereby we appear to give the client what they want, while we work to our own conception of what they need."[8]

In other words, what is required is a trick, a form of deception by which it appears as if the client is getting what he/she wants, while what happens is exactly what management education deems necessary. Yet this is anything but desirable because if it leads to an educational agenda which is separated from management practice, we are back to where we started.

The essence of the process under discussion is strikingly worded in one of La Fontaine's fables:

> "The children (presumably) were too lazy to earn a living by working in the fields, as their father wanted them to. So he told them instead that there was a treasure buried in the ground. Eager to get rich in a hurry, they overturned the soil in an unsuccessful search for the treasure, and in doing so made it so fertile that they did indeed get rich."[9]

In relation to what we pointed out earlier about the effectiveness of managers in practice and the (supposed) contribution made to this by management education, expectation and effect analyses would be able to provide more insight into original aims and their ultimate realization, and also into what happens to positive and negative results that had not been envisaged beforehand.

MANAGEMENT EDUCATION AS A PROCESS

Academic thinking on management takes place in a hall of mirrors. Management theories usually originate in a setting of public institutes that are themselves the result of a basic planning or management process. According to Chia, management theories are a socially "managed" claim on a body of knowledge whose component parts contribute to the reinforcement of the very same dominant planning principle which they want to help to unmask. In fact, both the management of an organization and the organization of management thinking are mirror images of each other. They reflect and reinforce the surrounding system of dominant values and prevailing symbols. This mutual relationship is neither readily recognized nor acknowledged. Neither is there much attention paid to what this might mean with respect to either theorizing about or educating for management.[10]

The majority of current management theories are dominated by a frame of reference with a fixed arrangement of space, time, and subject matter. This determines the delineated or rather the limited image one has of reality. According to Chia:

". . . the belief that theories are attempts by intellectual elites of society to accurately describe and represent reality as it is in itself. When this accurate mirroring is achieved, theories are then deemed to be true and hence carry the full weight of scientific authority along with them. Univocality of assertion and, hence, universality of application is arrived at by systematically undermining and killing off competing views much in the same way military strategists manoeuver to first isolate and then pick off opposing forces."[11]

In this Newtonian vision, causational thinking and the state of rest and stability determine what is considered normal and what should remain so. Movement is nothing more than the transition from one stable state to the next. In this view, change, movement, and transformation are merely stepping stones and side issues; they do not form an essential part of true reality. Much current thought on planning, management and knowledge thus represents a reality it has created itself.

The poet Wordsworth depicts this self-limitation most poignantly as:

". . . *That false secondary power*
By which we multiply distinctions, then
Deem that our puny boundaries are things
That we perceive and not that which we have made."[12]

How different is the view that everything flows and is in motion; where everything is in a state of becoming and is continuously coming into being. This mode of thought turns up repeatedly as a countermovement, albeit in the shape of a vague intuitive generalization. "Panta rhei: oude menei" from Heraclitus is a pre-Socratic philosophical proposition, which has since been re-adopted by Bergson and Whitehead, among others. Both deserve a moment for us to dwell on their importance and possible contribution to management education.[13] We once again have to become familiar with the fundamental mobility of reality: "It is movement that we must accustom ourselves to look upon as simplest and clearest, immobility being only the extreme limit of the slowing down of movement, a limit reached only, perhaps, in thought and never in nature."[14]

If one takes as the premise the primacy of movement and process above that of static entities and permanence, this will have radical consequences for grasping and understanding the process of managing, and for the pedagogical agenda of management education. The idea that management is concerned above all with delineated achievements, whereby management knowledge is a commodity of which one could have any number, is based on the presuppositions of existential ontology ("this is the way it is") and a representational epistomology (". . . and these are the knowledge labels we work with"). The objection – even from one's own learning programs – that attention is really paid to insight and vision induces one to have a further look at what new elements Bergson and Whitehead have to add (note that both published their findings at the beginning of this century).

Bergson sees intelligence and intuition as two fundamentally different types of knowing and acquisition of knowledge. Intelligence scans a particular object, while intuition explores it from the inside. The first observes and compares and the second enters and wishes to learn as much as possible from within. Intelligence puts its faith in what is known, whereas intuitive knowing is intellectual empathy, i.e. one is keen to grasp that which is unique and for that reason not yet readily put into words. In a sense this requires a reversal in how we have been accustomed to thinking: "To philosophize . . . is to invert the habitual direction of the work of thought."[15]

Language labels and other well-known paired concepts are no longer central. It is too tempting to use them as a means of viewing things in the old way. Wittgenstein says: "The limits of my language means the limit of my world."[16] According to Rorty there is no way to describe the world independently of the manner in which we do so.[17] By striving to think beyond that which is already known, one is entering what was unknown territory until then, and looking with eyes open for what is new and uncertain. At any rate, one is not going to avoid it, but will be prepared to allow oneself to be infused by a reality other than the familiar one.

By rebelling against existing concepts, one creates the necessary space to formulate personal insights, from which an individual management vision may develop: "a creative advance into novelty."[18] Negative capability is exactly what keeps Alice on her feet in the turbulence and insecurity of Wonderland, where every familiar concept is turned upside down and new concepts turn out to be usable only if (à la Whitehead) they are understood beyond familiar knowledge categories.[19]

Cultivating vision or foresight is of crucial importance to being successful in a world which is increasingly characterized by fluidity and the continuously shifting and changing activity of business. It is vital for future orientation and vision to be rooted in the recognition and control of routines. Routines are of absolute importance. They prove themselves if one conforms to them, looks after them, and when necessary develops new ones. Social life, just like an organization, is embedded in and flourishes under routine. A community needs stability (as does working together), vision itself presupposes stability, and stability is the product of routine.

But no matter how fundamental this may be, acceptance and trust in routine is not sufficient. To be successful as a manager one also has to develop the ability to understand the continuously complex variety of societies, one has to get a grip on trends and social movements, and also be able to give a quantitative assessment of such qualitative changes. It is above all this complementary

> *To be successful as a manager one also has to develop the ability to understand the continuously complex variety of societies, one has to get a grip on trends and social movements.*

165

aspect of both, the power of routine and the instinctive grasp of patterns of interconnectedness, which together form vision or foresight.

For Whitehead, vision or foresight is a general aptitude "for eliciting generalizations from particulars and for seeing the divergent illustration of generalities in diverse circumstances."[20] If one has the ability to see similarities in differences and differences in similarities, one can also reverse and redefine certain kinds of management situations: "the conduct of business requires intellectual imagination!"[21] If management education can promote this, at the same time accentuating creative and intuitive knowledge and knowing, one would be better able to see alternative possibilities in specific management situations and circumstances.

The key question still revolves around the degree to which situation-specific or contextual knowledge is a determining factor in the final result. It is becoming increasingly clear that a proportionate, reflective, and therefore pragmatic management approach would be the most effective and valuable. There are no dispensaries any more, we have all become citizens of Wonderland. The configuration of political, technological, cultural – but also ideological – developments is in constant motion.

All the more reason why every management situation should be viewed as charged with the way it originated; with mistakes, adjustments, good and bad assessments, but also with a series of possibilities for future results. Observation of such processes and a constant eagerness to learn makes one realize that the way in which events originate affects and is affected by how one observes and what has been perceived. The manner in which we grasp a situation inspires a specific kind of approach, while at the same time the choice of a particular reaction in turn influences the shifting pattern of who, what, how one observes.

There is no more vivid, optimistic way of illustrating the success of this dynamic and substantial interaction than by quoting Goodwin on how the Amazon area was able to come into being. "Trees modify and enrich the soil by dropping their leaves and producing organic compost that retains water, so forest systems such as the Amazon developed on originally poor soil creating conditions for the stunning variety of species that has emerged in this vast ecosystem."[22]

Management education as a process-philosophical activity proves itself by asking probing questions and by putting into perspective what has for too long been the accepted norm and which has seeped into management thinking. This theory of knowledge based on process makes its own justified demands on management learning.[23] By holding on tightly to an experience, one can elicit as much out of it as one wishes. Such situations can be understood fully only by looking to see how burdened they are with the weight of their past. It is then that one can perceive the specific fabric of an event or circumstance. Mutual and reciprocal influencing, as opposed to supposed linear causality, is of more help in seeing clearly how and why things, events, and results become what they are; new insights rarely come about through pure and simple experimental activity.[24] Reciprocally, this process is possible only if, like Peter Pan, one is prepared to engage in battle with one's shadow without seeing any image other than the one reflection.[25]

TECHNICAL RATIONALITY

More understanding needs to be cultivated of the social processes of organizations and, in particular, the role of one's own behavior in the production and reproduction of organizational life. For it is true that ". . . management is too potent in its effects upon the lives of employees, consumers and citizens to be guided by an instrumental form of rationality."[26]

MBA programs strongly advise students on the importance of safeguarding their careers. Almost everything and everyone is seen as a stepping stone or an obstacle in realizing this end. This attitude is still being reinforced by insecurity in business and on the labor market, though to a slightly lesser extent in recent years. To oppose it would only invite resistance. Read how elegantly MBA-director Peters expresses his criticism: "I would like to teach a class on strategy and business integration. I would like to use material that is at a minimum 25 years old and preferably reaching the stage of early antiquity. I would like to remove the copyright dates on the material, and I would like to think that I can get away with it, without the least bit of suspicion among the class."[27]

In education and educational matters it helps to explicitly discuss the tendency people have of avoiding emotions or discussions on power problems and underlying dynamic processes. The thing that makes experimental learning so very valuable is not possible until there is no escape route left. Students and other participants in the program will initially be opposed to expressing their emotions and will also feel ill at ease, but getting over this helps and facilitates their learning. It is no less important to stimulate the capacity to doubt the truth of perceptions.[28] For truth is made, not discovered.

Things do not have to be what they seem at first glance. Let me illustrate this. Two children are playing and they both fall into the mud. One of the children didn't get a dirty face and when he sees the soiled face of his friend, it is understandable that he should run inside to wash. The other, the one who actually is dirty and could do with a good wash, stays sitting there quietly. He didn't get a fright at all; after all, his friend looked the same as always. However, it is far less understandable if it is managers who become the unwitting prisoner of a supposed "instrumental" perception.

The technical view of management practice can be criticized from both inside and out(side). In the latter case it is the attempt to dominate others which is criticized. Looking at the instrumental apparatus from the inside, there is absolutely no proof that control techniques actually lead to the desired control. Drucker has already recognized that "control weakens control."[29] In other words, even within one's own frame of reference, purely technical views on management practice are not particularly moral or effective.

A far more complex picture is to be seen in practice. Nevertheless, it seems as if a large portion of management teaching is playing along with insecurity and greed, and therefore with the idea that "being managerial" can (technically) do everything. What's worse is that a lot of energy goes into the attempts to keep up the illusion on an organizational level. The alternative is to acknowledge that management practice is primarily of a socio-relational and political nature; and to learn to be able to muster the discipline to act within that restriction (or is it in fact an opportunity?). This means an education plan which emphasizes that a manager will always be a tangible, approachable person instead of simply having a managerial role. The very things managers will have to learn to deal with are insecurity, doubts and mysteries.[30] The lecture hall will often be a safer place than one's place of work for thinking, experimenting, testing, and questioning. It is a good place to practice and to learn to be alert in everyday work situations.

The role of management education is therefore more inclusive, and is also concerned with accepting daily dilemmas, both moral and instrumental, and no longer believing that a technical approach can be neutral, even though it seems to be taught that way.[31] The past 20 years, which have been characterized in the West by a modern neo-capitalistic political climate, have increasingly validated the usefulness of management education. On the one hand, education is considered as socially valuable to the extent to which it adds to economic welfare and international competition. On the other hand, within the framework of an individualistic consumer culture, education is considered personally valuable in so far as it enhances the economic position and career of the individual.

> *The role of management education is concerned with accepting daily dilemmas, both moral and instrumental, and no longer believing that a technical approach can be neutral.*

Business studies and management education score well on both criteria. However, this will remain true only if people continue to feel there is a positive relationship between management education, results in management practice, and managers' individual achievements.

WHAT IS RATIONAL AND WHAT IS MODERN?

One interesting case in point is the dominant role of rationality in and by organizations, and rationality in and by markets, which is under quite heavy attack. If it is true that rationality and linearity are invalid models, as is suggested by critical research, management education programs will have to be purged of them. But shouldn't just as many linear and other quantitative techniques, and above all the underlying way of thinking, undergo critical and careful scrutiny? What does this mean with respect to the relationship between management practice and management education, at least in the way this relationship is regarded by those in practice and those requesting management education?

This problem about the nature of rationality is in itself an arena for different research and disciplinary traditions. Indeed, as everyone is well aware, it doesn't look as if this dispute can ever be definitively won by one or other of the approaches. Because right under the surface lies the relativistic criticism: even if it is possible, should we consistently want to do it? It is much more valuable to regard this type of dispute as an incitement to be able to use them again and again in management education in order to illustrate that there are always different perspectives, and that they will continue to be generated as long as one keeps relying on suppositions that are certain. This is an invitation to the managerialists to become acquainted with critical studies, but also in reverse, so that critical research keeps starting with the established traditions in management thinking.

Management knowledge deserves to be properly managed. Accepting differences and cherishing pluriformity is a paradoxical must. One is after all invited to think about the complex and disputable nature of both management knowledge and management practice.

Critical remarks were made about managerialism being functionalist in essence. In addition, arguments were put forward against positivism and the Newtonian stress on cause and effect reasoning. In my view, process thinking and the acceptance of pluriformity offer an alternative. What I am talking about is in effect a relativistic and postmodern approach. I choose this on the basis of Latour's analysis of the results of the ambition of what is modern. In the same year, it appeared that not only did the Berlin Wall succumb in the East but nature, which so determines the quality of our existence, was crumbling under our feet.[32] Latour says:

> "The perfect symmetry between the dismantling of the wall of shame and the end of limitless Nature is invisible only to the rich western democracies. The various manifestations of socialism destroyed both their peoples and their ecosystems, whereas the powers of the North and the West have been able to save their peoples and some of their countrysides by destroying the rest of the world and reducing its peoples to abject poverty. Hence a double tragedy: the former socialist societies think they can solve both their problems by imitating the West; the West thinks it has escaped both problems and believes it has lessons for others even as it leaves the Earth and its people to die. The West thinks it is the sole possessor of the clever trick that will allow it to keep on winning indefinitely, whereas it has perhaps already lost everything."[33]

A different orientation is needed, one that begins with each individual, every manager, and every company. It is not acceptable to choose only for shareholder value, at the cost of the value of job opportunity. Neither can one choose to just keep on going when nature is demonstrably going down the drain. This generation has to leave something of life for those who come after it. The quality of responsible management lies in the acceptance of and the need to balance different interests and consequences.

KNOWLEDGE MANAGEMENT AND LEADERSHIP

The most important problem posed by the existence of different interests, that is to say different mental models and paradigms about and within organizations, is how to tackle their (potential) incompatibility. In order to manage the cognitive and normative differences and preferences as part of organizational practice, knowledge management and thus management education will have to detach themselves from a functionalist management ideology, and the positivistic idea of knowledge and rationality which is associated with it.[34] Such concepts as deutero leaning, n-th order changes, and innovation (instead of improvements) do not fit into the latter approach. Functionalism has a marked preference for unity above diversity, for harmony above conflict, for (functional) integration, and it chooses order above the potential chaos of continuous change.

> *The most important problem posed by the existence of different interests is how to tackle their (potential) incompatibility.*

Incompatibility or incommensurability are then seen as a grave threat to vested interests. Functionalists in particular react too emotionally and with disgust at the idea of (apparent) unreconcilable differences which adhere to incommensurability. If, however, knowledge management and therefore also management education wish to be able to pride themselves on the fact that they aspire to continuous innovation and learning in organizations, then the management of irreconcilability and pluriformity will be an unavoidable and indispensable prerequisite for its success.

". . . postmodernism belies all grand narratives like those of positivism and even Habermas's theory of rationality, that (. . .) try to force people into the mold of a specific way of thinking and acting (. . .). Postmodernism explains this tendency of grand theoretical systems (. . .) by positing two central characteristics of human reason: first, there is the fundamental and inalienable freedom of reason to conceptualize 'the world' in different ways, while second, each of these conceptualizations has a built-in and irreducible claim to universality."[35]

Management of incommensurability and heterogeneity in organizations expressly demands a postmodern epistomological perspective. Such concepts as incommensurability and internal differences have a prominent place in postmodernism. As is evident from the above quotation, postmodernism belies all great narratives on the levels of both epistomology and social philosophy. Positivism and even Habermas's theory of rationality, which under the guise of universality attempted to force people into a certain way of thinking and acting, as history has so adequately demonstrated, do not shrink from a totalitarian approach.[36]

Postmodernism shows that the incompatibility of grand theoretical systems is to be traced to two central features of human reason: first, the fundamental freedom of thought with which to view the world in one's own and therefore different way, and second, the inbuilt claim to universality, i.e. that one considers one's own point of view to be the best.[37] It is for this reason that in practice it is not enough to minimalize the differences between alternative perspectives (which could lead to a kind of pluralistic indifference); neither would it do to resolve the conflicts between them in a forcible manner (this would lead only to dogmatism). Managing differences will therefore be a challenge for knowledge management to find which leading element would be helpful in steering the ship of organization past the rocks of totalitarian rule and then around the cliffs of indifference.

Putting into context

Knowledge leadership actually contributes to innovation and learning on account of the way incommensurability and pluriformity are taken seriously, and thereby enlarge that very freedom of choice in favor of the organization and its members. If, on the other hand, knowledge leadership were to want to find out what fellow workers in organizations think and do and would want to be able to specify (and perhaps even check) this, its future role would be bordering on the absurd, both morally and practically: Big Brother would still be with us, but this time in the next millennium.

From a functionalist point of view the danger is real enough, considering the innate preference for unity and order. Where, historically speaking, information management has left the integrity of the human mind intact, one wonders whether a control-oriented interpretation of knowledge leadership will do the same.[38]

It goes without saying that one would choose management of pluriformity. Considering the pace of change and innovation in world economy and business, knowledge leadership and management education are making a considerable contribution to the strategic business aims of safeguarding organizational flexibility, adaptability, and creativity. And so the question has become all the more pressing as to the extent to which modern technical rationality can be seen as separate from the postmodern need for a management of change and diversity.[39]

13

FUTURE LEADERSHIP DEVELOPMENT

ROBERT M. FULMER AND MARSHALL GOLDSMITH

The mantra of the nineties has been: "Learning may be the only source of sustainable competitive advantage." When it comes to developing leaders, smart chief executives are making strategic investments to ensure their executives can produce strong results. Companies spent an estimated US$60.7 billion on training in 1998, according to the *Training Magazine. Business Week* estimates that companies spend US$15 billion annually on executive education and leadership development alone. Budget isn't the only commitment. Executives such as Roger Enrico of PepsiCo and Larry Bossidy of Allied Signal are spending significant portions of their business day personally teaching and mentoring future leaders within their organizations. It is becoming increasingly clear that developing executive talent is not a luxury, it is a necessity to remaining competitive.

The need for executive education is apparent. Key questions include: how can we learn from today's best practitioners to understand the trends and challenges that will become the norm in the future? Are there "best" ways to develop current and future leaders? How will we pick our leaders? What process will transform managers into leaders ready for strategic action? Who will design, manage, and deliver world-class leadership programs?

LEADERSHIP DEVELOPMENT: SCOPE AND PROCESS

Focus on corporate strategy

Leadership development is becoming closely aligned with and used to support corporate strategy. Issues such as globalization, decentralization, and the rapid pace of today's marketplace have forced companies to evaluate the way they operate. Paradigms that have worked for years are no longer effective when an organization's largest customer is thousands of miles away. Realizing the need for change is important. Determining exactly how to turn these challenges into opportunities is, however, a task that keeps many CEOs awake at night. In some cases, bold strategic initiatives are under way to revamp the way organizations do business while re-creating the workforce undertaking these efforts.

Best-practice organizations view the leadership development process as an increasing source of competitive advantage. GE Crotonville is described as a "staging ground for corporate revolutions." From 1981 to 1997 General Electric more than tripled its revenues while decreasing its worldwide employment from 404 000 to around 240 000. Naturally, this type of growth caused an enormous cultural shift within GE, including Crotonville. The central education function even changed its name from Corporate Management & Development to Corporate Leadership Development (CLD).

With the need for change apparent, James Wolfensohn joined the World Bank as president in 1995. Acknowledging both the internal and external challenges, he also felt the World Bank offered a number of great opportunities. The fall of the Berlin Wall meant that many new clients and potential funders could join the organization. The information revolution enabled knowledge to be transferred at a much more rapid pace, both with the member countries and the clients of the World Bank. Wolfensohn saw new leadership development efforts as one of the tools he could use to reshape the culture of the organization.

Aligning leadership development with corporate strategy

If the leadership development process is to be an effective piece of the change process, it must be aligned with all of the strategic objectives of the organization. Leadership development initiatives have gone to great lengths to understand and help implement overall corporate strategy. Only by aligning their efforts will new leaders be able effectively to meet business challenges and global market constraints.

Arthur Andersen's Partner Development Program must link closely to the firm's business strategy to stay in sync with current objectives and therefore help meet the needs of a business that continues to diversify and globalize. PDP constantly reviews strategy documents from not only the business but also the four service categories when conducting needs analyses.

Johnson & Johnson believes it is critical to start any discussion about education and development with the business objectives of the company. The company has focussed on three basic objectives:

- *top-line growth* – the company's history of double-digit, top-line growth requires innovation, whether it be through heavy R&D investment, new alliances, or mergers and acquisitions;

- *enhanced competitiveness* – Johnson & Johnson believes that enhanced competitiveness must come through aggressive cost reduction and not increased prices. The organization has had around 90 000 employees for the past five years but has still managed double-digit growth during this period;

- *organizational excellence* – Johnson & Johnson has to focus on finding great people and then developing them.

Meanwhile, Shell has long understood that developing leaders is a significant source of competitive advantage. Working within the context of its core business strategies and values – integrity, professionalism, respect for people, long-term focus, and pride without arrogance – became the foundation for planning these leaders' development. Shell admitted that it did not know exactly what its future leaders would look like. The company simply knew that a transformation must happen for it to remain competitive in the constantly changing global economy, and dedicated itself to the pursuit of breakthrough performance to realize the full potential of opportunities.

Focus on core issues

Corporate leadership development will focus more on core issues such as values and strategic change that are vital to the entire organization, while business units focus on challenges specific to their operations. A corporate leadership development function focusses on leadership skills and often leaves the management skills and business-specific skill development to the businesses. Management skills tend to deal with the basics – skills and behaviors that enable employees to make their numbers. Leadership development builds on these core attributes. At GE the ability to influence peers is critical. With Johnson & Johnson, building leaders involves giving employees the tools to make tough ethical decisions. Corporate leadership development efforts seem to focus on applying corporate values to specific strategic initiatives. Teaching management and supervisory skills is usually handled at the business level.

This split of responsibility seemed to work well – corporate leadership efforts complement those within the business, as opposed to competing with them. Generally, the business operations are much better equipped to handle their own management/training needs. However, the corporate leadership programs are providing the decision-making framework to effectively use the tools provided by the businesses.

Johnson & Johnson feels that the expertise for management development in a particular operating company often resides within that business. As a result, it makes no sense for corporate level to have full responsibility for this activity. Leadership development, on the other hand, is consistent across the company and as a result it makes sense to have a central group take the lead on this issue.

Focus on human resources development and business experience

Excellence in leadership development will involve teams that emphasize the importance of both human resources development and business experience. At Arthur Andersen, Johnson & Johnson, and Shell International, the heads of the leadership development process had senior-level business experience before assuming responsibility for this function. The use of business leaders in key human resources development positions does not imply a lack of respect for unique aspects of the discipline. Rather, it is based on a feeling that the presence of business leaders in the functions will help ensure buy-in from the businesses and the practicality of programs.

> *Excellence in leadership development will involve teams that emphasize the importance of both human resources development and business experience.*

Building on the concept of "hiring from the field," a number of best-practice organizations found innovative ways of bringing additional business experience on board. General Electric and Shell International bring in high-potential individuals on two-year rotational assignments. Hewlett-Packard recruits key people from line positions to ensure that knowledge of the "HP Way" and the pragmatic needs of the business are addressed in an adequate manner. These assignments help the leadership development function in its attempts to ground its efforts in business realities and help those individuals who come in from the business. Often, a person will start an assignment with knowledge of only a particular line of business but leave with an understanding of the entire organization.

Focus on internal and external factors

Leadership development efforts should be internally focussed and externally aware. New business demands dictate the need for change but certainly do not provide a framework for how to create the change. Whether started by the CEO, or bubbling up throughout the organization, the focus on building the skills of current and future leaders surfaces as a potential enabler of change. Creating a process to build leadership skills, abilities, and techniques has pushed organizations to look internally and externally for answers.

Organizations should realize that for the leadership development process to enable change, it must fit the culture of their organization. A first step for those designing the leadership development process was to ensure this linkage by soliciting the direct input of their customers. Input from key customers has become an ongoing process for the organizations. To conduct a proper needs analysis, organizations rely on a number of tools, including:

- the use of line executives in key human resource development positions
- program steering committees
- formal links with strategic planning efforts
- extensive conversations with business leaders
- internal and external customer surveys.

These formal needs assessments may seem like an obvious step in creating a leadership development process, but they are by no means done universally.

IDENTIFYING THE LEADERSHIP POOL

Competencies rather than past successes

Confidence in identifying leadership competencies is more important than formal studies about past successes. Any discussion about competencies can easily become controversial. Many contend that the identification of competencies helps organizations to understand those qualities, characteristics, and skills that lead to outstanding performance and outcomes. Others question whether competencies can be defined at all.

The vast majority of organizations believe that once competencies are defined, the results should be consistent throughout the company – regardless of position, business unit, or geographic location. For example, Johnson & Johnson sent a team around the world to make sure that what made a successful leader in the United States, for instance, would translate to Europe or East Asia. Although the company found that some of the wording for its competency model had to change from location to location, the behaviors were, in fact, consistent.

General Electric is perhaps the most skeptical of the partner companies in its take on competencies. Consistent with the CEO's emphasis on "Speed, Simplicity, and Self Confidence," GE does not spend time on formally defining leadership competencies. This does not mean, however, that leaders at GE are working without a road map. The following GE value statement serves as a guide to the traits being assessed and developed.

GE leaders . . . Always and with unyielding integrity:

- have a passion for excellence and hate bureaucracy
- are open to ideas from anywhere
- live quality, and drive cost and speed for competitive advantage
- have the self-confidence to involve everyone and behave in a boundaryless fashion
- create a clear, simple, reality-based vision, and communicate it to all constituencies
- have enormous energy and the ability to energize others
- stretch, set aggressive goals, reward progress, yet understand accountability and commitment
- see change as opportunity, not threat
- have global brains, and build diverse and global teams.

GE's values play a key role in determining each person's performance. All employees discuss with their managers their performance and career goals during a review meeting. The organization has a famous chart for rating people: their performance (i.e. the "numbers") is rated on one axis, and their adherence to GE values is rated on the other. Those who make the numbers and have demonstrated GE values are the most highly prized (those who do neither are the least prized). Those who don't make the numbers but adhere to the values are given a second chance. In fact, they are valued more than those who make the numbers but do not demonstrate the values.

Growing leaders rather than buying them

Growing leaders will be more effective than buying them. Aspiring companies want to know the secret of making "leaders their most important product." Organizations must emphasize that their top leadership came from within the company. Senior executives tend to be products of the leadership development system, groomed from the beginning to take on increasing responsibilities. In stark contrast to the situation at many companies today, buying top-level talent is done occasionally but not emphasized. The best-practice organizations lean toward internal leaders because of the powerful and distinct cultures in which they work. The best-practice organizations see their strong culture as critical to their continued success but realize that not everyone can thrive in these unique situations. Executives who are brought in from other organizations may have all the right experience and skills, but they may not be a good fit with Johnson & Johnson's credo or Hewlett-Packard's decentralized structure. Leaders who have come up through the organization are a proven fit – they have demonstrated the ability to successfully accomplish assignments in the way the organization has determined for its leaders.

Organizations should also realize that some executive positions must be filled externally to avoid stagnation and "inbreeding." In some cases, buying talent is a competitive must. As organizations transform themselves to deal with new markets, technology, or customers, hiring externally is often the fastest way to expand competencies and skills. When organizations hire from outside, they must rely on the development function to fill the role of cultural assimilator by exposing learners to the organization's culture and values.

Getting the right people into the right program

Tomorrow's organizations will emphasize getting the right people into the right program. Organizations should have a good idea of both the type of individual and the type of program they want as part of their leadership development process. Organizations must look to the goals of their leadership development process to determine who would be selected as a participant. At Shell International, the goal of the program is to create leaders at all levels, therefore LEAP programs are open to anyone within the organization (even though certain programs are aimed at individuals with the highest potential). The World Bank's Executive development program and Arthur Andersen's partner development program focus only on those at the leadership level. Others, like General Electric and Hewlett-Packard, are more selective with entrance into their key leadership programs as they want to focus only on the "A players," those individuals who have the potential to move quickly through the ranks.

Whatever the specific criteria may be, organizations should spend a great deal of time deciding who needs to be involved in leadership development. It is very important for an organization to bring a diverse population into the leadership development process. In future each successful organization will operate in the global marketplace and consequently must look to the leadership development process to help its organization build a more diverse workforce. Moreover, the diversity of the classes adds different perspectives that improve learning. Most top organizations say they try to get a mix of different countries, cultures, and business skills into their corporate development efforts.

> *Whatever the specific criteria may be, organizations should spend a great deal of time deciding who needs to be involved in leadership development.*

GE Crotonville's leadership development opportunities are for high-potential individuals (the organization's "A players" who are identified through the succession planning process). The organization feels it should spend most of its time developing its best and brightest. The company employs approximately 240 000 people worldwide, and each year Crotonville trains about 10 000 of them.

At Arthur Andersen, each program team is responsible for managing vendors and working with them to modify existing courses. Johnson & Johnson prefers to partner with a fewer number of suppliers whom they respect and know. The company looks for suppliers who fit in well with its culture and seeks to develop long-term relationships with them. Besides the external consultants and universities used in the development of Shell's programs, there simply weren't enough staff members to handle delivery.

At the World Bank, all the modules of the executive development program are delivered by the university consortium (Harvard Business School, John F. Kennedy School of Government, Stanford Business School, INSEAD, and IESE). These programs have been tailored to meet the specific needs of the bank's managers, but all are influenced by the universities that deliver them. This was precisely what the bank had in mind when it decided on these universities. Since the World Bank operates in a culture in which many employees hold advanced degrees, the organization needed to provide a program delivered by highly regarded faculty.

ENGAGING LEADERS IN THE PROCESS

Action rather than knowledge

The primary purpose of corporate education and leadership development is action, not knowledge. In preparing leaders to make critical decisions, leadership development functions have realized a need to do more than simply provide their leaders with knowledge and information. Disseminating the right knowledge can build a strong foundation, but the leadership development process must equip participants with the skills, qualities, and techniques necessary to apply that knowledge in ambiguous situations.

Organization should focus on using action learning, and take advantage of real-time business issues as the basis for learning and development. Content is not sacrificed for simplistic solutions, but in this new model, the answers to tough questions are not in the instructor's head but must be developed on the spot by learners.

Arthur Andersen uses a great deal of small problem-solving groups in its program activities. Each course has prescribed content, and other learning techniques include:

- case methods
- simulations
- action learning
- experiential learning
- executive coaching.

GE chairman and CEO Jack Welch chooses the action learning topics for each business management course (three per year) and executive development course (one per year). As a result, when individuals/employees hear that a certain initiative was a recommendation from the BMC or EDC, they go the extra mile to make sure it becomes a reality. In most instances, recommendations made by participants have been implemented.

Technology and interaction

Technology is growing in importance but will not replace the importance of bringing leaders together to deepen the learning experience. Companies across the globe acknowledge that technology has enormous potential in creating a learning organization. Top companies use technology to:

- disseminate knowledge
- keep people connected throughout the organization
- expedite and facilitate team learning
- allow access to the knowledge capital of the organization.

On the other hand, the experience of getting leaders away from their jobs and providing face-to-face exposure to colleagues from across the world is an essential part of the best programs. William James once said: "Genius is simply the ability to see the world from a different perspective." Corporate programs can provide learners with this capacity.

Best-practice organizations feel they cannot fully achieve the benefits of networking via technology. Their favorite method of delivery is face to face. At present technology is often seen as a plug to fill gaps in the learning process. For instance, part of Johnson & Johnson's strategy is to create an organization of 90 000 leaders. The company realizes, however, that it cannot put 90 000 people through its top development programs. But it can provide the technology for employees across the world to interact and learn from each other. In this case, technology is seen as a potential bridge to touch leaders at all levels within the organization.

As Johnson & Johnson moves towards using technology more in leadership offerings, it has created a four-point strategy for implementation:

1 *100 percent access* – every employee worldwide should have access to what he or she needs to know to be effective on the job;
2 *experiment* – since it is not clear what the best educational technologies are, it must experiment with various design and delivery modes;
3 *benchmark and partner* – internally, CED links up with the information technology function and the advanced communication group to leverage resources and determine the best strategies for using educational technology.

Externally, the organization does a significant amount of benchmarking to keep up to date;

4 *business value* – learning and experience have to focus on compelling and critical performance issues.

Realizing constraints such as cost and time, Shell has begun to use existing technologies. Laptop computers, e-mail, and Internet forums are all used by the various teams, but no efforts have been made to replace the face-to-face workshops with distance learning.

Succession planning

The leadership development process is becoming closely linked to succession planning. As part of the alignment between leadership development and other corporate systems, organizations should tie educational efforts and the formal succession process. Top development functions should discuss the usage of 360-degree evaluations as a part of their leadership development process, whether it be simply for development or for actual selection purposes. Coaching and developmental plans growing out of this feedback are encouraged as part of the executive conference progress, but the results of the assessment are not fed directly into the succession planning process.

Organizations should tie assessment, development, feedback, coaching, and succession planning into one aligned, integrated system. In this new model, leadership development becomes an important part of maintaining a steady flow of information throughout the organization to ensure that top talent is tracked and continues to grow. General Electric ties the leadership development process directly to succession planning and is open in making that distinction. All GE managers participate in a mandatory annual performance review with all their employees. The review includes discussion about performance and adherence to GE values and is later interpreted by someone at a higher management level to ensure fairness and accuracy. As part of GE's human resources planning process, all employees are rated in a nine-block system. This system incorporates the high (or low) potential of the employee and the quality of his/her yearly performance. The chairman believes that "corporate owns the top 500 people in the company and just rents them out to the businesses." To encourage the sharing of business talent, GE includes a negative value variable in its performance appraisals for managers who hold back talent. Outstanding business performance and leadership development go hand in hand.

ASSESSING THE IMPACT

The leadership development process is increasingly recognized as a symbiotic tool of effective leaders. Top-level support is a consistent key to developing leaders and sustaining the process. Without that support the processes would flounder. Yet the success of leadership development engenders even more high-level support. As top leadership development functions help their organizations meet current and future competitive demands, they win further support from the organization's leaders. Corporate executives are more likely to support leadership efforts that are clearly helping them get the results they seek. Through a strategy of monitoring the effectiveness of the leadership development processes, capitalizing on quick wins, and communicating their successes throughout the organization, the best-practice organizations keep this "virtuous cycle" going.

Groups such as Arthur Andersen's PDP and GE Crotonville remain successful with a customer-focussed strategy where careful listening, diligent crafting of programs, constant monitoring, and communications all play a role in creating senior management buy-in. This makes it much easier for senior executives to understand how the leadership development process has helped to shape and disseminate their organization's culture, overcome resistance to change, and achieve strategic goals.

General Electric's leadership development process is an effective tool for keeping GE at the top of its competitive game. Reasons for this include:

- culture
- top-level support
- operational-level support.

To maintain a high level of buy-in, the corporate leadership development center surveys GE's leaders around the world to ascertain future business needs and the requirements of future leaders. Additionally, the center identifies and uses "early adopters" of the leadership process. Throughout GE, certain developmental initiatives excite some business leaders sooner than others. By identifying these champions and leveraging their support, the company has been able to attain a critical mass of support for its efforts. This early identification and rallying was used with both the Work-Out™ program and the Change Acceleration Process (CAP).

Hewlett-Packard has garnered support for its leadership development process by involving both the CEO and senior management as participants in its programs. These executives serve as mentors, faculty, and

> *Hewlett-Packard has garnered support for its leadership development process by involving both the CEO and senior management as participants in its programs.*

sponsors in the process's design and programs. For example, HP's CEO Lew Platt opens and closes every accelerated development program with a dialog session about the HP way and the expectations of those participating in the process. The chief financial officer Bob Wayman is the sponsor of a planned worldwide broadcast and will facilitate a panel discussion. Executives also serve as teachers during the programs and as mentors to program participants.

The World Bank's executive development program was initiated after president Jim Wolfensohn created the strategic compact with the board of directors. In the compact, he outlined a number of integrated initiatives, including increased focus on executive and management talent. This compact began the movement toward the present-day EDP, so Wolfensohn's support was evident from the beginning. As initial positive results have been attained, this support continues, even though the program is costly. Senior-level support for the executive development program is further engendered by executives' participation as champions and coaches of the EDP's project teams.

Focus on assessment and measurement

Assessment and measurement is becoming increasingly important. All organizations should be concerned with the perceived value of their efforts. Shell International reported that members of the LEAP staff do not feel their program is adding value unless the team projects generate revenues of at least 25 times the project costs, and even that goal may be too low. Johnson & Johnson does follow-up research to determine whether subordinates and peers could see significant improvement in key performance areas after an executive conference. Arthur Andersen has found that graduates of its partner development program have higher levels of client satisfaction and higher per-hour supervised net fees than partners who have not attended the program.

Assessment should also be seen as a means of generating buy-in and keeping efforts focussed on the right objectives. The type and intensity of assessment depend on the objectives of the leadership development process and the culture of the firm. To collect this vital information, the best-practice organizations use a number of tools and techniques. While the Four Level Model of Evaluation (participant reaction, knowledge acquired, behavioral change, business results) is but one of the means that organizations use to determine the impact of leadership development efforts, it is nonetheless common and important.

For instance, Arthur Andersen has found self-assessment to be very accurate:

- *impact research* – the firm has compared partners who have attended the partner development program with those who have not (on a course-by-course basis). The results show a link between PDP and both increased client satisfaction and higher per-hour supervised net fees. Impact research is done in a two-year cycle; information is gathered on partners a year before the program and extends to a year after the program is completed;

- the use of both participant satisfaction and impact research helps provide a balanced set of results. For instance, Arthur Andersen found that one of its programs was not getting a high participant satisfaction rating, but impact analysis showed that the program was having a greater impact than any of the other courses.

GE's leadership development process is not driven by typical measures such as cost and ROI. Steve Kerr, chief learning officer, suggests that "Crotonville may be the only unmeasured and uncontrolled cost center in GE." Instead of traditional attempts to measure impact, the organization relies on feedback from a number of sources to make sure it is staying on the right track. For example, more than half the senior executive development courses at the company are run by the leaders of the corporation. They are a great source of feedback about the effectiveness of course design. The organization also relies heavily on student feedback.

In terms of measurement, Shell has a unique situation in that all the LEAP programs have goals and real deliverables. During the initial contracting process, a member of the LEAP staff and the leader within the business determine project outcomes. As a part of this discussion, the business leader expresses his/her objectives in sending the candidate to the program, and in many cases that defines the program and the problem the team or candidate will address. These specific goals are tracked by the LEAP staff, and the results are reported by the teams to the business leader. In addition to this, LEAP looks at the financials at the start and the end of the program to identify any changes, as well as scanning for factors that may have played a role in any changes.

Focus on value rather than cost

Leadership development is becoming more costly – and a better investment. The old adage, "you get what you pay for," seems to apply to the leadership development processes within the best-practice organizations. If organizations encounter change, they should see value in investing in their future leaders. Costs must be considered in the process, but the larger focus must be on the value that the program could provide. For example, when we have been asked to rank the importance of certain criteria while selecting an outside partner or vendor for the leadership development process, "fees" tended to be ranked as one of the least important factors.

Leadership development must be viewed as a long-term investment. The payoffs take time. In 1997 Arthur Andersen invested $306 726 651 in education, approximately 6 percent of total revenue. The firm spends this amount because it believes that if you want to deliver a "best-practice" program, you must focus on value and not cost (cost is important, but it is not the driving factor). General Electric has an extremely high level of buy-in for corporate leadership development. Crotonville has proved its worth time and time again, so the

Leadership development must be viewed as a long-term investment. The payoffs take time.

company has few qualms about investing in corporate training efforts. The World Bank realized that to foster a strategic cultural change and re-create a new language for leaders, the price would not be low. As Jim Wolfensohn laid out the strategic compact to the board, he stated that creating real change would take a large investment.

CONCLUSION

Leadership development will be an important tool for organizations in future. Each organization should require a unique commitment and should build a superb program (and process) upon the solid foundation. This excellence must be based on two key pillars. First, the overall tone of quality must be anchored with the commitment; second-best should simply not be acceptable. At the same time, good value for money is important. Second, the leadership development process is created to fit the specific organization. This chapter combines our experience with the methods of some of the world's best practitioners of leadership development. None of them will be a perfect fit with the needs of your organization, but they may suggest alternatives or stimulate ideas that might fit your specific challenges. Read, reflect, and use the parts that are applicable to your situation. Above all, keep listening and learning.[1]

14

COMMUNITIES OF LEADERS OR NO LEADERSHIP AT ALL

PETER M. SENGE AND KATRIN H. KÄUFER

Faced with profoundly new business realities – unprecedented demands from global competition, new technologies, emerging markets, possible mergers and alliances, and growing environmental pressures – many companies are falling back on old leadership habits. In particular, they seek to create more adaptive and flexible enterprises through turning to hero CEOs who can deliver shareholder value. Ironically, these CEOs, in turn, are typically asked to distribute authority and business accountability more widely, so that the enterprise is more able to recognize and respond to dynamic marketplaces. But many soon discover that it is not possible to create less hierarchical organizations solely through better hierarchical leaders.

This is the leadership paradox of our times: enterprises must become significantly more flexible and adaptive and this will undoubtedly require deep cultural changes and strong leadership, but powerful bosses may actually impede the increased creativeness, risk-taking, and innovation required to become more adaptive. The success rate for top-driven changes is not encouraging: according to studies by Arthur D. Little and by McKinsey & Co., two-thirds of total quality management (TQM) programs "grind to a halt because of the failure to produce hoped-for results."[1] The same is true for reengineering, where the success rate falls between 20–50 percent.[2] On the other hand, it is hard to imagine that the answer is less leadership.

Our experiences with many significant change efforts over the past ten years suggests that the only resolution to this paradox lies with a fundamental rethinking of what *we mean by leadership*. So long as we cling to the notion that leader means top manager and strong leadership means powerful executives, the perpetual search for the hero CEO will continue. Indeed, worshipping the cult of the hero-leader may be the primary cause for maintaining change-averse institutions. An alternative is to re-establish an older notion of a leader as someone who steps ahead, who has the courage, capability, and credibility to inspire change at many levels. This notion leads inevitably to seeing leadership as a distributed phenomenon and to posing a key question: how can we better understand and nurture leadership communities, people in diverse positions who collectively help the members of an enterprise shape their future? Rather than making executives less important, we argue that understanding leadership communities brings the unique roles of executive leaders into much clearer relief, as it does the roles for other types of leaders – all of whom will ultimately depend upon one another in creating successful 21st century enterprises.

> *Rather than making executives less important, we argue that understanding leadership communities brings the unique roles of executive leaders into much clearer relief.*

THREE TYPES OF LEADERS

The views expressed in this chapter stem from experiences within a consortium of companies, the first chapter of an emerging global network of learning communities, the Society of Organizational Learning (SoL). This first SoL (formerly the MIT Organizational Learning Center) involves about 20 US-based enterprises, mostly Fortune 100 corporations, but also including the World Bank, the Urban League, and several agencies within the US federal government. Since 1991, many long-term projects have been undertaken within these organizations aimed at implementing new processes and structures to accelerate and deepen organizational learning. These initiatives have differed in terms of their objectives and specific business context, but all have been focussed on crucial business issues, typically involving the redesign of workplace environments so that day-to-day work activities also involve opportunities to develop core learning capabilities:

- individual and collective aspiration: clarifying personal vision and values and building shared visions;
- reflective conversation: increasing personal reflectiveness, especially regarding individual and shared mental models, and developing capabilities for dialog and productive discussion within work teams;
- understanding complexity: developing systems' thinking abilities to conceptualize highly independent issues and distinguish high-form, low-leverage strategies.[3]

As a non-profit research and education association, SoL provides an infrastructure that helps people to learn from each other's experience and to engage consultants who help with change efforts and researchers to better understand those efforts. In particular, making sense of successes and failures during these profound change projects has led to identifying three distinct types of leaders: local line leaders, executive leaders, and internal networkers or community builders.

Interestingly, in some SoL member companies there have been many examples of significant change efforts that have lasted ten years or longer with neither top management support nor knowledge; yet there have been no examples of successful sustained change efforts without committed local line leaders.[4] The reason local line leaders are so essential to innovation is simple. All genuine management or organizational innovation is concerned with enhancing the processes whereby value is generated. If an enterprise does not enhance its capacity to create value, either through greater efficiency or effectiveness in current activities, or learning how to generate new sources of value, there are no consequences for those whom the organization serves, its customers. Local line leaders are essential to innovation because they operate near to where value is actually created, at the front lines where products are designed, developed, produced, and sold, where services are generated and relationships with customers built. As executives know only too well, line managers shape how new ideas become or fail to become new organizational practices. Many grand strategies fail to be implemented because local line managers are not committed to executives' change initiatives. Even while paying lip service to changes driven by executives, and complying with their requirements, uncommitted line managers have great latitude to undermine those changes. On the other hand, committed line managers are instrumental in actually establishing the new practices and processes whereby broad change goals are translated into action and results. But we have found that the role of local line leaders goes beyond implementing or failing to implement executive strategies. They are a critical source of innovative ideas themselves, both operational and strategic.

Conversely, at their best, executive leaders make unique contributions as designers, mentors, and role models or stewards.[5] Over the long term, they can have profound influence on the overall environment for innovation in an organization. As designers they can focus on guiding ideas – values, core business strategies, long-term visions and purpose – that orient and give meaning to day-to-day activities, on governance systems, and on other deep structural impediments to innovation. As mentors, they help line leaders relate immediate challenges to long-term aims and can play crucial roles in developing the leadership capabilities of others. As stewards or role models, they embody commitment to change through demonstrating their own vulnerability and continual learning.

Yet executives who endeavor to initiate important changes often find that there is little they can accomplish without the assistance of local line leaders able to translate new mandates into new practices. "Anyone who thinks you can drive this sort of change from the top is wrong," says Rich Teerlink, retired CEO of Harley Davidson.[6] "When I first came in as CEO," says Shell Oil's Phil Carroll, "everyone thought, 'Phil will tell us what to do.' But I didn't have the answer, thank goodness. If I had, it would have been a disaster."[7]

As it turned out, both Teerlink and Carroll were highly successful in helping to develop networks of talented local line leaders, as a result of overt strategies (e.g. Shell's annual top 200 leadership conference) and their persistent encouragement to others to take initiative. Nearing retirement from Shell, Carroll reflected on his experience as CEO and commented about vulnerability: "You need a healthy dose of humility . . . The truth is everyone can see your flaws . . . if you try to hide them, they wonder what else you are hiding."[8]

Lastly, internal networkers represent a type of leader who is all but entirely neglected, both in the literature and by many managers. Internal networkers come from many formal roles: they may be internal HR or training staff, engineers, or even local managers. What distinguishes them is their mobility, their ability to move freely within the informal networks which operate in all organizations. They play the key function of connecting predisposed but isolated line managers to new ideas and practices, and to other like-minded managers. They serve as mentors, internal consultants, and "thinking partners," helping local line leaders deal with the host of day-to-day practical issues that otherwise thwart change. Yet their importance is often overlooked, even by those with whom they work closely, because they usually do not occupy important positions in the managerial hierarchy.

Why do we call the internal networkers "leaders?" Because without effective internal networking we have found that large enterprises have great difficulty sustaining significant change. Internal networkers are crucial to the diffusion of innovative practices, as shown by research on "communities of practice," the informal networks through which most innovations diffuse.[9] Without effective internal networkers, there may be many "pockets" of innovation but these changes rarely add up to organization-wide changes. Most of all, we call internal networkers "leaders" because of our favored definition of leadership: the

> *We call internal networkers "leaders" because of our favored definition of leadership: the capacity of a human community to shape its future, to sustain significant change.*

capacity of a human community to shape its future, to sustain significant change. To not regard internal community builders as leaders would be to ignore a critical dimension of an organization's capacity for large-scale change.

In order to better understand and develop an organization's capacity to sustain significant change, it is essential to understand the dynamic interactions between these different types of leaders and the challenges they are facing. This requires a systemic view of the change processes.

LEADERSHIP AND THE CHALLENGES TO SUSTAINING CHANGE

In 1993, we began a series of research workshops with SoL members using systems thinking to better understand the forces that shape significant change efforts and how different types of leaders deal with these forces.[10] The premises underlying this ongoing study have been:

1 the types of change required of Industrial Age institutions unfold at the "outer" and "inner" levels. They involve changes in the systems, processes, and practices that define how organizations function; but they also involve changes in beliefs, assumptions, and habits that are social and ultimately personal. In other words, the changes are personal, interpersonal, organizational, and even inter-organizational – the essence of truly systemic change. Failing to understand the multi-dimensionality of profound change is why so many "change efforts" fail;

2 leaders in such systemic change can be thought of as growing new ways of working together, rather than changing old ways. This is not just a semantic distinction. Effective leaders do try to change people, they seek to demonstrate that something new is possible. They lead through creating the new and specifically through their willingness to change themselves, rather than through convincing others that "those others" need to change. This is true regardless of the organizational position such leaders occupy;

3 thinking of change as growing something new means that processes of institutional change can be understood by analogy to growth processes in all natural systems. All growth processes in nature are governed by the interaction of self-reinforcing (positive) and balancing (negative) feedback. For example, if a biological population grows it is because there is a reinforcing process whereby more adults lead to more births, which eventually leads to more adults and still more births. Similarly, the growth of new organizational practices involves self-reinforcing processes, such as new approaches leading to new results, leading to increased commitment and willingness to extend these new approaches. But every growth process in nature is counterbalanced by balancing or "limiting processes." Such limiting processes represent a system continually seeking balance points – a human body's homeostatic state, an ecosystem's balance of predator and prey, or a

company's historic sense of identity and continuity. As Chilean biologist Humberto Maturana puts it: "All growth occurs while it is being inhibited;"

4 leaders at all levels sustain change by helping create the energies (vision, passion, imagination, commitment) that generate self-reinforcing growth processes, while simultaneously attending to the forces that limit change;

5 in most situations, the greatest leverage lies in understanding and attending to the limiting processes. While many would-be leaders try to overcome these limits by pushing harder on the growth engines, artful leaders pay close attention to the challenges they encounter, knowing intuitively that therein lie their most effective strategies;

6 understanding the diversity of limiting processes that profound change efforts encounter can reveal the variety of leadership strategies *and* leaders needed to sustain such change. In particular, it provides an initial insight into how executive leaders, local line leaders, and internal networkers depend upon one another.

So far, ten distinct challenges or sets of forces that impede significant organizational change have been identified. Each challenge arises as a consequence of some measure of success in building momentum in a change process. If no momentum develops, then these challenges are never encountered, just as the limits to any growth process in nature arise only as a consequence of growth occurring.

However, despite the predictability of these challenges, many leaders are unprepared for them, and react in low leverage ways when they arise. Herein lies a key insight for leaders of all types: success will breed forces opposing further success; sustaining change requires understanding the sources of these forces and having workable strategies for dealing with them. This is "The Dance of Change,"[11] the inevitable interplay between forces producing innovation and growth and forces conserving stability. Great leaders understand this and learn how to work with the full range of forces crucial to long-term change. Ineffective leaders disregard these forces, and simply keep trying to push their agenda, believing that their mission is to "overcome resistance to change" rather than seeing such resistance as an inevitable by-product of their own efforts, and ultimately a source of great leverage for sustaining change.

The following list summarizes these challenges, grouping them in a typical sequence in which they are encountered by a pilot group at any level, including a top management team.[12] "Challenges of initiating" concern forces that come into play at the earliest stages, arresting movement before it ever achieves any significant degree of change. "Challenges of sustaining" develop somewhat later, often after innovative pilot groups have achieved what they regard as significant accomplishments, only to find themselves encountering new problems, both as their pilot effort draws in more people and as it encounters difficulties within the larger organization. "Challenges of redesigning and rethinking" concern deep limits to transformational change within most Industrial Age organizations, limits such as the concentration of power and centralized control in shaping strategy and purpose. These challenges, while pervasive and ever-present, often become most evident well into the life cycle of highly successful change initiatives.

Challenges of initiating

- time: "We don't have time for this stuff"
- help: "We have no help" or "We're wasting our time"
- relevance: "This stuff isn't relevant"
- walking the talk: "They're not walking the talk."

Challenges of sustaining

- fear and anxiety: "This isn't good"
- measurement: "This stuff is not working"
- true believers and non-believers. "We have the way" or (from the non-believers' perspective) "They are acting like a cult."

Challenges of redesigning and rethinking

- governance: "They (the powers that be) never let us do this stuff . . ."
- diffusion: "We keep reinventing the wheel ..."
- strategy and purpose: "What are we here for?"

We are not saying that all change initiatives necessarily encounter all these challenges. For example, those which never surmount the challenges of initiating are unlikely to be retarded by the subsequent challenges. But most eventually do, especially those which achieve some degree of success. Our experiences within the SoL community have shown that each of these challenges has the capability of bringing otherwise promising efforts to a halt.

LEADERSHIP STRATEGIES

In *The Dance of Change,* practitioners, researchers and consultants map out these challenges and offer their experiences and reflections on strategies that have helped them meet those challenges.

Challenges of initiating

Time

The first challenge that many pilot projects confront is the lack of time. Trapped between the daily workload and aspirations to change the workplace, leaders quickly realize that even ideas which have broad appeal never get implemented because there is simply no time for people to even think seriously about possible change, let alone engage in serious change efforts.

An example of a creative and successful strategy to deal with this challenge was developed by MIT professor Lotte Bailyn and her team of action researchers involved in multiple change initiatives aimed at helping people balance work and family life.[13] Bailyn and her colleagues developed the distinction between "thinking time" and "communication time." They found that much time was wasted each day by the fact that people could not sit down and work on one task without being interrupted. With their help, work groups established "thinking time" with the status of a meeting: they reserved a certain part of each day for individual work.

Strategies to cope with the "no time" challenge depend on identifying ways that time is being wasted and striving to enable people to regain greater control over their time. The following list summarizes strategies of how to meet the "no time" challenge:

- integrate initiatives and set a focus instead of running a high number of different initiatives
- trust people to control their time
- value unstructured time for reflection, dialog, skillful discussion, practice and learning
- find ways to eliminate unnecessary work
- say "no" to political game-playing
- say "no" to non-essential demands
- consciously experiment with time as a managerial practice.

Help

The "no help" challenge stems from the fact that developing new learning capabilities is no trivial task. It takes time. It takes persistence. And it usually involves coaching or mentoring from people with prior experience. This can be from outside consultants. But it can also involve internal consultants or managers with significant experience from similar initiatives. The important point is not to underestimate the help needed. If it was easy to develop capabilities for reflection and dialog, to raise complex and controversial issues that were previously ignored to protect people, to understand complex interdependencies among diverse organizational processes and activities, and to build shared aspirations, everyone would already be doing it. It is precisely because they are difficult that they carry significant potential for improvement. Pilot groups often have access to numerous sources of help but the quality of help matters. Not every consultant or senior manager can offer the right experience and advice. The "no help" challenge has two sides: leaders in pilot groups must accept the fact that help may be essential for success, and they must learn what kind and quality of help is needed. Finding effective help requires a team to understand its goals and aspirations and to be able to articulate specific needs. Strategies for coping with this challenge are:

> *Pilot groups often have access to numerous sources of help but the quality of help matters. Not every consultant or senior manager can offer the right experience and advice.*

- investing early in help
- creating internal capacity for coaching
- finding partners who can counsel one another
- building coaching into line managers' responsibilities
- reflecting on your attitude about seeking help.

Relevance

The challenge of relevance stems from the fundamental question, "Why is a change initiative important for people's specific business goals and their job requirements?" Managers often seem to think that because a change is relevant to them, or simply because they declare that "this is something we must do," the relevance is clear to others too. Yet change initiatives championed by executives are routinely undermined when local managers do not see their relevance for their own goals and business objectives. If a change effort is not significant for people's practical needs, a commitment gap arises. Strategies for meeting the challenge of relevance within a pilot group are to:

- build awareness among key team leaders
- explicitly raise questions about relevance in the pilot group – make the subject open and discussable
- make more information available to pilot group members
- keep any type of training linked tightly to business results
- inquire openly if perceptions arise that some people are getting carried away: people can become so enthusiastic about particular changes, like developing dialog, that they alienate other, less enthusiastic team members
- revisit relevance periodically.

Walking the talk

Ultimately, all change involves risk, and many people will commit themselves only to the extent that they have confidence in the people advocating the change. Whether advocates are local line managers, internal networkers or executives, their personal credibility and perceived integrity are inseparable from the credibility of their change aspirations. If leaders are perceived as not walking the talk, this will severely limit people's willingness to commit to any change initiatives. This limit is especially important, in our experience, as it pertains to local line managers because they are the most immediate contact point in the management hierarchy for most people.

Leaders' credibility must be built continually, but people especially look to periods of stress as indicators of what a person really stands for. David Marsing, Intel vice president, describes one such experience during a difficult business situation earlier in his career as a local line manager:[14]

> "In the mid-1980s, I became the plant manager of an Intel fabrication plant in Livermore, California, the facility at which we produced the 386 processor, which launched Intel's spectacular revenue growth of that time. This plant was also the site of remarkable technical improvement, but as an 18-year-old facility, it could not stay competitive with new, more advanced facilities. In 1989, we were told that we would have to shut the operation down. We senior managers made a commitment that whatever we did, everybody working there would have a job. We would find them a job in the area or, if they could relocate, somewhere else at Intel. We spent two years relocating more than 700 people. This was a phenomenal task, but it created a core group of people, scattered throughout Intel, who helped do some phenomenal things later. At other facilities, employees would say, 'You can't trust management.' But people who had been at Livermore would say, 'You can trust these managers, because they'll go to the mat for you.'"

Marsing's story illustrates how trust and shared responsibility built in difficult times can carry over into the future. Conversely, failing to trust when it matters eventually limits many change initiatives. Strategies for addressing the challenge of walking the talk include:

- develop espoused aims and values that are credible in terms of the living qualities of the organization;
- build credibility in organizational values and aims by demonstration, not by articulation – remember the old adage, "I can't hear your words, your actions speak too loudly;"
- don't go it alone – work with partners who can help you see how your behavior may communicate messages of which you are unaware;
- cultivate patience under pressure;
- develop a greater sense of organization awareness;
- think carefully about your beliefs about people;

- make room for talk about the individual's values;
- cultivate patience with bosses;
- practice shuttle diplomacy.

Challenges of sustaining

Fear and anxiety

The challenge of *fear and anxiety* arises because, to some degree, everyone has fears of exposure, of making a mistake, of showing ignorance, or of accidentally hurting others through inappropriate candor and behavior. These are very reasonable concerns and they inevitably grow as significant change processes reveal more of the deeper issues that have usually been buried for many years. In some sense, all change efforts can induce fear of the unknown. But deep change processes that eventually call into question long-held beliefs and attitudes, and habitual ways of acting (such as deferring to bosses, or bosses not having to reveal their reasoning), can be especially threatening. If fear and anxiety are not acknowledged, they become powerful limits to change. People may say all sorts of things, ranging from "this is a waste of time" to "these new ideas are great" (because they are afraid to say what they really think), but their fear will make them withdraw their emotional involvement and operate defensively rather than imaginatively.

However, fear and anxiety do not have to be insurmountable limits – some leaders appreciate fear as a potential source of awareness. As mountain climbers say, "those without fear are the first to die." Fear is a healthy reaction to the unknown, especially when there are real dangers. Fear becomes counterproductive only when it is unacknowledged and then begins to occupy people's minds. But fear and anxiety must also be dealt with gradually. Trust is not built in a day. When not appreciating the natural dynamics in building the trust needed to overcome fear, impatient managers often want to "solve this trust problem" in the way that they would attack other, technical problems. Several years ago, a CEO in a SoL company learned from consultants about several difficult issues which members of his team considered undiscussable in his presence. He was upset at hearing this and declared, "We will solve this problem. We'll put each of these issues on the agenda of our next staff meeting." Needless to say, this did not improve matters. The fear that was making these issues undiscussable in the first place was only intensified by the boss confronting his staff and demanding they discuss the issues in his presence.

Strategies to cope with fear and anxiety include:

- start small and build momentum before confronting difficult issues
- avoid "frontal assaults" on people's anxieties

- set an example of openness
- learn to see diversity as an asset
- use problems as opportunities for learning
- do everything possible to ensure that participation in pilot groups and change initiatives is a matter of choice, not coercion
- remember that skills matter
- as a manager, work to develop a link between vision and reality
- remember, and remind others, that fear and anxiety are natural responses to the precariousness of a learning situation.

Measurement

The challenge of *measurement* arises for two reasons. First, soon after a change initiative begins, some people expect to see improved business results. However, there are usually significant time delays – anywhere from a few months to even years – in implementing new business practices. The "result gap" between expected and actual results often creates negative assessment within a pilot team, and especially outside it. In addition, negative assessments can arise because traditional means used to judge performance may be inappropriate to new ways of working together.

The Epsilon product development team, developing a new car model, achieved significant improvements in cost, quality and timing.[15] Yet there were also side effects from their improvements that made things look worse through some traditional measures. For example, they set a new record for on-time completion at an important prototype stage. The Epsilon team had 88 percent "parts on time," compared with a company-wide average of under 50 percent. Team members regarded this as a great achievement and evidence that the changes in how they worked together were paying off. However, completing more of the prototype on time also created problems; notably, it led to a subsequent surge in "change request" (CR) or "concerns," official documented reports by an engineer that something might need to be changed. CRs increased because all the engineering sub-assembly teams could now see the work of the others, and they quickly discovered many potential problems that would have otherwise only shown up much later. The team members regarded the increased CRs as a positive development but outside the team they were seen as a major problem.[16] The program was regarded as "out of control" because no one had ever seen so many change requests.

Strategies for meeting the challenge of assessment and measurement include:

- appreciate the time delays involved in profound change;

- build a partnership with leaders on assessing progress, as well as checking on the assessment process itself;

- become proactive around assessment: make assessing progress, and developing new abilities to assess, a priority among advocates of change, rather than leaving it to bosses wondering "how things are going;"

- learn to distinguish the needs of those participating in a change effort to assess their own progress so as to improve, from the needs of outsiders who have to judge progress for other reasons (such as resource allocation).

True believers and non-believers

It is common for team members involved in highly innovative pilot efforts to split into *true believers and non-believers*. When this polarization occurs, not only do those committed to the project find themselves in difficulty, but the likelihood of their vision spreading more widely declines considerably.

Confidence is vital for innovators. But it can also have a dark side, breeding arrogance and isolation. As transformation initiatives achieve significant changes, the innovators' confidence grows. This comes about for two reasons. First, as new learning capabilities develop, team members find they are confronting important issues in new and more effective ways. Second, improved business results are evidence they are enhancing their capabilities. However, there is a thin line between confidence and arrogance, and it is often hard to know when this line has been crossed. The more time pilot group members spend only with one another, and the more they develop their unique ways of operating, the more isolated and distanced they can become from the rest of the organization. Dynamics on both sides of the gulf reinforce this isolation, and make the gap wider. Both sides can feel an almost irresistible pressure to defend themselves. Ironically, the deeper the changes that occur in a pilot group, the more easily members can feel disconnected from the larger organizational mainstream. To a certain degree, these problems are inevitable, as Art Kleiner shows in *The age of heretics*;[17] they have existed throughout corporate and industrial history.

Because innovative pilot groups create sub-cultures with ways of working that differ from the organizational mainstream, a clash between insiders and outsiders is inevitable. But it need not escalate to dysfunctional polarization if leaders recognize the danger and develop strategies for dealing with it. Some of these strategies include:

- leaders becoming bicultural: developing capabilities not only to operate effectively within new sub-cultures but to cross boundaries and operate effectively within the mainstream organizational culture as well;

- seeking mentoring from other leaders, especially those with high credibility within the mainstream culture;

- building the pilot group's ability to engage the larger system from the beginning;

- cultivating openness;

- respecting people's inhibitions about personal change;

- developing phraseology that is understood inside and outside the team;

- laying a foundation of common values.

Challenges of redesigning and rethinking

Governance

Innovative groups sooner or later find themselves caught up in issues of accountability and power; these represent the challenge of *governance*. It may happen when they press for more autonomy, feeling they have the ability to make decisions on their own due to their increased capabilities. It may happen when they cross organizational boundaries; for example, initiating changes to better serve customers but inadvertently undermining established practices which other managers rely on. Sooner or later, pilot groups with high levels of autonomy will expand their activities and affect other parts of the company for which other people are accountable. When this happens, pilot groups will encounter the organization's governance system, outlining who has the power to make what sort of decisions. Issues concerning governance are not just necessary for pilot groups, they also involve many executives designing enterprises for today's marketplaces. Indeed, the pilot group may actually be the top management team, wrestling with such design issues. "We're not trying to eliminate control in our organizations," says former Hanover Insurance CEO Bill O'Brian. "The movement of increasing localness is really about replacing hierarchically imposed control with increased self-control. This is a far more difficult challenge than merely giving people authority to make decisions."

Strategies for meeting the governance challenge are different for the pilot group and the executive leadership:

The pilot group should:

- pay attention to boundaries, and be careful about the way it crosses them;

- articulate the case for change in terms of business results;

- make executive leaders' priorities part of the team's creative thinking;

- experiment with cross-functional, cross-boundary teams, if the hierarchy is prepared to back them.

Executive leaders should:

● promote a coherent philosophy regarding the sources and uses of power; without clear governing principles, power tends to be exercised in the form of unilateral decisions by executives, reinforcing the perception that it is wielded arbitrarily;

● develop specific structures that guard against "authoritarian drift," the gradual concentrating of power in higher levels (this can happen both because of executives exercising power and because of middle level managers shirking responsibility);

● deploy new rules and regulations judiciously;

● be prepared for a long journey if they are sincere about the orderly distribution of power and authority. And don't embark alone: make sure you have supporters within the executive group and/or your board.

Diffusion

The challenge of *diffusion* is one many executives wrestle with: the persistent concern that there is much new knowledge being generated within the organization that never escapes local "pockets of innovation." This concern is one of the major reasons for investment in knowledge management systems, typically, efforts to deploy information technology to capture, store, and retrieve organizational knowledge. The fact that many such investments are major disappointments reflects the reality that the deeper challenges of diffusion are social, not technical. This can be caused by a feeling among innovators that no-one really cares about their efforts. Diffusion of knowledge won't just happen because the CEO says it should, or because new information technology is ordered by management.

Ultimately, meeting the challenge of diffusion effectively depends on creating an organizational climate that encourages risk-taking and sharing, that values the diversity of ways in which people learn, and fosters a healthy balance between competition and collaboration. None of this is easy, but leaders can start by concentrating on tangible changes in learning infrastructures that encourage people to cross functional boundaries and to engage in a mutual learning process. Strategies for meeting this challenge are:

> *Meeting the challenge of diffusion effectively depends on creating an organizational climate that encourages risk-taking and sharing, and fosters a healthy balance between competition and collaboration.*

● learn to value network leaders as carriers of new ideas and as coaches; leaders with hierarchical authority are often too focussed on their immediate tasks to be effective at sharing what they are learning;

- pay attention to existing communities of people in an organization as chan-nels for diffusing knowledge and information; learn how they function and how they can be nurtured;

- release information about innovations more freely;

- periodically, gather people from across functional boundaries for collective inquiry into mutually important topics;

- design more effective media for internal information exchange;

- cultivate "appreciative inquiry."[18]

Strategy and purpose

Lastly, the challenge of *strategy and purpose* arises in different ways for dif-ferent types of leaders. Today, the field of strategy and strategic planning is in a state of turmoil. Traditionally the domain of top management, their strategic planners and strategy consultants, many leading thinkers, including many within executive ranks, now realize markets are too dynamic to "figure it all out from the top." Even if the top could figure it out, by the time their brilliant strategy reaches the front lines, often everything has changed. As leading strategist Gary Hamel puts it: "The bottleneck is at the top of the bottle."[19]

For top management, the challenge of strategy and purpose means rethink-ing the strategy process. It is not that senior management has no responsibilities, or that all strategic thinking should be left to people at the front lines who are often taken up with short-term concerns. But the crafting of strategy, or the nurturing of effective emergent strategies, must become more of a two-way street, with more give and take among all levels of man-agement. From the standpoint of pilot groups, those that sustain their efforts for some time and achieve significant practical successes, invariably find new aspirations emerging. They begin to live with basic questions like: "What do we really want to create?" But if local groups articulate new business visions, they may be seen to be significantly overstepping their mandate. Moreover, they may be unaware of many things, from market and technology trends to internal political dynamics, vital to pursuing new strategies. Lastly, lying behind many questions regarding strategy are even deeper questions about the purpose of business enterprises. The taken-for-granted belief that the purpose of the business is to maximize shareholder investment is becoming more ques-tionable in marketplaces with abundant financial capital, and increasingly scarce natural resources and increasing pressures for social accountability.

Strategies for meeting this challenge include:

- use scenario thinking to investigate blind spots and signs of unexpected events;

- develop stewardship as an organizational ethic and practice;

- engage people at all levels around questions of organizational strategy and purpose;
- expose and test the assumptions behind your current strategy;
- focus on developing better strategic thinking and ethical thinking capabilities.

THE DANCE OF CHANGE

When one considers the range of challenges described above, it would take a true flight of fancy to think that all an organization needs is a great hero CEO to create change. In fact, creating change means dealing with the diverse challenges of initiating, sustaining, and redesigning, of which those described above are undoubtedly a great simplification. This diversity of challenges creates a background for understanding leadership in a new way, as a complex phenomenon with diverse players working with the diverse forces. Specifically, we think this picture adds substance to the belief that significant change occurs only through the actions of a community of leaders, that focussing on leaders as individuals with certain traits and skills is incomplete at best and dangerously misleading at worst, and that it really is possible to think about leadership more systemically.

In particular, the challenges identified above represent a good starting point for seeing the specific roles that different types of leaders play in initiating and sustaining deep change. For example, local line leaders are crucial for dealing with the challenges of initiating, especially the challenges of time, relevance, and walking the talk. By and large, only local line leaders are in a position to help people prioritize their efforts so as to create the time needed for new initiatives. Likewise, they need to "make the case" for the relevance of particular change efforts for people's practical goals. Lastly, people will look to those championing change as local role models, and if local line leaders do not measure up, many will disengage. Internal networkers are also important for dealing with the challenges of initiating, first through identifying genuinely predisposed line leaders and encouraging their interest and curiosity (for example, often through introducing them to peers already engaged in such processes) and later through serving as coaches and mentors to team members. But they also help to keep innovative teams from becoming too isolated from other teams, and within the overall processes of diffusion. Lastly, executive leaders can play an initiating role when they begin transformational initiatives within their teams.

Conversely, executives bear special responsibility for the way local innovations lead to broader organization-wide learning, dealing with challenges of sustaining and especially the challenges of redesigning and rethinking. For example, there is little that local line leaders can do about measurement systems that might thwart the spread of innovative practices, but there is much that executives can do – they can help those outside understand the nature and significance of new practices, thereby addressing the challenge of "believers and non-believers." Similarly, questions of governance and strategy are distinct executive domains of inquiry and leadership.

Where there are overlaps in leadership activities, the different types of leaders tend to provide important complementary perspectives. For example, local line leaders and other team members need mentoring and coaching. Both internal networkers and executives help in this way. But executives tend to focus more on dealing with larger organizational issues, such as the ways that an innovative team may be misperceived by those outside the team or the way the standard metrics may create misleading indicators of team performance, whereas the coaching of internal networkers tends to be more focussed on developing team capabilities. Similarly, both internal networkers and executives tend to play an important part in how local innovations diffuse – internal networkers through informal systems, and executives more through confronting specific structural barriers, like reward and measurement systems, and through creating organizational learning infrastructures such as investing in research capabilities to better understand new work practices.[20]

Thinking systemically about leadership also means nurturing the understanding of systems principles within such leadership communities. A systems principle that all leaders should understand is "compensating feedback," the natural tendency of a complex system to resist efforts to change behavior.[21] Compensating feedback reveals a common flaw in the strategies of leaders of all types who find themselves fighting blindly against resistance to change. Leaders who are obsessed with overcoming such resistance usually have little appreciation of the forces they are fighting and how to work with, rather than against, such forces. When they encounter difficulties, they naturally work harder to overcome them. But the harder they push, the harder the system pushes back. For example, consider the predicament of a local line leader who fails to understand why people seem not to be committed to a new initiative. She entreats them to the task, telling people how important it is. Yet the harder she tries to convince them, the more they seem unconvinced. Somehow pushing harder on commitment does not make people more committed. She must address the limiting process at play, and recognize that the real issue is her "walking the talk," and the credibility of her values and aims.

Lastly, this emerging systems theory of leadership highlights ways in which different types of leaders are critically interdependent. Often to people within a complex change process, these interdependencies are far from evident, especially given the hero-leader myths which focus attention on individual actions and often cause people not to see how they depend on one another.

Consider the four basic challenges to initiating – time, help, relevance, and alignment of individual and organizational aims and values. Not only does each require particular types of leadership, but as each type of leader contributes in their unique way, the contributions of the others become more important. For example, if local line leaders and internal networkers are successful in getting transformational initiatives started, executive leadership then becomes *more* important. This happens because, if a transformational initiative is sustained for some time, people start to realize the degree of commitment required. They then begin questioning management's values and commitment. If executives have been championing the need for such initiatives, people will begin to look more and more carefully at the executive's behavior and apparent commitment to such changes. This is why it is often better to have executives who are disengaged than those who are superficially championing ideas like "learning organizations."

Such systemic interdependencies between the different types of leaders become more subtle – and more difficult for people to see – when they are displaced in time. This is why so many otherwise highly successful local line leaders often see themselves as more independent than in fact they are. For example, local line leaders tend to focus all their attention on the success of their local transformational initiatives, not realizing that the more successful they become, the more they will need the help of executives and internal networkers in dealing with the challenges that will arise in future outside their team or business unit.

This illustrates a crucial reason why thinking systemically about the forces underlying profound change is so important: if leaders understand the systemic interrelationships that shape these forces, they do not have to wait until problems actually arise to deal with them. They can anticipate problems in advance *because* they understand the play of forces that operate in such change processes. They can prepare for difficulties and often take action to prevent them arising at all. They can cultivate personal relationships in advance of when they will actually need others' help. This is the dance of change that artful leaders know intuitively, working with the continual interplay of forces that shape change. Moreover, it is a dance done together, by an ensemble of leaders in many places and roles, collectively determining the capacity of an enterprise to sustain transformational change.

What has been presented here is merely the beginnings of a theory. What is important is not its absolute truth, for surely there are many ways in which it can be improved, but the way of thinking about leadership that it proposes – seeing the phenomenon of leadership as embedded in webs of interdependencies that shape change. Translating this theory into practice means developing the capacity of people engaged in real change processes to think systemically, so that they can better see and appreciate the interdependencies within which they operate, and to act more and more in ways that truly support the whole.

III

21C

ORGANIZATION

The organization of the 21st century will be characterized by unprecedented complexity and will require a different breed of leader. The challenge for management will be to absorb the diverse and changing needs of individuals and to investigate employee-driven flexibility. Hamid Bouchikhi of Essec, France and John R. Kimberly of the Wharton School open the final part of the book by saying that organizations must transform into *customized workplaces* to suit the needs of both customers and workers. They strongly believe that 21st century managers will have to put customization not only at the core of their external strategies but also at the heart of their relationships with those who work for them.

Many organizational structures in the 21st century will depend on co-operation as well as competition. Corporations will work together to expand the value that is added by others. This set of corporations will strive to create unique goods and services. Professor David Conklin and Dean Lawrence Tapp of Richard Ivey School of Business in Canada believe managerial success will depend on the development of a *creative web*, in which innovation will require ongoing co-ordination among all the points of the web. They point out that success in the new millennium will be achieved by the corporation that can stimulate innovation not only within its own organization but throughout the overall creative web of which it is a member.

Organizations will aim to identify and nurture a handful of critical capabilities. They will continue to shift from focussing on structure to capability – what the organization is able to do and how it does it rather than who reports to whom and what rules govern work. Human resources guru Dave Ulrich gives his observations about the contextual factors impacting on organizations, how organizations will operate, and how individuals must prepare themselves today to respond tomorrow.

"Kaleidescope thinking" is the weapon to help leaders meet challenges of the 21st century. In a very unique style, eminent thinker and Harvard Business School Professor Rosabeth Moss Kanter takes the reader through a true global tour of the new business landscape. She has also identified three intangible assets in examining the strategies and cultures of worldclass organizations – concepts, competence, and connections. In this concluding chapter, Professor Kanter confidently nominates "the Kaleidescope" a symbol for the global information era.

15

THE CUSTOMIZED WORKPLACE

HAMID BOUCHIKHI AND JOHN R. KIMBERLY

It is 1 December 1998. As we contemplate the organization of the 21st century, our eyes fall on the front page of today's edition of the *Financial Times*. One headline screams "5500 jobs to go in Deutsche takeover of Bankers Trust," another reads "Volvo to cut 5300 jobs in attempt to lift profit margins," while a third announces "Total set for PetroFina takeover." In this same edition, we also read about the Hoechst/Rhône-Poulenc and Exxon/Mobil mergers. At the very top of the front page there is another headline, set in somewhat smaller type, which says: "Young people want a life, not long hours." This clearly illustrates the coming collision between the economic imperatives driving firm-level strategy and the changing nature of people in the workplace. The challenge for the organization of the 21st century, we argue, will be to balance these two apparently contradictory forces.

Over the latter half of the 20th century, firms have been caught between increased shareholder demands for higher returns and mounting pressure from competitors on price, quality, and product differentiation. These pressures have led many companies to develop customer-focussed mass customization strategies, and the most aggressive among them permit clients to customize a particular product or service within a wide range of options.[1]

Thanks to the application of information technology to manufacturing, and to the growth of electronic commerce, people will increasingly be able to personalize a car, a computer, or a holiday package to fit their particular budget, tastes, personal and family characteristics, and time availability. A hallmark of the end of the 20th century is thus the emergence and increasing power of the consumer-entrepreneur. As a consequence of this trend, and of developments in other spheres, a gap has developed between the power and choice enjoyed by individuals as consumers and citizens on the one hand, and that available to them in the workplace on the other.

The core argument of this chapter is that this gap, which is becoming increasingly noticeable, cannot be maintained in the long term. Reducing this gap will be a major challenge for management in the 21st century and a potential source of radical managerial innovation. We strongly believe that managers will have to put the logics of customization not only at the core of their external strategies but also at the heart of their relationships with those who work for them. In parallel with the customization of products and services, management will have to customize the workplace.

To explain what we mean by the customized workplace and how it differs from more commonly accepted approaches to management, we begin with a brief historical caricature comparing how the dominant managerial paradigms of the 19th and 20th centuries have dealt with the important issue of flexibility and why the new paradigm must be based on flexibility from the perspective of the worker as well as the firm.

We next lay out the case for the customized workplace. We will argue that it is a necessary response to significant changes occurring in the world outside the firm. The theories of personhood that have underpinned management models and practices to date are out of sync with these changes. To maintain its legitimacy as a core social institution, the firm will have to invent ways to meet the changing needs and demands of those who work for it. Whereas historically these individuals may have been more or less content with a relatively passive role in relation to company strategies, policies, and incentives, they are becoming much more proactive architects of their own *strategic life planning*[2] and their connections to the world of work.

In the third section we contend that such managerial innovations of the eighties and nineties as participative management, empowerment, total quality management, and pay for performance are unlikely to be adequate responses to the demands of person-as-architect. The cycle of incremental adjustments, inaugurated by the human relations movement and driven by the needs of the firm, will be replaced by a new management paradigm better suited to accommodating an individual who has radically changed during the course of the 20th century.

The very notion of the customized workplace rules out the possibility of *a* management model. However, a few basic principles should apply irrespective of the specifics associated with any particular model. The final section discusses some of these principles and explores their pragmatic implications.

MANAGEMENT THEORY IN CARICATURE: FROM THE STANDARDIZED TO THE CUSTOMIZED WORKPLACE

More than specific tools and techniques, it is the firm's flexibility and responsiveness to various stakeholders that differentiates 19th, 20th, and 21st century management paradigms (*see* Table 15.1).

The 19th century paradigm, still alive in many industries and areas around the globe, is typically not responsive to shareholders, customers, and employees together. The firm is often family-owned and managed as a closed system. Customers buy whatever it makes available to them. Employees are viewed as interchangeable and replaceable, are hired and fired at will, and have little voice and choice. For them, opportunity lies in finding a paternalistic capitalist who offers some benefits to make life a little less painful and the constraints of work a little more tolerable.

Over the last half of the 20th century, customers and shareholders have been more proactive and management has needed to become more responsive to them. Market driven strategies and flexible organizations have developed as a consequence. In contrast to the 19th century paradigm, 20th century management is more open. The firm actively listens to its customers and shareholders and involves them, through different mechanisms, in a variety of decision processes.

In 20th century management, customers are the main drivers of the firm's needs for flexibility and employees are on the receiving end, being required to adjust their work schedules, tasks, vacation periods, geographic assignments,

Table 15.1 Managerial paradigms of the 19th, 20th, and 21st centuries

Individuals' demands for flexibility	Low	High
Organizations' needs for flexibility		
Low	**19th century management** Responsiveness to neither customers nor people Manufacturing-driven organization	
High	**20th century management** Responsiveness to customers Market driven organization	**21st century management** Responsiveness to customers and people Customized workplace

and jobs in light of these needs.[3] Because they are on the receiving end, workers often complain about the constraints it puts on them. Management's efforts to respond through improvements in the "quality of work life," while highly visible, are a product of the 20th century paradigm and will not be sufficient for the future.

The challenge for management in the 21st century will be to fully internalize the diverse and changing needs of individuals and to invent employee-driven flexibility. The challenge is significant, because management will have to customize the workplace to suit the needs of both customers and workers simultaneously. To do this effectively, the firm in the 21st century will have to apply the logics of marketing, developed for its customers, to its relationships with workers.

"Our people are our most important asset." This slogan, often articulated by 20th century firms but not always accompanied by consistent management practice and hence subject to much cynicism, does not capture what will be required in the 21st century. Rather than putting customers or workers first, we believe that management will have to put "shareholders, customers, and workers first." Whether the individual is acting as customer, investor, worker, spouse, parent, or community activist, she is less and less willing to let others make decisions for her. Institutions that fail to take notice of this

> *Rather than putting customers or workers first, we believe that management will have to put "shareholders, customers, and workers first."*

trend do so at their peril. Just as management does not have a choice on whether to acknowledge or ignore shareholders and customers, it will also have to cope with the demands of autonomous and proactive individuals whose collaboration and commitment can no longer be taken for granted.

THE SOCIOLOGICAL CONTEXT OF 21ST CENTURY MANAGEMENT

To envision the challenges that will face firms in the 21st century, we need to move beyond conventional business discourse and consider the managerial consequences of some already visible sociological trends.[4]

The foundations of business management were established in the 19th century, with the birth of the modern factory, and systemized by Frederick Taylor, Henri Fayol, and automobile entrepreneur Henry Ford, among others, in the first decades of the 20th century. The theories and prescriptions of the 19th century management paradigm are built on a view of the worker as a reluctant individual whose efforts need to be predefined, monitored, and sanctioned.

While it reflects the social order of early capitalism – antagonistic relationships between capital and labor – and still underpins managerial action significantly, this view will need to be replaced by one that is more consistent with life in what Giddens calls post-traditional societies.

The distinctive feature of life in a post-traditional order, according to Giddens, is the declining role of tradition and hierarchy in governing individuals' attitudes and behavior. While being disenfranchised from tradition, the individual discovers a new form of autonomy and discretion in making life decisions. In this new context, the individual draws on an extensive body of knowledge about social life, available as a consequence of the increasingly reflexive character of modern societies, and actively develops a sense of self-identity through strategic life planning. People are making choices in areas where before they did not or could not. For example, individuals are deciding about their physical appearance, their sexual life and gender, parenting, living alone or with a partner, their eating habits, living places, and membership of various communities. If the 19th century witnessed the emergence of the business entrepreneur, the late 20th century has seen the birth of the life-entrepreneur: an individual who is actively participating in building and sustaining a self-identity.

At the macro social level, the emergence of the autonomous and reflexive self precipitates and is reinforced by the parallel crisis of traditional institutions such as marriage, the family, parenthood, geographically defined communities, the church, and the military. It is interesting to note that the latter two core traditional institutions have both been criticized in recent years because of how they have dealt with homosexuals and women, two social groups that exemplify the proactive new world which firms will face.

At the same time that many traditional institutions are in crisis, new social forms and norms are emerging: Gay Olympic Games, virtual communities, weight watchers, pro-choice groups, same-sex marriage and genetic engineering legislation, to name just a few. Irrespective of the specific area in which these forms and norms grow, they correspond to what seems to be a universal need for more democratic institutions that can reflect and support increasingly democratized, reciprocal interpersonal relationships in post-traditional societies. The development of alternative forms of socializing is furthered by the availability of education and technologies, enabling individuals to have instantaneous access to great amounts of information, and to communicate beyond traditional time-space boundaries.

Caught between rapid changes at the micro and macro social levels, the firm, a core intermediate institution, faces a number of challenges to its legitimacy as the 21st century approaches. It is no longer perceived as favorably as it has been. It is being criticized for perpetuating hierarchy and domination, perpetuating inequalities between the sexes and ethnic groups, destroying natural resources, polluting the environment, stressing and sacrificing individuals, and breaking up families and communities. The proportion of people for whom a traditional career is no longer the natural path is increasing and many of those who work for established firms are distancing their self-identity from that of the firm. Successive waves of restructuring and downsizing, and the concurrent development of the discourse on employability, are inducing individuals to dissociate their fate from their firm's and to explore alternative work models.[5]

The labor market in developed countries is already affected by these trends. Firms in traditional sectors, hampered by their image as unprogressive, are finding it increasingly difficult to hire adequate numbers of people. In other industries, firms are competing for a limited pool of talent and are investing considerable time and money in recruitment. Younger people seem to be increasingly attracted to self-employment, entrepreneurial opportunities and the professions. And the business press regularly contains reports of high-flying executives who quit comfortable jobs to start their own business, work as independent consultants, or more simply to spend more time with their families.[6]

These trends reflect the growing effort by individual people to reclaim control over their lives. They want to have a say in what they do; where, when, how, and with whom they do it; and, perhaps most importantly, why. As the firm listens to and involves people in these decisions, in the same manner that it has internalized the needs of customers, customization of the workplace will inevitably emerge.

In 19th century management, individuals were taken for granted and had no choice or voice. Its foundations were built on an asymmetrical relationship between employee and employer. Because they do not seriously question these foundations, 20th century management and the managerial innovations of the eighties and nineties will not enable the firm to cope effectively with the life-entrepreneur and personal architect of post-traditional societies.

THE COLLISION BETWEEN 20TH CENTURY MANAGEMENT AND THE LIFE-ENTREPRENEUR

Earlier in this chapter, we argued that a hallmark of 20th century management was the increasing responsiveness of the firm to customers' needs under growing pressure from shareholders. Another hallmark is the growing awareness of the importance of people issues. Ever since the Hawthorne experiments of the thirties, management has been aware of the importance of a motivated and involved workforce for the achievement of organizational goals. Successive "managerial innovations" were designed to enhance motivation and involvement, including job enrichment, semi-autonomous work teams, flexitime, participative management, pay for performance, total quality management, and empowerment.

Interestingly, however, in spite of this sustained flow of managerial effort, independent surveys continue to show low employee satisfaction and morale and little trust in management. In a report on employee satisfaction in European firms, based on a survey conducted by International Survey Research Corp., The *Financial Times* writes:

> "At the other end of the satisfaction stakes, British workers were among the most discontented. 'Despite significant attempts at corporate restructuring and re-engineering, employee attitudes towards the organization and the efficiency of their work are among the least favourable in Europe,' says the (ISR) report. 'Despite a strong commitment to total quality management in many companies, attitudes to the quality of work performance are more critical than in any other country.'"[7]

Unless we think, as some senior managers may, that people are never grateful, these data may point to a more serious problem.

The managerial innovations of the late 20th century have a limited impact because they are primarily driven by the firm's need for effectiveness and flexibility. Even the most progressive management books, such as *Liberation Management*,[8] *The Individualized Corporation*[9] or *The Human Equation*[10] start with the firm's needs for flexibility, innovation, and/or competitiveness and go on to plead for more people-oriented management. Isn't it somewhat ironic that the most popular management book of the day, *The Dilbert Principle*, is a parody of "innovative" management?

People are not easily fooled. They are, in fact, well placed to understand that these "innovations" are not always motivated by a genuine desire to respond to their own needs. They well know that management's loyalty increasingly goes first to shareholders and customers and that, in times when difficult choices are to be made, people don't come first. Even in a company like Levi-Strauss, long praised as an employee-friendly workplace, people ceased to come first when profitability and estimates of returns declined.

The long record of downsizings, restructurings, and other lay-offs is no doubt largely responsible for the deep and widespread distrust in management. *Business Week* reported the findings of another survey by *International Survey Research Corp.* showing that employees' trust in management has been declining in the nineties (under 50 percent in 1997).[11] Even more telling, 70 percent of senior managers thought that employees trust management. The gap suggests that the reality of the workplace may not match the promise of conventional management discourse. Meanwhile, the *Financial Times* used the headline "Disgruntled mice turn on fat cats" to report the results of another survey by ISR, this time of 450 companies in 18 countries.[12]

How many people can turn down an assignment without jeopardizing their career chances? How many executives, to say nothing of their lower-level employees, find it better to give the impression of agreeing with the boss rather than speaking their mind? How many people are able to take parental leave without being moved to the slow lane? How many people are able to adjust their workload to fit in with their personal life circumstances? How many people are able to develop a set of skills they need to move on their own initiative to a different job? How many people are asked for a consequential opinion about how effective their leaders are? These are only some of the questions we regularly discuss with executives in management development programs and the answers show that people issues are generally still handled and decided unilaterally. Contrary to the popular management discourse of the day, the only real choice for people in many of today's firms is between compliance or exit. But will this be adequate for the firm in the 21st century?

After thriving on marketing and product mass customization in the 20th century, firms will have to transfer what they learned in dealing with customers to their relationships with their employees. Management will indeed make a radical leap into the 21st century only when it acknowledges that its object – the individual – has changed dramatically and is no longer willing to be solely at the receiving end of managerial policies and incentives. The individual today is, and will increasingly be, willing to take an active part in decisions regarding life in and outside work. In 21st century management, the individual will no longer be the object but a subject of management. This evolution will require a genuine co-exercise of power.

> *After thriving on marketing and product mass customization in the 20th century, firms will have to transfer what they learned in dealing with customers to their relationships with their employees.*

Co-exercise of power as we understand it is very different from empowerment. The latter notion conveys the idea that power resides with one party and it delegates a portion to the other. Empowerment, in other words, does not change the hierarchical and asymmetrical nature of the workplace.[13]

Our purpose here is not to dismiss several decades of managerial efforts to improve the quality of work life. There are still many workers, around the globe, who would certainly be happy to enjoy the same treatment as their American or French counterparts. Our point, though, is that treating people well is not enough when people are, in fact, asking to be reckoned with.

THE CUSTOMIZED WORKPLACE: A NEW PARADIGM FOR THE 21ST CENTURY

Because it represents a radical departure from commonly accepted management principles and techniques, the contours of the customized workplace cannot be envisioned without a paradigm shift and a new mindset. We have summarized the main differences between 19th, 20th, and 21st century management in Table 15.2.

Table 15.2 Contrasting the paradigms

	19th century	20th century	21st century
Theory of personhood	Interchangeable muscle and energy	A subordinate with a hierarchy of needs	Autonomous and reflexive individual
Information and knowledge	The province of management alone	Management-dominated and shared on a limited basis	Widely diffused
The purpose of work	Survival	Accumulation of wealth and social status	Part of a strategic life plan
Identification	With the firm and/or with the working class	Identify with a social group and/or the firm	The disenfranchised self
Conflict	Disruptive and to be avoided	Disruptive but tolerated and can be settled through collective bargaining	A normal part of life
Division of labor	Managers decide, employees execute	Managers decide, employees execute thoughtfully	Employees and managers decide and execute
Power	Concentrated at the top	Limited, functional sharing/empowerment	Diffused and shared

In contrast to the traditional organization design process where organizational structures and systems are derived from a pre-defined strategy, the design of the customized workplace, as we view it, will seek to balance what matters for the firm (its strategy) and what matters for individuals (their life strategies).

The sociological trends summarized above suggest that the individual in the 21st century organization will reclaim some control over some fundamental aspects of her work life: over what to work for, the content of the work, when and where to work, how to accomplish the work, with whom and for whom to work, for how long to work, direction of career plan, and skills needed to pursue it.

While individuals' needs and aspirations have been viewed as disturbances in 19th and 20th century management, they represent the starting point for the design of the customized workplace. Balancing firms' needs for predictability and effectiveness with diverse individual needs requires a new employment contract, one where management and employees confront their strategic and life plans and seek common ground.

Although fully fledged examples of the customized workplace are yet to appear, a few business organizations across the globe already display some of its characteristics. At Semco, the Brazilian company made famous by Ricardo Semler's book *Maverick*,[14] employees are involved in deciding the location of new facilities and the acquisition of machinery, have substantial freedom in deciding their work schedule, and enjoy total discretion over the investment of a portion of the profits. At Metanoiques, a French mid-size company specializing in collaborative software and created by an unconventional founder, there are no employees. Every member owns an equal share of the company and acts as an independent entrepreneur with profit and loss responsibility. The company has no head office and people are free to organize their own schedules. Internal collaboration is carried out through extensive use of information and communication technology.

The founder of Compagnie Française de Défense et de Protection (CFDP), a small French insurance company, went so far as to sell the company to employees and partner insurance agents and dismantled the head office. Through this move, he hopes to transform the organization into a "community of independent entrepreneurs" where associates are free to conduct their local business and use network-like mechanisms to co-ordinate with other members of the organization.

Therese Rieul, the founder manager of KA-L'informatique douce, a mid-size computer and software retailer, has always refused to write formal job descriptions because she believes individuals should be allowed to design their own jobs. She is driven by the belief that management should be concerned primarily with outcomes and leave people free to figure out the best ways to perform the tasks.[15]

Independent of the specific features it can take, the customized workplace is, first and foremost, a philosophical attitude vis-à-vis people management issues. It entails a replacement of the traditional hard-nosed, macho, and "I'm the boss here" attitude with one that is more open to individuals' needs and more tolerant of conflict and divergence. This attitude is today more likely to be observed among women and minority managers than among their male and majority counterparts.[16]

The customized workplace requires a recognition that individuals are life-entrepreneurs who do their own strategic life planning. In 20th century management, even in its most enlightened versions, the firm is the only strategic planning agent. Management first elaborates a corporate strategy and then wonders about the optimal organizational and incentive structure to motivate people to implement the firm's strategy. In a context where individuals are less easily inclined to work harder for more money or social status, it is important to involve them, upstream, and to give them an opportunity to influence business strategy in a sense more consistent with their own life strategies. This evolution will be hard to accomplish given the deeply-seated belief that strategy is a top management's exclusive privilege and that inviting input from lower levels would only yield mediocre ideas and, perhaps more threatening, challenge management's competence and authority.

Sharing information and responsibility for the firm's situation with employees is another ingredient of the customized workplace. Contrary to the idea widely held in management circles that people never make decisions that can hurt them, some companies have proved that sharing the burden of the situation with employees can be a very effective turn-around strategy, as the case of Bertrand Martin and Sulzer France demonstrates. Martin joined Sulzer France, a company specializing in diesel engines, as CEO at the height of a severe financial crisis. Instead of formulating an action plan unilaterally, he told the employees that they should not expect him to come up with a miraculous solution, that the company's fate was in their hands, and that his role was to engage a process whereby together they could develop an effective turn-around strategy. Today, this case is often cited as an exemplary bottom-up turn-around story in France and Bertrand Martin, now retired, is a sought-after speaker.

Everyday experience shows that individuals are able to commit a great deal of their time, resources, and self-identity in trustful relationships. After being pushed to the background by the logic of "scientific management," the centrality of trust in business life is being rediscovered. The literature on inter-organizational alliances and joint ventures, for example, stresses the critical role of trust for the effective maintenance of these relationships.[17] We believe the challenges of management in the 21st century will require that trust be put at the core of the employment relationship. The importance of trust is revealed most clearly in times of hardship. Only a trusting workforce can voluntarily make sacrifices and explore with management every option to improve the organization's condition.

But trust must be built before the hard times come, and for trust to grow between two parties, reciprocity is required. People would be willing to put a part of their fate in management hands only if management also put some of its fate in the hands of people. Reciprocity develops only when each partner in a relationship is potentially

People would be willing to put a part of their fate in management hands only if management also put some of its fate in the hands of people.

vulnerable to the decisions of the other. Managers who need to keep things and people under control can never establish trusting relationships.

In the customized workplace, the individual actively plans and negotiates her present and future employment. Managers will find this transition difficult to live with because they have historically managed individuals through policies designed for aggregate groups: blue-collar workers, hourly workers, part-timers, white-collar workers, high-potential executives, women, minorities, etc. In the customized workplace, people can no longer be managed as members of a given group; they need to be treated as individuals. The biggest challenge for management will be to achieve sufficient predictability with individuals whose behaviors are less subject to direct control.

Achieving organizational predictability in the customized workplace will not be possible without notions of mutual commitment and accountability. The customized workplace is not viable if it is made up of free electrons who can change their behavior or withdraw from the game at any time. Organizations that have always relied on the co-operation of autonomous and powerful individuals, like professional sports teams, have long since placed mutual commitment and accountability at the heart of the employment relationship. Professional athletes and team managers are bound together for an agreed number of seasons and early termination of the contract by a party entitles the other to substantial compensation. In the business arena, this sort of arrangement has been mainly reserved for the employment of senior executives of large public corporations. In the 21st century, it will have to be extended to every employment relationship. When the employment relationship eventually binds the parties for a predetermined period of time and makes them accountable for opportunistic termination, people can no longer suspect the firm of treating them as disposable assets and the firm can count, in return, on their collaboration for the duration of the contract.

Because it is based on participation, power sharing, trust, negotiation, reciprocity, and commitment, the customized workplace will require adult, as opposed to charismatic, leadership. Contrary to the underlying adult/child pattern implied by charismatic leadership, adult leadership relates to individuals as adults and requires skills for listening, understanding individuals' self-identity, anticipating, mediating, compromising, trusting, and committing.

The organization of the 21st century will be buffetted by multiple and contradictory forces and will be characterized by unprecedented complexity.[18] It will require a different breed of leader. The leader of the 21st century will not be a "god" but a mortal who helps other mortals to awaken the "god that is in all of us."

CONCLUSION

Although fully-fledged versions of the customized workplace may not yet be apparent in the real world, some of its main features are, although they tend to be applied to an elite minority of highly sought-after professional workers. The core thesis of this chapter is that the 21st century firm will have to extend the treatment offered today to this small minority to the entire workforce.

Because in the customized workplace shareholders, customers, and employees are equally important, it will most likely require a different governance structure where the interests of these stakeholders can confront and balance each other. Corporations with significant employee ownership and those operating within more democratic societies will find it easier to make the transition toward the customized workplace.[19] It is probably not too much of a stretch to say that the dominant organizational form of the 20th century, characterized by the separation between ownership, management, and labor, is not the end of history and that other forms of co-operation and governance structures will emerge with the development of the customized workplace.[20]

We have stressed throughout this chapter that the major challenge posed to management by trends in the world outside the firm is one of openness to individuals' needs and democratization. Without substantial and sincere efforts in this direction, the firm may well experience the same loss of legitimacy and marginalization that other social institutions have experienced in the course of human history.

Do we believe that economic imperatives will somehow suddenly diminish and "enlightened" management will be less prone to base major strategic decisions solely on economic criteria? Not any time soon. That shareholders will be willing to accept lower returns on invested capital to allow the customized workplace to flourish? Not until they see how their lives as shareholders and as people in the workplace are connected. Are we hopelessly romantic and out of touch with the harsh realities of the marketplace? Perhaps. But the kinds of changes we have described in this chapter have been developing over decades. We mustn't forget that capitalism needed the better part of the 20th century to win the battle of free enterprise. It will now have to demonstrate that it can also accommodate the free person.

16

THE CREATIVE WEB

DAVID CONKLIN AND LAWRENCE TAPP

Corporate structures are being broken down and decentralized, and these trends are adding a new complexity to the innovation process. Large corporations are outsourcing a wider variety of components and services, relying on smaller supplier firms. Large corporations are also placing greater decision-making responsibility on individual units within the firm, flattening the traditional hierarchical pyramid. The academic literature has begun to address these transformations.[1] In the 21st century, we expect to see an increase in the importance of this subject, with more attention devoted to organizational structures that may enhance innovation among the network of interrelated decision-making units. Fresh analytical frameworks will be needed to address the new types of decisions that management will face. In the 21st century, managerial success will depend upon the development of a creative web.

In the past, the size of the corporation was largely determined by the transaction costs and transportation costs that would arise if activities were conducted in separate firms. The telecommunications revolution has reduced transaction costs among corporations, and has facilitated the inter-corporate flow of information. To an ever-increasing degree, autonomous business units will be able to integrate their planning without the need for a single hierarchical organization. The transportation revolution has reduced shipment costs, as has the decrease in physical components as a percentage of the final value of a good or service. The nature of economies of scale has changed as a result of these transformations. While final assembly and marketing will still leave a key role for large corporations, success will depend on stimulating and coordinating continuous improvement among a wide array of individual business units.

The simplest traditional value chain was one in which a firm supplied parts to an assembler who then sold to a retailer or an end user. In the 21st century, the connection a firm will have with its suppliers, their suppliers, and its customers is more like an interconnected web, rather than a sequential chain. A chain implies a unidirectional exchange along a distinct flow, whereas a web suggests the interconnectedness and multidirectional, multilevel relationships that can lead to better and faster innovations. Innovation today requires that all parties interact on an ongoing, extended basis. If the initial producer of the components knows the needs of the ultimate user of their products, they can better design for that purpose. If there is a free exchange of information and communication, all parties benefit from decreased development times, assured market acceptance, and continual, planned offerings.

Globalization adds a complication to innovation and this creative web. With current communications and transportation technology, outsourcing can involve any country in the world, and as such, each corporation has a wide selection of alternative potential suppliers. Here, the creative web becomes a geographical web. Co-ordinating this complex network so that it involves an ongoing innovation process has become a key determinant of company success. To achieve innovation, a corporation can no longer simply accept the components or products it is offered by export agents or distributors from other countries. Corporations must create organizational structures that facilitate an ongoing international collaboration focussed on the innovation process. This may require an exchange of personnel among corporations on a regular basis, as well as ongoing dialog and exchange of research information.

> *The creative web becomes a geographical web. Co-ordinating this complex network so that it involves an ongoing innovation process has become a key determinant of company success.*

A considerable amount of literature has developed in regard to "clusters" that are geographically concentrated in particular regions. Some authors have focussed on the advantages of geographic proximity. For example, Mick Carney, in the article "The competitiveness of networked production: The role of trust and asset specificity," has suggested that "proximity fosters norms of trust because there is a greater probability of future interaction among neighbouring businesses and because reputation signals are more reliably transmitted over short distances." As we look at the 21st century, an important subject will be organizational structures that can achieve such trust without geographical concentration.[2]

To understand these new organizational structures requires a fresh analytical framework. In recent decades, Michael Porter's "five forces" – which we will outline – have been used to analyze industry structure, focussing on the

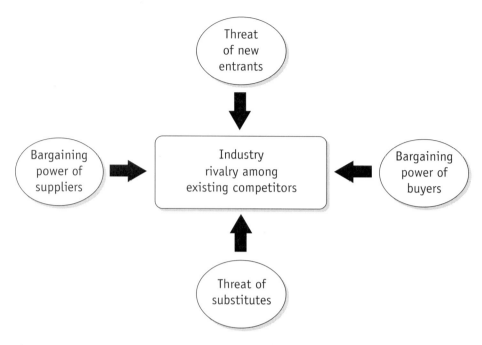

Fig. 16.1 Porter's Five Forces

division of the value chain among various suppliers and competitors. Game theory has presented an alternative analytical framework, resting on the reality that each industry participant's decisions impact on other participants and their decisions. Each organization must evaluate a chain of reactions in order to determine its best decision path. Furthermore, various players within an industry may co-operate in such a way that everyone's economic outcomes are improved. Analysis of the creative web builds upon these frameworks.

LIMITATIONS OF MICHAEL PORTER'S FIVE FORCES

Michael Porter developed a framework for analyzing each industry structure by focussing on five forces within each industry: rivalry among existing competitors, threat of new entrants, bargaining power of buyers, threat of substitutes, and bargaining power of suppliers. A certain value is created as the good or service moves from one corporation to another and on to the ultimate customer along a chain of suppliers. This perspective concentrates on how the value that is added within the industry will be divided between a particular firm and the other industry participants. Here one examines the relative "strength" in the relationships in order to determine how the value added by the industry will be allocated. This perspective draws attention to an existing set of goods and services that are produced in the industry, and so the availability of substitutes is important. Porter's framework places in words the elements that underlie the demand and supply relationships used in microeconomics analysis. Figure 16.1 illustrates Porter's five forces.

We wish to suggest that many organizational structures in the 21st century will rest on co-operation as well as competition. A set of corporations will work together to expand the value that is added by their group. In particular, this set of corporations will strive continually to create unique goods and services so that potential substitutes are further removed from the final customer's purchasing decision. While the group as a whole faces competition from other groups, the organizational dynamic within each group seeks to improve the outcomes for all participants. Thus Porter's Five Forces are not particularly helpful as an analytical framework for the creative web.

BUILDING ON GAME THEORY

In the latter years of the 20th century, the concept of game theory came to be applied to business relationships. It was emphasized that participants within an industry may be able to increase their industry's added value, or at least the financial profits, by collaborating rather than competing. In the simplest instance, competitors might collaborate to raise prices. Business can be viewed as a game in the sense that the actions of one participant will impact on the profitability of other participants. Decisions must be undertaken based upon an evaluation of a series of possible outcomes, where each outcome depends upon the reaction of others in the industry. Brandenburger and Nalebuff have suggested the diagram in Figure 16.2 as a useful framework for the analysis of an industry.[3]

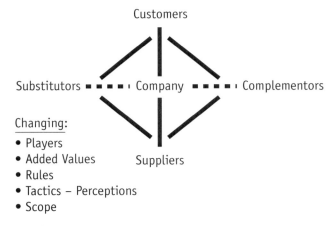

Fig. 16.2 The value net

Participants may alter potential outcomes by changing the industry structure in any one of a variety of ways. In particular, Brandenburger and Nalebuff suggest that each corporation should use what they refer to as "PARTS as a comprehensive, theory-based set of levers" to help generate strategies. Each letter in the phrase "PARTS" represents a lever for changing the industry structure. A corporation may threaten to change the number of players (P) by indicating that it intends to enter an industry. The mere threat may result in compensation being paid to it, thereby altering the allocation of the value-added element among the participants. A corporation may change the "added values" (A) by lowering the added value of others, as well as by increasing its own added value. A corporation may change the rules (R), for example, by developing new pricing policies. A corporation may change tactics (T) in ways that alter other players' perceptions and therefore their decisions. A corporation may change the scope (S) of the game by severing links with other companies or building new alliances. Unlike Porter's five forces that analyze an existing industry structure, this game theory approach examines ways to change the industry structure.

The analysis of the creative web builds upon the game theory framework in that it focusses on the ways in which individual corporations may impact on the success of each other. However, it sees this relationship as one where the objective is for all participants to win through innovation that increases the web's value-added element, enabling all participants to increase their financial gain. Furthermore, the analysis of the creative web leads to new managerial issues about decision-making forms and processes, new agreements in regard to research, development, and marketing, and new arrangements in regard to investments, incentive structures, and allocation of rewards.

NEW ORGANIZATIONAL STRUCTURES: A NEW ANALYTICAL FRAMEWORK

The creative web presents a new organizational structure, and it may be helpful for management and academics to consider a new framework for its analysis. A series of attributes deserve consideration:

1 The focus of the creative web is on innovation and continuous improvement. A central purpose is to increase the value added within the group by creating new goods and services and/or by devising methods to lower costs and improve efficiency. The members of the group may still attempt to negotiate a particular share of the total value created by the group, but the success of the group requires that all participants receive compensation that they consider to be satisfactory in return for their contribution to the success of the group as a whole.

2 The creative web involves dynamic rather than static analysis. The best "answers" to managerial questions will change over time. In fact, a purpose of the group is to create change. While the game theory perspective focussed on a particular corporation achieving success vis-à-vis other corporations by changing one or more of the "PARTS," the creative web focuses on the group as a whole changing the "PARTS."

3 There is continual collaboration in regard to the group's production process. In terms of the game analogy, all members of the group are on the same side for purposes of increasing innovation. In this regard, there may even be no obvious competitor in striving to achieve this purpose. To a greater degree than the game theory analysis, this perspective emphasizes the dependence of each member of the group on the creativity of the group as a whole. This radically changes the traditional customer-supplier concepts.

4 The creative web generally has a central organizer. In this sense, the organizational structure is not "a net." There is a concentration of decision-making power in the hands of a single corporation near the centre of the web. Co-ordination is necessary for success, and a central question in the creative web is: "Who will do the co-ordinating?" Often this will be a retailer or a final assembler, each of whom seeks to develop a differentiated set of goods and services that give the co-ordinator – and hence each web – a unique place from the perspective of the ultimate customer. Neither the retailer nor the final assembler can achieve success by itself. Each such co-ordinator relies upon a web of relationships.

5 At the end of the web of relationships, there may be individual corporations that have no direct relationship with each other. In this sense, such corporations are not part of a net but rather are the final threads of a web. The success of the web must be a shared success, and in this sense there is an ongoing and permanent mutual dependence, even on the part of those furthest removed from the central co-ordinator.

6 The nature of the relationships involves much more than a unidirectional flow of components or partially completed materials. The reverse flow involves decisions concerning the objectives and procedures of R&D&M (research, development, and marketing) and often financial assistance towards achievement of these objectives and procedures. This reverse flow may be crucial to the success of the creative web. Hence dependence runs in many directions throughout the web, as is shown in Figure 16.3.

With the approach of the new millennium, a substantial body of literature has discussed the modification of traditional business hierarchies.[4] Many companies have recognized the importance of "employee empowerment" and of new managerial techniques for stimulating the positive involvement of all the employees in the achievement of corporate objectives. For many years, North

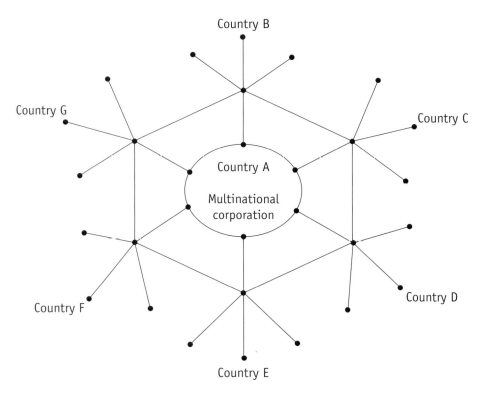

Fig. 16.3 The creative web within a single corporate structure

American writers pointed to Japan as a nation that pioneered such concepts as "quality circles," where employees participated actively in discussing how they could modify their procedures to better satisfy the company's customers. The incentives of profit sharing and employee ownership of shares, together with the process for creating profit centers within the corporate structure, have become common. These shifts in organizational structure have resulted in decentralized

With the shift of responsibility from a hierarchical corporate structure to separate but related work groups, a central issue is the set of systems that can best foster "intrapreneurship."

decision-making units operating with some independence within the overall corporate structure. For such organizations, strengthening the creative web is an internal challenge. With the shift of responsibility from a hierarchical corporate structure to separate but related work groups, a central issue is the set of systems that can best foster "intrapreneurship."

THE INTERNATIONALIZATION OF THE CREATIVE WEB

For many reasons, the creative web has become international, with participants in a variety of countries. This adds a complexity that is not present in the Brandenburger game theory model. The geographic dispersion is an important element of the creative web. This is far more than Michael Porter's "cluster theory" where geographical proximity may stimulate creativity among corporations.

Several powerful forces have stimulated the internationalization of corporate strategies, including international agreements that have reduced trade barriers, liberalized foreign direct investment, and protected intellectual property, together with the new technologies that have facilitated this trend. For much of the 20th century, corporations were able to succeed on the basis of national strategies with relatively little regard for the political, economic, societal, and technological forces in other countries. As the 20th century came to a close, corporations restructured in response to their new global strategies; and the analysis of environmental forces in other countries attained a new significance.

For much of the manufacturing sector, the corporate structure of the multinational corporation (MNC) provides a nearly automatic shift of business activities out of high-wage developed countries to less developed countries with lower wage rates. The international product cycle literature was developed to explain the growth of the MNC, in which production and trade are linked to innovation and the international diffusion of new technology. For subsidiaries of MNCs, the development of global mandates for new products and components has become a continual necessity. While these "rationalized production processes" have been analyzed by academics, the implications for the role of the creative web will attract increasing attention.

John Dunning has pointed to two features of 20th century hierarchical capitalism that he believes deserve re-examination in the context of internationalization:

> The first is that it implicitly assumes that the prosperity of firms depends exclusively on the way in which their management internally organizes the resources and capabilities at their disposal . . . The external transactions of firms are assumed to be exogenous, rather than endogenous, to their portfolio of assets and skills, and to the way in which these assets and skills are combined with each other to create further valued-added advantages. The second characteristic of hierarchical capitalism is that firms primarily react to endemic and structural market failure by adopting "exit" rather than "voice"-type strategies.[5]

Dunning suggests that both these features should be questioned, as multinational corporations find success through external relationships and as they attempt to change the industry structure that confronts them, rather than just "exiting" or not entering the country where that particular structure exists.

A vast array of articles has examined corporate experiences in regard to international joint ventures and strategic alliances.[6] Much research has focussed effectively on technical "how to" issues, such as those involving cross-cultural challenges and the development of "trust" in business relationships. What lies ahead is the need to conduct more effective research in regard to the environmental forces in other countries, as they relate to foreign-owned corporations. The generalizations about globalization need to be focussed on particular sectors and particular nations and regions.[7] The analysis of "country risks" and how to manage them still has far to go.

NEW MANAGEMENT ISSUES IN THE CREATIVE WEB

The creative web brings with it a series of new management issues. These include:

1 Each corporation must decide which web to join, and whether it should join more than one. The decision is similar to an investment decision in the sense that there will be a commitment of resources to the success of the new organizational structure. An important set of issues concerns the criteria and terms and conditions for leaving a particular creative web, or for dismissing a member of a particular creative web. The degree to which the creative web should devote resources to research, development, and marketing is crucial for the success of each member of the group. A decision to join one group as opposed to another may be impacted by a corporation's evaluation of the creativity of the web. Conversely, the web must make decisions about whom to accept into the web, and in this regard an important criterion for acceptance is innovative capability.

2 For both the sets of decisions described in the above paragraph, the issue of trust is crucial. This, however, is not the same focus as one finds in much of today's literature about trust, where the focus is on whether one can believe another party's commitment to fulfill a promise. Here the concept of trust involves an evaluation of the ability of the various participants to work together in order to achieve effective R&D&M in the long term. The outcomes are uncertain, and trust concerns the faith that one's fellow participants will be able to achieve success. In this sense, the organizational structure drives trust; whereas for many social scientists, such as Fukuyama, the degree of trust drives organizational structure.[8] For Fukuyama, organizational structures differ among countries because the

> *The issue of trust is crucial. Trust concerns the faith that one's fellow participants will be able to achieve success.*

degree of trust differs among societies. Our perspective suggests that the creative web will become a common organizational structure throughout the world in the 21st century. It is not that people are more comfortable with the creative web than with Porter's five forces or Brandenburger's value net, it is simply that the creative web promises them much more success than either of these traditional models.

3 Of central concern will be the nature of financial relationships in the context of substantial R&D commitments with uncertain outcomes, or the need for effective marketing in order to maximize these outcomes. Incentives for successful innovation must be offered to each member of the web. It is in the interest of all members that each should feel appropriately compensated. How should the success of a particular member be evaluated in the context of group success? It is likely that derivatives will be used to gear compensation at one moment in time to outcomes that will occur later.

4 For some corporations, entry into a creative web may require the initiation of subsidiaries that do not carry the baggage of the past. The creative web requires a mindset very different from that of the traditional hierarchical corporation, and it may simply be impossible to include the latter in the former.

The creative web requires a mindset very different from that of the traditional hierarchical corporation.

In the context of allocating global mandates and evaluating the success of profit centres, "value management" approaches to the decentralized corporate structure received increasing attention in the nineties. However, in order to achieve higher growth, management in some companies has chosen to concentrate blindly on size and market share to the detriment of return on capital. A value management approach which has come to the forefront of the business community is Economic Value Added (EVA), the registered trademark of Stern Stewart & Company.[9] EVA creates a common language to be used within an organization as well as with external stakeholders. EVA integrates financial planning, capital budgetting, performance measurement, compensation levels, and goal setting. This one measurement tool attempts to account accurately for all the complexities involved in creating value for the shareholders. The failure of managers to account properly for the cost of capital in their decisions, and hence the difficulty in holding managers accountable for those decisions, can be avoided through the use of this financial tool. EVA permits managers to concentrate on the importance of generating incremental earnings above the capital costs, thereby creating economic profits. A linchpin to a successful comprehensive EVA financial management system is in the proper execution of the incentive compensation program. The compensation system is designed to encourage managers to act as though they are owners of the company. To ensure that management is creating value, they are evaluated and compensated in accordance with their EVA performance.

While the concept of EVA has been developed for use within a single corporate structure, an important question is whether evaluation systems such as EVA can be applied to the creative web. It is clear that new concepts must be instituted in regard to success criteria and incentive systems for individual organizations that have developed internal creative webs. The inter-firm creative web introduces a second related objective to the maximization of shareholder value within each firm: adding all web shareholders to the organization's group of shareholders as a focus of value maximization.

ANALYSES AND EXAMPLES OF THE CREATIVE WEB

Towards the end of the 20th century, academics began to discuss various aspects of the decomposition and decentralization of the corporation. Figure 16.4 illustrates a continuum involving the degree of hierarchy and co-operation. We suggest that as the 21st century advances, corporations will be shifting from a lower left quadrant towards the upper right quadrant, from A to B.

In *Blueprint to the digital economy: Creating wealth in the era of e-business*, Don Tapscott et al. have provided an extensive set of references to corporations that have changed their structure in response to new communication technologies. Business sectors where such transformations have been common include banking, publishing, pictures, and education. Tapscott et al. have emphasized the issue of innovation in these new relationships.

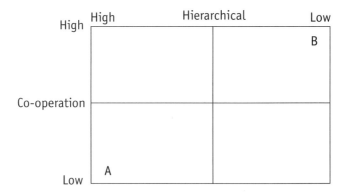

Fig. 16.4   The shift in organizational structure

As competition intensifies, innovation cannot be attained solely within the integrated industrial enterprise, or even the so-called virtual corporation. Rather, companies must work together to create online networks of customers, suppliers, and value-added processes. The result is what we call the e-business community, or EBC.[10]

In the software industry, the leading EBCs are Wintel (led by Microsoft and Intel) and Java (led by Sun, IBM, Oracle, and Netscape). Often, a single company is a member of two or more competing EBCs; Microsoft and Intel, for better or worse, are involved in the Java community. Meanwhile, IBM, Oracle, and Netscape are active players in the Wintel EBC. The term "competition" best describes these dynamics.[11]

In a *Harvard Business Review* article entitled "When is virtual virtuous?" Henry W. Chesbrough and David J. Teece point to the literature about virtual corporations: "Champions of virtual corporations are urging managers to subcontract anything and everything. All over the world, companies are jumping on the bandwagon, decentralizing, downsizing, and forging alliances to pursue innovation."[12] The authors raise a concern about the relationship between such organizations and the capacity to innovate. They suggest that different types of innovation call for different types of organization, and so choosing the right organizational design is important. "Because so many important innovations are systemic, decentralization without strategic leverage and co-ordination is exactly the wrong organization strategy."[13]

Some authors have expressed the view that innovation within a web of corporations poses much more severe difficulties than does innovation within a single corporation. "Knowledge-based arguments suggest that organization knowledge provides a synergistic advantage not replicable in the marketplace."[14] These authors have raised several management issues that are important in the design and implementation of a creative web, particularly a web that involves a number of corporations. Resolution of these issues will form an important subject in 21st century business literature.

In their 1993 *Harvard Business Review* article, Richard Normann and Rafael Ramirez discuss what they refer to as "a new logic of value."[15] They point to IKEA as a corporation that has transformed an existing set of activities along a value chain into a new configuration that has improved outcomes for both customers and itself. They also refer to Danish pharmacies that have altered their retailing operations to involve private customers and healthcare institutions in new relationships and offerings. They suggest that a new challenge of value constellations is to integrate knowledge and relationships, and French corporations Compagnie Générale des Eaux and Lyonnaise des Eaux Dumez have achieved this. A series of commentaries on the Normann-Ramirez article has offered additional perspectives on these new organizational structures.[16]

In their 1997 *Sloan Management Review* article, Michael Weiner et al. discuss the impact on the structure of the electricity industry of three sets of forces driving change: deregulation, a variety of market forces, and techno-logical forces. As a result of these, "electric utility companies will have to reinvent themselves to change from vertical to 'virtual' integration based on value networks segmented into six areas: generation, transmission, distribu-tion, energy services, power markets, and IT products and services."[17] This shift will pose radically different challenges to the electricity industry in regard to arrangements within the new value network.

In their 1995 *California Management Review* article, Gianni Lorenzoni and Charles Baden-Fuller discuss the role of a strategic center in creating value:

> Typically each of these partnerships extends beyond a simple subcontracting rela-tionship. Strategic centers expect their partners to do more than follow the rules, they expect them to be creative. For example, Apple worked with Canon and Adobe to design and create a laser jet printer which then gave Apple an important position in its industry. In all the cases we studied, the strategic center looked to the partners to be creative in solving problems and being proactive in the rela-tionships. They demanded more – and obtained more – from their partners than did their less effective counterparts that used traditional subcontracting.[18]

Lorenzoni and Baden-Fuller present a series of suggestions through which the strategic center may be able to improve its effectiveness in strengthening the creative web. They emphasize the need for new structures as well as new strategies. A 1998 *Sloan Management Review* article by John D. Kasarda and Dennis A. Rondinelli points to the need for new infrastructure support systems and knowledge centers to stimulate innovation by providing a reliable source of personnel capable of achieving such success.[19]

A good example of the creative web is found in the automobile industry. Changes in consumer demands, government regulations, and competitive pres-sures from Japan have combined to create an innovation revolution in North American automobile production. Innovation has achieved reduced vehicle weight, increased fuel efficiency, improved safety, and enhanced durability and performance. Some of these have involved the substitution of aluminum and plastics for steel, the creation of smaller and more efficient engines, the use of computers to control vehicle systems, and the need for new approaches to instrumentation. How many of these innovations can be credited solely to the large assemblers? It is clear that numerous supplier firms have played key roles in this innovation revolution.

Often it is the so-called "tier one" firms supplying the assemblers with com-ponents that have made the innovations that give the entire creative web a competitive advantage. And often the "tier two" firms that supply the tier one firms are also intimately involved in the innovation process, usually basing their product modifications on R&D from tier one level firms. The development of these innovations has come from ongoing relationships with the assem-blers and the end users. At times, a parts producer may look directly to the end users, skipping over the assemblers to see what the market wants, and adjusting its products accordingly. The assembler may encourage this kind of interaction, as it facilitates innovation.

Creative webs are widening to include suppliers to the suppliers. More and more, responsibility for research, design, development, and testing is being pushed out along the branches of the web, so that every firm within the web is looking for new ways to innovate, lower costs, and meet the needs of their direct customers and the ultimate consumer. Tier one suppliers are becoming systems integrators that combine the innovations of their tier two and tier three suppliers into product offerings that take into account the needs of the entire web. Even small service firms are relying increasingly on other firms for their ongoing innovation. As the 20th century drew to a close, the large-scale manufacturing sectors of Western economies were ceasing to be the main contributors to GDP. The service sector of the economy is now the main employer, and most of the jobs created are in firms with fewer than 100 employees. In many cases it is the interconnectedness of small-scale creative webs, allowing for more creative innovations in their offerings, that increases their appeal to the final customer.

> *Responsibility for research, design, development, and testing is being pushed out along the branches of the web, so that every firm within the web is looking for new ways to innovate, lower costs, and meet the needs of their direct customers and the ultimate consumer.*

For a retailer, the creative web has also become a key to success. The retailing process today involves extensive dialog with manufacturers on customer needs and product modifications, requiring that the retailer become knowledgeable about potential innovations, and manufacturers are continually encouraged to make improvements in product construction and upgrades. The retailer's personnel travel regularly to manufacturers around the world.

For an increasing number of companies, innovation includes university-level research, and many research parks have been created to strengthen corporate-university research links. Firms often find there is more value earned for their investment by outsourcing their R&D since they avoid the additional costs of owning the facility. While academics have pointed to the success of university corporate research parks, much remains to be written about the procedures that can enhance the effectiveness of these relationships. The analysis of this subject will no doubt form an important component of business school research for the 21st century, and prescriptions will no doubt differ among regions and business sectors. Furthermore, it appears that business schools have rarely played a key role in such research parks, and we might expect that such a role will be explored and expanded in the years ahead.

For business schools, it has become increasingly important to develop their own creative webs, enhancing the effectiveness of various types of corporate links. Here, as well, creative webs are likely to involve international alliances in order to enhance learning experiences. To create executive development programs tailored to the needs of each corporation, semi-permanent relationships have become necessary. While business schools have traditionally used case studies as a mechanism for bringing reality into the classroom, one may expect a proliferation of new kinds of communication flows, with corporations playing a greater funding and advisory role.

> *Success in the new millennium will come to the corporation that can stimulate innovation not only within its own organization but throughout the overall creative web of which it is a member.*

There is a paradox that small size facilitates the specialization, expertise, and creative flexibility that underlie the innovation process. Yet, at the same time, innovation requires ongoing co-ordination among all the points throughout the creative web, no matter how big that web may be. Resolving this paradox will continue to be a central focus for corporations. Success in the new millennium will come to the corporation that can stimulate innovation not only within its own organization but throughout the overall creative web of which it is a member.

17

CONTEXT, CAPABILITY, AND RESPONSE

DAVE ULRICH

In 1964, I attended the World Fair in New York City. I have two clear memories. One exhibit displayed the helicopter and promised how this relatively innovative travel machine would solve most of the highway congestion problems. With confidence, the exhibitor proclaimed "In 20 years, we will have helicopters in every driveway." A second exhibit talked about technology and leisure. It showed the evolution of technology in the home and claimed that the newly burgeoning technological revolution would result in enormous leisure time.

My experience with predicting the future is not unique. A number of either true or apocryphal stories have come to me in the past few years about our ability to predict the future:

"Nothing will ever replace carbon paper." A report by IBM marketing assessing whether to buy Haloid, which later became Xerox.

"Who the hell wants to hear actors talk?" H.M. Warner, Warner Brothers, 1927.

"There is no reason anyone would want a computer in their home." Ken Olson, president, chairman, and founder of Digital Equipment Corporation, 1977.

"Heavier-than-air flying machines are impossible." Lord Kelvin, president, Royal Society, 1895.

"I think there is a market for maybe five computers." Thomas Watson, chairman, IBM, 1943.

All of these predictions suggest that no one can fully predict the future.[1] Helicopters have not shown up in most driveways; technology, while expanding, has not given us more leisure time (in fact, we could argue the opposite, as we now can log on and work 24 hours a day). Business predictions that speculate with confidence often miss the mark and backtrack with less vigor. However, if we do not anticipate and live for a future, we live doomed to repeat and be bound by experiences of the past. Pondering and envisioning the future gives us hope for what we might become and confidence in how we might act today to get there. A sign of maturity is recognizing that today's deeds determine tomorrow's outcomes. Projecting the future may change what I need to do today to both create positive and avoid negative outcomes. Since I spend my time thinking about and trying to improve organizations, I will suggest some observations about the contextual factors impacting organizations, how organizations will operate, and how individuals must prepare themselves today to respond for tomorrow. My hope is that these observations, while clearly speculative, may help the individual think about, prepare for, and have fun in an unknown future. After all, even if it is unpredictable, it is coming anyway.

CONTEXTUAL FACTORS IMPACTING ON ORGANIZATIONS

A number of authors have cataloged the drivers for the future of organizations.[2] Let me merely highlight six of those drivers which will have a profound impact on how organizations operate and individuals behave.

Global

We live in a global village. Because of 24-hour worldwide news, citizens of the world feel remorse for the death of a British princess, experience first-hand the devastation of a flood in China, and live the hourly trauma of armed conflict in Ireland, Iraq, and Africa. The Internet enables colleagues around the world to be more accessible than those next door. The Asian economic crisis affects stock prices in Europe and the United States. As businesses like automotive, banking, energy, and airlines engage in global mergers, large domestic companies become giant global companies, often with the scope and influence of mid-size countries.

Any successful organization must acquire global leverage and awareness. Global leverage will enable lessons in product design, marketing, and distribution in one country to be adopted around the world. Global awareness and sensitivity will enable firms to adapt products to local conditions and cultures. Simultaneous global homogeneity where things become the same (e.g. food, fashion, and tastes) and heterogeneity where cultural differences are respected (e.g. food, fashion, and tastes) will continue to challenge companies and executives to live in the paradox of being both global and local.

Technology

Technology, particularly fueled by digitalized hardware and software, will make the world smaller and faster. One morning between 6am and 7am, I shared a chapter we are authoring with colleagues in Hong Kong, Australia, and Utah. We commented in our own time zones, and by evening had made revisions to this work. What would have taken days before (with overnight mail) now takes hours. As technology gets more sophisticated (e.g. voice recognition, live video transmission) we can only envision how this will connect people more quickly. While the downside of technology (e.g. personal and emotional isolation, loss of privacy, debates about who owns what information) will need to be addressed, it would be hard to conceive of a world without technology. As technology proliferates, those who have it (as countries, companies, and individuals) may have a significant advantage over those who don't have it or are slow to acquire it, thus creating not only affluence gaps but information access gaps.

Technology will affect both where and how people work and the type of work people do. With technology, an office becomes less defined by physical place and more by connection and contact. Colleagues don't need to see each other to connect; virtual offices may exist at home, in hotels, or shared offices as long as people are able to connect and share information. Technology also adds a fundamentally new distribution channel for products and services. The Internet potential has begun to be tapped, with firms like Amazon becoming the world's largest bookstore, and Dell Computer selling nearly $2 billion per year through this distribution channel. As people become more comfortable with and confident in the Internet, more products and services will pass through this channel, disintermediating the channel of distribution.

Speed

Speed will become a major determinant of organizational success. Judgements about television programs, clothing styles, or movies will be made much more quickly. Product life cycles will shorten and first-mover advantages will become ever more important. Because Sun Microsystems was first with Java, an integrative Internet computer language, it won great market share, only to be at risk when the next generation of products emerges. With speed comes the requirement for agility to change, adapt, and learn more quickly.

Speed means changing from a mindset of accuracy and precision to one of innovation and risk taking. One executive said: "We used to wait until we had it 98 percent right before we launched a product; now we have to go out with 80 percent right and fix the rest as we go." Speed means shorter cycle times for designing training programs, restructuring companies, and implementing new products or services. Agility means taking advantage of opportunities that arise as soon as they present themselves, or losing out to a competitor who has the knack and will to move quickly.

Customization

Consumer customization exists when the marketing research focusses on individual households, not consumer segments. A grocery chain now gives its preferred customers a frequent shopper card that enables them to check out of the store by going to cashiers with no lines and by running their preferred card through a card reader. Two years later, this chain sends the customer a printout of buying preferences, including brand, price, and duration. The chain offers this preferred customer the option of having these items delivered to her home within a week or two of them being required, as evidenced by the buying pattern in the previous two years. While intrusive and risky in terms of privacy, many busy customers appreciate the more hassle-free grocery shopping. This grocery chain does not have market segments, but accurate data about each target customer which enables the firm to customize its offerings for that customer. Customization will likely occur in any business where customer data may be accumulated, then used to track and serve each customer in a unique way.

Employee customization will also occur more frequently. To attract top talent in a firm (either a leading scientist, executive, athlete, or analyst), special deals are cut which may include vacation time, stock options, cash bonuses, stock options to a spouse, access to private schools, housing allowances, car allowances, investment advisers, and legal counsel. As employee talent becomes more scarce at all levels of the firm, such customized deals will need to be crafted throughout an organization. Currently employee customization occurs with top talent (e.g. the best athlete may receive special or unique treatment in his contract), but over time will migrate through an organization.

> *Employee customization will occur more frequently. To attract top talent in a firm, special deals are cut.*

Organizations which customize for both employees and customers must focus on flexibility more than rules, service more than systems, and commitment more than consistency.

Intellectual capital/knowledge workers

Intellectual capital and the knowledge that employees possess will become increasingly the critical asset for firms. Knowledge is more than power and who is in charge; it represents the underlying values and soul of an organization. Firms that access, leverage, and create knowledge will win; those that don't will play a never-ending game of catch-up. Knowledge directly affects the growing service sector (e.g. professional service firms which sell knowledge as their primary product, financial firms which depend on knowledge to create products and induce greater commitment) and the traditional manufacturing sector.[3]

Organizations must learn to continually access knowledge and ideas. They must become learning organizations which generate and generalize ideas with impact. They must become thought leaders within their industry so that they set the rules of the game rather than be constrained by being strategic followers. Employees must be able to forget in order to learn, to give up old ways to try new, and to constantly experiment. In my work as a professor, I have required myself to have 25 percent new material each year. This may seem easy, but after a few years the ongoing challenge requires asking questions to which there are not answers and to taking risks with new material rather than teaching tried-and-true cases and lectures. Managers must be challenged to constantly have new approaches, insights, and processes to accomplish work. Knowledge is the only asset which must regenerate itself. When knowledge depreciates, value is destroyed; when knowledge grows, value is created. In the future, as Thomas Stewart suggests, knowledge becomes the hidden wealth of nations, organizations, and employees.[4]

> *In the future, knowledge becomes the hidden wealth of nations, organizations, and employees.*

Profitable growth

Survival of the fittest will continue to apply in the business jungle. Firms that do not meet financial goals will fail. Financial success will become not just reducing cost but creating growth. Cost-reduction pressures will continue as evidenced in attention to improved processes, avoiding redundancies, and higher productivity. An agenda for growth will continue through attention to global distribution (selling products and/or services to new markets), customer intimacy (selling more to existing customers), and innovation (creating products and/or services).

Organizations must continue to balance the short and long-term requirements of employees, customers, and investors. They must sustain credibility by meeting quarterly goals and having long-term visions which excite possibilities. They must find ways to continue to increase revenue while managing cost. Leaders of tomorrow will have a clear strategy for growth and cost simultaneously.

CRITICAL ORGANIZATIONAL CAPABILITIES

The organizational implications of the above contextual trends will require a shift in thinking about organizations. Formal organizations as a way of accomplishing work are a relatively new phenomenon in the overall scheme of things. As Alfred Chandler points out in his classic review of organizational growth, large bureaucratic organizations evolved from the late 1800s to their dominance in society as we enter the 21st century.[5] For most of these 100 years, we have held a view that organizations were defined by their structure – the roles people play, the rules created to govern work, and the chain of command within the organization.[6]

With the rapidly changing and dynamic contextual factors described above, the essence of organizations has shifted and will continue to shift from focussing on structure to capability. Capability represents what the organization is able to do and how it does it rather than the more visible picture of who reports to whom and which rules govern work. When we think of Disney, for example, we don't think about the number of levels in the hierarchy, how much decision making is delegated to each employee, or how pay is allocated based on experience, but about Disney's ability to give guests a fun experience, to create a safe and wholesome atmosphere, and to continually create guest experiences.

Organizations will operate in the future to identify and nurture a handful of critical capabilities. While these capabilities will clearly differ by industry (a pharmaceutical firm is more worried about innovation and cycle time whereas a utility is more interested in consistent delivery in a deregulated world), a handful of central capabilities may comprise the essence of how organizations will operate.[7]

Flex-everything

In a world where change occurs rapidly, organizations must be able to master the capabilities of speed, agility, culture change, reducing cycle time, and transformation. Underlying all these capabilities is the notion of flex-everything. Organizations will have more flexible employment practices (part time, full time, contract employees), compensation practices (flexible pay and rewards), and ways to get work done (work at home or from the office). Executives will want their organizations to have an identity of the most innovative, quickest moving, and most adaptive in the industry. They will create flexible management practices that encourage capacity to change. This means that organization structures are likely to be more fluid and dynamic. For example, rather than be hired to work in one department or function for an extended period, employees may work in ever-changing task forces, assigned projects and colleagues depending on the requirements of the customer.

Such organizations exist today in professional service firms. Consultants in any of the large consulting firms exist in a fluid organization. Each employee may represent a competence, which, when joined with other competencies, or team members, delivers value to the clients of the consulting firm. In practice, this means that consultants' careers are organized around a series of projects, or client engagements, where they collaborate to create value to individual clients. Future organizations committed to lean manufacturing or focussed factories will have similar organization flexibility.[8]

Human (intellectual) capital

Recent work on intellectual capital shows that the workforce within a firm becomes a critical predictor of overall firm success.[9] At a broad level, intellectual capital represents the collective knowledge, skills, and abilities of all employees within a firm. Economists track intellectual capital by the calculation of market value divided by replacement value.[10] This equation offers a broad insight into the importance of knowledge and people within a firm. For example, tradition- ally large capital-intensive firms like General Motors have much less intellectual capital than high-tech, knowledge-creating firms like Dell Computer. The market value/replacement value ratio offers an overall indicator of intellectual capital, but it does not translate to specific managerial actions to create it.

More recent work on intellectual capital assesses the competence and com- mitment of employees within a work unit.[11] For example, McDonald's has found that when restaurants increase the competence and commitment of people who work within a restaurant (a measure of each establishment's intel- lectual capital), they find these restaurants reach higher performance goals. HR practices may clearly be used to increase both competence and commitment of employees. By hiring, training, incentivising, and governing employees with the right set of skills and in the right way, firms may increase their human capital.

Leadership depth

A recent study by the McKinsey consulting firm has found that CEOs believe there is a "war for talent," particularly in finding successors for senior man- agement positions. Companies with leadership bench have the ability to continue to adapt and change with new business conditions. Johnson & Johnson has invested heavily in building the next generation of leaders through formal training programs and stretch job assignments. These investments pro- duce leaders who have the capacity to make bold and difficult decisions and to shape an organization for the future. HR practices may be used to create lead- ership bench. When more talented leaders are hired, and when the organization is governed in such a way to give them profit and loss accountability, they build depth and capacity. These organizations seem to have long-term, not short-term success; create strategies for changing business conditions; and be built to last.[12]

Creating leadership depth implies that a firm produces a unique brand or identity for its leaders. Traditionally, brand has referred to products that a firm produces (e.g. Coke), then brand referred to the firm, or the identity a customer might associate with a firm (e.g. Nordstrom). If leadership brand can be created, a firm's leaders will embody not only the values of the firm but ensure delivery of results the firm requires.[13] Firms which invest in leadership brand have leaders who stand out. At a professional conference, the leaders of firm X will stand out and everyone at the conference will recognize that this individual must come from firm X because of how she or he approaches problems, thinks about issues, defines results, and accomplishes work. Such leadership branding may occur throughout the organization.

Learning

In recent years, learning organizations have been identified as central to a firm's success.[14] Organizations that learn seem to have the capacity to reinvent themselves, to manage knowledge, and to adjust to changing competitive conditions. In our research, we found learning organizations had the capacity to both generate and generalize ideas with impact.[15] Coca-Cola, for example, has invested heavily in a learning consortia where innovative ideas from one country are codified and shared with other countries facing similar issues. By learning to share and implement ideas, Coke has become more of a learning organization.

> *Organizations that learn tend to be more innovative, able to manage knowledge workers, and able to create strategies.*

Investments in HR practices increase this capacity to learn by innovative training, compensation, and communication efforts which encourage sharing ideas. Organizations that learn tend to be more innovative, able to manage knowledge workers, and able to create strategies.

Successful organizations will have the capacity to regenerate themselves by both generating ideas and generalizing those ideas. Generation of ideas may come from running experiments, benchmarking, hiring from outside, training, and continuous improvement efforts. However, merely having a new idea is not enough to be a full learning organization. The idea must be generalized or shared with others. This means that events (e.g. an off-site meeting where candid information about customers and competitors is shared) must

> *Successful organizations will have the capacity to regenerate themselves by both generating ideas and generalizing those ideas.*

become a pattern (where the same level of candor exists in day-to-day operations). Success in one unit must be shared with other product, functional, or geographic units. Leaders of learning organizations must relish change and experiments and build discipline to share ideas from unit to unit.

Customer connection

Many firms have discovered through customer value analysis that 20 percent of customers account for 80 percent of business performance. These target customers become critical for a firm to compete and win. In some firms, the focus on target customers has led to a definition of success as the "share of target customer." For example, Royal Bank has identified wealthy clients and has targetted these clients. With dedicated account managers and account teams, they have worked to gain a higher percentage of these clients' business. Success is measured by "share of client" rather than absolute revenue. This means that Royal Bank works to get a high share of targetted accounts, managing the stock, bond, loans, equity, insurance, pension, and other financial transactions of targetted customers. HR practices may increase this customer connection by forming account teams, building compensation programs based on account performance, and including key customers in HR practices. These practices increase customer connection which in turn leads to business results because of repeat business, customer loyalty, and lower costs to create revenue.

Creating customer connection may come from databases which identify and track each individual customer's preferences. For example, when I enter the Amazon.com website, I am told of books that might be of interest to me based on my past purchases, such as authors who have a new book out, or a similar genre of book that has received good reviews. Customer connection may come from dedicated account teams which build long-term relationships with a targetted account. Public accounting firms often assign a lead engagement partner to sustain client relationships over time. Customer connection may also come from involving a customer in the firm's HR practices. When a restaurant I often frequent wanted to hire a new chef, they invited target customers to interview possible candidates and sample their cuisine. By participating in the hiring decision, I became more committed to the restaurant. Likewise, many firms are including customers in staffing, training, compensation, and communication practices, the net result of which is customer intimacy.

Shared mindset

Shared mindset, or common culture, represents the extent to which employees have a collective agenda. When a shared mindset exists, employees have a common focus and commitment to how to work to meet goals. A shared mindset helps a company set an agenda and make sure that it translates to employee behavior. When Continental executives worked to turn around the airline, they chose a shared mindset which started with key customers, business travelers who paid full fare. Business travelers wanted Continental to be known as the "on time" airline so that they could have a predictable schedule. With "on time" as the desired shared mindset, Continental executives worked to make sure that HR practices focussed employee behaviors on this. This meant building training programs so employees understood how to make on time happen; creating compensation which incentivised employees to be on time; and introducing suggestion systems whereby employees could share their ideas on how to be on time. Shared mindset leads to business performance because employees are focussed, attentive, and engaged in a common agenda.

Shared mindset also becomes an important predictor of a firm's success.[16] When employees throughout a firm share both the goals of the firm and a commitment to the processes required to meet those goals, shared mindset exists and the firm wins. Called in layman terms "being on the same page," it is quickly evident when a shared mindset exists.

Strategic clarity

If a random set of employees was asked to identify a firm's probability of success with a single question, a pertinent one would be: "What is the strategy of this business which sets us apart from competitors and helps us win with customers?" When employees have common answers to this question, strategic clarity exists. This clarity helps customers know how to differentiate a firm and helps employees know what is expected of them. Southwest Airlines has strategic clarity. Employees throughout Southwest know that it wants to be the low-cost, high-touch airline. Multiple management decisions support this strategy, e.g. one aircraft to save money on gates and turnaround time at airports; no frills on the airline; cheaper tickets without using travel agents; and the ticket technology: point-to-point departures, no assigned seating, etc. This strategic clarity helps Southwest create a distinct niche. It also commits employees to a clear agenda and purpose. HR practices of who is hired, how they are hired, and how they are trained play a critical role in making strategic clarity real to employees.

Accountability

Many firms make promises – to investors, customers, and employees. Accountability increases the probability of meeting promises. Firms that meet those promises are more likely to be successful because they have long-term commitment from customers and investors. Allied Signal has created a culture where discipline and accountability matters. When Allied removed sectors and organized itself around business units, it was able to assign clear profit and loss accountability to business unit leaders. These leaders know they have to deliver business performance and they have the necessary resources to make it happen. This accountability culture has helped Allied leaders make difficult decisions and accomplish what they promise.

HR practices build accountability. When goals are set and achieved, good things happen; when goals are set and missed, bad things happen. At times this accountability lies with individuals and at other times with teams. Accountability also comes from clear and standard processes for doing work which may come from mastering quality and other processes.

Boundaryless

Over time, most firms create multiple boundaries.[17] Vertical boundaries separate lower from higher level employees. Horizontal boundaries separate functions or units from each other. Geographic boundaries separate countries. External boundaries separate a firm from suppliers and customers. These boundaries cost time and money to cross. Removing boundaries makes an organization both more efficient and quicker. General Electric has worked hard to remove many types of boundaries. It encourages information sharing, talent movement, teams, and rewards to be shared from top to bottom, side to side, inside out, and around the world. The removal of boundaries comes in part from HR practices which provide forums to share information (e.g. workout), have team-based compensation, and communicate clearly the removal of boundaries.

Organizational diagnosis and assessment

The above capabilities are not inclusive, but indicative. There may be other organizational capabilities for the future which will be central to business success. Regardless of which capabilities are more or less critical, thinking about organizations through a capability lens changes the way organizations are assessed and improved.

Executives charged with building better organizations will worry less about structure and more about capabilities. They will not judge their organization a success by the number of levels, people, or systems, but more by the extent to which their organization demonstrates critical capabilities. Identifying, measuring, and improving these capabilities will become the standard for organizational assessment. This will require innovative metrics that shift attention to the types of capabilities an organization must possess to win. It will require executives to continually probe and hold managers accountable for the capabilities they create.

HOW INDIVIDUALS PREPARE TODAY TO
RESPOND TO TOMORROW

In the context and organization of the future, where organizational capabilities matter more than hierarchy, individuals will be expected to think and behave differently. They will be required to be as flexible, committed to learning, boundaryless, and able to join and work in teams as the organizations in which they work. Employees essentially have to consider themselves as a company of one. As the CEO of one's own company, the employee must deal with five issues and respond to five questions.

Self-reliance: How do I assume responsibility for my own career?

My mentor Bonner Ritchie taught me that "you can never make organizations safe for people, you have to make people safe from organizations." Each individual bears primary responsibility for what a career looks like and how the individual wants to interact with the organization. This means clearly understanding the skills you bring to the organization, how you want those skills to be used, and how you want to be treated by the organization. My recent experience is that organizations have the infinite capacity to take, and at times, abuse employee skills until the employee defines the parameters of the employment contract. Employees who are self-reliant are aware of their skills, of what they want from their work in the organization, and willing to be accountable for making good things happen within the organization and to them without blaming others.

Self-reliance comes from employees having the discipline, self-confidence, and self-esteem to conduct honest career assessments. Employees have ultimate responsibility for their career and need to perform period career check-ups to see if it is working best for them. A colleague in her early forties as a single mother with two children at home had been one of the most successful officers of her firm. As she assumed responsibility for both her career and her life, she chose to leave full-time employment and spend time as a mother. This was a conscious, careful, and flexible decision. In time, she realizes she may move in and out of work in a variety of ways – full time within a company, part time with a company, independent consulting, public service, and family care. She accepts responsibility for her career choices, realizing that today's choices influence but do not inhibit tomorrow's opportunities.

Resilience: What is the life cycle of my knowledge?
How do I stay current?

As knowledge moves more rapidly through invisible Internet space, each employee bears the burden of being current. Resilient employees are those who will learn, change, and constantly be literate in their area of expertise. These employees keep up on current ideas and innovations, are tied into a network of other employees at their career stage, and are willing to shed old ideas as they become obsolete. Resilient employees experiment with new ideas, learn from their failures and successes, and always think about what's next rather than what has been. They are likely to shift projects, work activities, or even careers when unplanned opportunities arise. They see risk as an opportunity to learn, not fail.

Resilience comes from the insatiable desire to ask: "What's next?" An old adage says: "If you do what you have always done, you will get what you always got." Employees of the future cannot stand idle, nor can they accept what they have always done. Discovering innovative, untried, and often risky ways to think about and carry out work will distinguish the successful employee. Getting to this point requires asking oneself questions such as, "what if?" "what are the questions to which we don't have answers?" and "how can I take learning from A and apply it to B?"

Results: Who are the recipients of my work and what value do I add to them?

Employees who deliver value will stay active. Since value is defined by the receiver not the giver, the first step in delivering results is to identify who the recipients are of the work you do. This comes by answering the question: "Who uses the ideas, products, or services I produce?" Then, once constituents are identified, it is important to learn what these recipients want (which they may know) and need (which they may not know) and how you can provide these wants and needs. Results come when value is created.

As customers and their needs change, desired results change. In one firm facing downsizing, the head of HR proposed that her department should absorb an inordinate burden of the downsizing. She felt, as she looked at the firm's strategies and requirements to succeed in the near term, that other departments were more important to the firm's success. This sacrifice on her part came because she knew the results of the firm and how those results were derived. This sacrifice also earned her enormous credibility over time as managers came to trust her recommendations as focussed on the firm rather than on herself.

Relationships: Who cares about me and who do I care about?

A major downside of the context and organization of the future is isolation, loneliness, and alienation. Technological connection may not replace the personal contact we need so desperately. In a fast-changing, technologically driven world, we still need to connect to others in intimate and emotional ways. This means that the successful employee of the future will recognize that she can't be all things to all people because intimacy is not created uniformly, but requires dedication of time and attention. Defining who we care about and how to nurture relationships will become a challenge for employees who are busy, globally focussed, and technologically attached. However, through relationships come communities where differences are respected, individuals are valued, and care for others ensures personal worth.

> *A major downside of the context and organization of the future is isolation, loneliness, and alienation. Technological connection may not replace the personal contact we need so desperately.*

Relationships come from building trust. Friendships matter. Intimacy counts. It behoves employees of the future to invest not only in professional growth but in relationship growth. Relationship equity comes as people spend time together, communicate concern for each other, sacrifice personal goals, confirm the value of each other, share warmth and personal concern, and work together for common goals. In a world of rapid change, continuity of relationships offers a stability so that change can occur.

Resolve: What do I want to do and what is my identity?

Personal resolve means having a clear identity, then making sure that all actions are congruent with that identity. A personal definition of success helps people avoid being all things to all people and as a result satisfying no one. The resolve which comes from a strong personal identity helps people master change rather than be mastered by it. An identity often comes when an individual sees personal action in the context of the action: how is what I am doing coming across to others? Is this congruent with the identity I want to be associated with?

Resolve comes from values and mission statements where the individual does a personal audit to continually ask: Is this what I want to be doing right now? In a chaotic external world of change, learning, ideas, globalization, technology, and customization, employees who succeed will have the capacity to find an inner peace. This peace comes from reflection about what matters most and from having the capacity to make one's own decisions and shape one's own identity. Employees with such inner compasses remain calm, instill confidence, and keep focussed on what matters most, even when times are difficult.

CONCLUSION

Some prophets envision the future and tell the people they are damned. Others see the future and tell the people to prepare. I like being in the latter category.

Since the future is unpredictable but coming anyway, we need to prepare as best we can by projecting about context, organization, and people. Some day my son or daughters may read this chapter and marvel at how far off my predictions were. For them, my views of the future may or may not become their realities. However, by having a point of view about the future, they can acquire perspective and purpose in relating to it.

18

KALEIDOSCOPE THINKING

ROSABETH MOSS KANTER

The scene was memorable. I was sitting in a Singapore ballroom when the British head of a global oil company told his top managers worldwide about what they needed to succeed in their company in the future. Like the other people listening, I squirmed in anticipation of the usual cliches about audacious goals, working in teams, and putting customers first.

"Brains," he said. "You need brains." And he sat down.

How unexpected. How refreshing. How appropriate.

Mental agility is essential when business itself is at a crossroads. Every place we look, received wisdom about how things always were or even how things ought to be is being challenged. New technologies and expanded market possibilities are revolutionizing industries. Trying to conduct business while the system itself is being redefined puts a premium on brains – to imagine possibilities outside of conventional categories, to envision actions that cross traditional boundaries, to anticipate repercussions and take advantage of interdependencies, to make new connections or invent new combinations. Those who lack mental flexibility and imagination will find it harder and harder to hold their own, let alone prosper.

Thinking across boundaries and creating new categories is the ultimate entrepreneurial act. Call it business creativity. Call it holistic thinking. Research has associated integrative thinking with higher levels of organizational innovation, personal creativity, and even longer life. Blurring the boundaries and challenging the categories permits new possibilities to emerge, like twisting a kaleidoscope to see the endless patterns that can be created from the same set of fragments. I call it "kaleidoscope thinking." It is the ultimate weapon to help leaders meet the challenges of the 21st century.

DRIVING THE NEED FOR MENTAL KALEIDOSCOPES:
A BRIEF TOUR OF THE NEW BUSINESS LANDSCAPE

The defining feature of the global information economy is not the flow of goods – international trade has been an almost constant feature of modern civilization – but the flow of capital, people, and, especially, information. Time and space are no longer a barrier to doing deals anywhere in the world; computer networks permit instantaneous transactions, and market watchers operate on a 24-hour basis. Consolidation in the financial sector puts control over the flow of money into fewer hands – indeed, it removes the need for the "hands" at all, as financial transactions are electronically mediated. International mergers and acquisitions are growing, especially as many countries have eased restrictions on foreign direct investment. Travel and tourism have increased dramatically. From 1960 to 1988 the real cost of international travel dropped by 60 percent; during the same period, the number of foreigners entering the USA on business rose by 2800 percent.

Information industries are quickly replacing tangible objects, physical environments, and labor-intensive contacts with information-packed products and services available over electronic networks. The growth of e-commerce over the past five years is only the leading edge of a much deeper phenomenon; e-services delivered over the Internet might be even bigger, from remote medical diagnoses to satellite-based systems that can tell a farmer the specific weather conditions or dampness on every part of his fields. Information technology now includes biotechnology; seeds given particular genes (a kind of "software" implanted in the seed) can result in insect-resistant crops with higher yields, replacing pesticides and the physical labor to spray them.

Information is even more mobile than capital or people. Information can now reach different parts of the world simultaneously. One landmark was passed when CNN offered live global broadcasts of the Gulf War as it happened; another when the United States Congress put the special prosecutor's report about President Clinton on the worldwide web. The Internet makes it possible for any design, any fashion, any idea, to be known anywhere in the world at the moment of launch; a New York apparel manufacturer put its spring line on the Internet and within days had five orders from Beijing. According to a report from ActiveMedia, business-to-business marketers are eagerly adopting products allowing immediate two-way communications with customers, including net phone, net videoconferencing, and workgroup products.

As global media and entertainment giants grow – Sony, Bertelsmann, Time Warner, and Disney – they seek products or concepts that travel easily over world communication channels, channels that themselves are increasingly controlled by global giants. Communication industries on both the content and the infrastructure sides are consolidating quickly in the USA., accounting for four out of five of the largest-ever mergers through 1997: WorldCom's $37 billion deal for MCI, Bell Atlantic's $25.6 billion deal for Nynex, Disney's $19 billion acquisition of CapCities/ABC, and SBC Communications' $16.1 billion acquisition of Pacific Telesis. Bell Atlantic's acquisition of GTE in 1998 for over $50 billion topped all of these. The rise of global communications encourages universal languages. Already, English is the preferred language of commerce, including e-commerce. According to a 1999 OECD report, "Communications Outlook," about 78 percent of all websites use the English language, and for websites with secure servers over 91 percent are in English. In Belgium, the use of English for electronic commerce far exceeds the use of the two national languages, French and Flemish. Even in linguistically-sensitive France, 20 percent of the secure-server-linked webpages under the national domain ".fr" are in English.

In key industries, business strategy has changed from a country-by-country approach to global lines of business in which the same products are sold in every part of the world at the same time, manufactured in fewer places that supply the world, and supported by global procurement. Consider Gillette's shift to world products a decade ago. Like many consumer goods companies, Gillette traditionally developed products a market at a time, with gradual roll-outs around the world based on their assumption of when a market was ready for something new or more advanced. Starting with the Sensor razor in 1990, Gillette created a global product with a global launch – the same advanced product conveyed by the same advertising message available in every corner of the world within months.

Other consumer products companies are following. Procter & Gamble's recently announced restructuring was designed to ensure global simultaneity, eliminating regional business units and putting profit responsibility in the hands of seven executives responsible for global product units. P&G's new fabric care product, Febreze, was launched first in the USA. with expected annual sales of $150 to $200 million. If it had been launched by the new global fabric care and laundry unit, it would likely have been rolled out in other countries at the same time, generating $500 million in annual sales, new CEO Durk Jager told the *Wall Street Journal.*

Disney cartoon characters once made their way around the world at a leisurely pace, following the popularity of the films as they were gradually translated and shown. Now licensing agreements are in place with toys available everywhere even before the films are released. This sets in motion a global cascade: global purchasing by these companies, which pressurizes suppliers to globalize or join global networks.

While large, established companies are reinventing themselves to become more global, newer technology companies are born global. The newest technologies are inherently border-crossing, such as computers and electronic communications, and the strong American companies that develop and use them are rapidly creating alliances and networks with numerous companies in many parts of the world. Companies in new technology fields such as software, biotechnology, medical devices or telecommunications tend to design their products with world standards in mind and partners in many places even before they are ready to ship a single item outside their home country market. Sometimes this stance is propelled by the partnership of these small firms with global giants in industries; small biotech startups find willing partners in the pharmaceutical industry, in which major players such as GlaxoWellcome, Merck, and Novartis have swelled through mergers and reorganized around global product lines.

> *While large, established companies are reinventing themselves to become more global, newer technology companies are born global.*

World commercial standards inevitably follow, along with a push for even greater transparency. (Lack of transparency was one problem that ultimately caused Asia's speculative bubble to burst.) More watchdogs, with ever-more powerful analytic tools and ever-faster communication channels – securities analysts, the media, government data collectors, international trade treaty overseers, issue-oriented activists – provide data to track performance. Electronic procurement systems permit rapid comparisons among many different purveyors of goods and services. UPS and Federal Express offer software and data links that enable customers to track the status of their order; such systems also permit customers to provide instant performance ratings. In the future it is likely that more conduct will be scrutinized, compared, and exposed along more dimensions, even when countries have different rules and practices and disagree about the standards. New businesses are springing up to collect and disseminate these data – witness the phenomenal growth of Bloomberg business news services, available through every form of media. Management by fact will increasingly embarrass those still engaged in management by corruption or cronyism. Inevitably, this exposure will be one more force spreading world standards. The European quality standard, ISO 9000 and beyond, became *de facto* world process assurance standards necessary for any organization that wanted to do business with the best industrial customers.

But globalization does not mean homogenization; it requires strategies and practices that accommodate the diversity that exists across countries. Some business processes lend themselves to greater uniformity and economies of global scope, while others require local differentiation. Production processes, technologies, and supplies are more easily globalized than distribution, which has to connect with local infrastructure. Even world products and concepts reach customers in different ways depending on country conditions. For example, in its initial entry into Brazil, Wal-Mart made some obvious merchandising mistakes, such as stocking American footballs in a soccer-playing country or leaf blowers in tree-less, yard-less, concrete-dominated Sao Paolo, according to the *Wall Street Journal*, and it also faced different competition (Carrefour from France). But the more difficult challenges involved local infrastructure. Wal-

Mart had 300 deliveries per day in Sao Paolo instead of the seven per day typical in the USA. The chain initially lacked clout with local suppliers, so it could not gain the same pricing or logistics advantages as in the USA. Its stockhandling system could not handle Brazilian pallet sizes nor its computerized bookkeeping system Brazil's complex tax laws. Local companies adapt to the presence of international competitors by creative upgrades, while foreign companies accommodate local practices. In Lima, Peru, a local seafood restaurant in the same shopping mall with Burger King studied and adapted the foreign chain's techniques to create fast-food-style ceviche (more popular locally than hamburgers). Meanwhile, global giant McDonald's incorporated into its menus in Peru a major Peruvian soft drink, Golden Cola, because it outsells international brands.

Business strategy thus means multi-dimensional and multi-local thinking. Globalization creates a world business elite – an English-speaking, highly-educated business class – but that managerial class must understand the differences among nations and markets while rising above them.

> *Business strategy thus means multi-dimensional and multi-local thinking.*

This brief tour of the macro-environment points to the forces creating a need for innovation everywhere. For consumers and customers, the global information economy offers more and faster information, fewer geographic constraints, and greater access to world products and services. For businesses, that translates to more competition, fewer protected quasi-monopolies, faster product obsolescence, higher standards, and the need to juggle global scope and local responsiveness. To succeed, businesses must tap the power in brainpower: mental agility, imagination, the ability to learn and then to challenge that very learning with a new idea.

KALEIDOSCOPES AND COMPANIES

Brainpower is to the global information economy as oil was to the industrial economy. Economic research proves that "soft" or intangible assets are becoming the most important sources of a company's value; a Brookings Institution study showed that physical assets (property, plant, and equipment) accounted for 62.8 percent of the total market value of US firms in capital-dependent manufacturing and mining

> *Brainpower is to the global information economy as oil was to the industrial economy.*

industries in 1982 but had dropped to only 37.9 percent of the market value of those firms by 1991. For service industries, intangible assets create nearly all of the value.

Three intangible assets, that I identified in examining the strategies and cultures of world-class companies, are particularly important. I call them the "3Cs:"

- *concepts* – the best and latest ideas and technologies, the result of continuous innovation;

- *competence* – the ability to execute flawlessly and to deliver value to customers with ever higher standards, as people learn and then teach others their best practices; and

- *connections* – strong partners that leverage a company's offerings, link it to new markets, and provide access to innovations and opportunities that, in turn, fuel the imagination to innovate.

The best companies, in short, channel brainpower into a search for significant new ideas. They build on knowledge residing in the organization and in its partner network, but they encourage people to go beyond received wisdom to create significant new ideas, twisting and shaking their mental kaleidoscopes.

Concepts are the ideas that guide the organization, that frame possibilities and result in the means by which it creates and delivers value. Concepts range from the macro and strategic – the grand purpose of the organization – to the micro and tactical. At the most sweeping level, companies can have a core concept or theory of the "business" – why the organization exists, what elements are essential to its model for delivering value. More tactically, conceptual assets include specific product or service concepts – what is offered and to whom – as well as concepts for the processes that support delivering value to customers and other stakeholders.

Fields or industries in the midst of competitive, technological, political, or regulatory upheaval are characterized by a large number of new core concepts – breakthrough stand-alone models or transformational innovations that represent very big twists of very big kaleidoscopes. New core concepts or theories of the business often come from entrepreneurs bypassing established channels dominated by current players – such as Dell Computers, which innovated by first offering computers through catalogs, building computers to customer orders; Salick Health Centers that started stand-alone full-service cancer treatment centers, contributing one more model to a conceptual revolution in US health care delivery; Amazon.Com, that transformed bookselling through its on-line Internet virtual bookstores offering any title, along with information customized to customer preference; or in American public education, charter schools. Innovators can build a better office product (high-speed Xerox copiers) or you can build a better way to distribute office products (Staples, among the first office supply superstores). Every industry, no matter how mature or routinized, has its kaleidoscopic thinkers. Air transportation, for example, could easily become a commodity – the same aircraft, seat configurations, pilot training, interline ticketing, travel bookers. Southwest Airlines found a niche in low-cost services through creativity. Founder Herb Kelleher's core concept for a different kind of airline was augmented by a try-anything mandate to staff which produced numerous small creative differences.

Innovation begins with someone being smart enough to sense a new need. Of course, being "smart enough" comes from focussing time and attention on things going on in the environment that send signals that innovation is needed – perhaps because key stakeholders are getting restless and starting to look for new ways to get their needs met, eyeing the offerings of competitors. Tuning into the wider world outside a person's own daily milieu is like filling a kaleidoscope with the bits and pieces that eventually get shaken up into a new mix. Imagination and intuition often depend on fragments of new and different experiences that can then be combined in new and different ways. Consider some simple forms of mental stimulation that organizations can encourage – all of which have been associated with higher rates of innovation:

- regular visits to other parts of the organization and exchange of ideas;
- trips to new places to experience things quite different from normal practice;
- discussions with critics and challengers, or just those who hold a different world view, have different beliefs, make different assumptions;
- trend-tracking by asking everyone what's new, what's changing;
- reading outside a person's field as well as in it;
- attending conferences on subjects that are new and unfamiliar.

This is why flexible organizations encouraging mobility and rich in external partnerships are more likely to innovate than rigid, bureaucratic hierarchies. Imagination is limited when people have conventional wisdom or existing assumptions reinforced by talking only to those who agree with them and think exactly what they think. This locks the kaleidoscope's pattern in place.

Customers, suppliers, and venture partners are important sources of ideas for innovation. Innovation and collaboration can work together, if partners provide a new and different set of ideas that represent a window on new developments and marketplace changes. The airlines entering into the Star Alliance (Lufthansa, United, Air Canada, Varig, AllNippon, and others) have made learning from each other an explicit goal, as all seek innovation in an industry where it is sometimes hard to distinguish one carrier from another. New kinds of business partnerships with government, community groups, or non-profit organizations can also stretch thinking in new directions. IBM's Reinventing Education initiative puts IBM engineers, systems integrators, and consultants on significant projects in partnership with public school systems in the USA. and countries such as Brazil, Ireland, Italy, and Vietnam to apply new technologies that can transform education; but these projects have also helped IBM teams develop new solutions with commercial applications, such as voice recognition technology based on children's voices or data warehousing for large groups of users.

In the global information age, learning takes place in many settings and in all directions, not just top-down or from-headquarters-out or within one organization. "Kids" teach their seniors; for example, distinguished editor Michael Kinsley is unlearning print magazine rules and learning the Internet from Microsoft managers decades younger, as he creates a new on-line magazine, *Slate*. Useful ideas might come from far-flung locations once labeled "backwards;" Nynex's joint venture in Thailand, before its merger with Bell Atlantic, taught American engineers about telecommunications technology not yet in use in the United States. Rather than holing up in headquarters bunkers, successful CEOs like Gillette's Alfred Zeien are on the road constantly to exchange ideas face-to-face in the field. For DuPont, networks enhance the idea generation process necessary for innovation and the knowledge transfer process necessary to solve problems or utilize best practices quickly. Its central research lab supports over 400 networks. Combining face-to-face meetings with electronic exchanges, they range from ad hoc exchanges to solve a particular problem to ongoing interest groups specializing in technology issues.

Innovation is stimulated by competition for customers who can signal their preferences and needs directly to businesses. It is hard to use imagination in a vacuum; reports and numbers may indicate that there is a problem or an opportunity, but they do not stimulate the mind to see new possibilities in the same way as immediate experiences of living in a potential user's world. "Going direct" is one way that companies enable their people to have direct end user contact even if they sell to other organizations along the value chain. Rubbermaid, which distributes its products through large retailers, uses its laboratory stores to provide observations of consumer reactions to new product prototypes and to identify unmet consumer needs. It is harder for companies loops away from end users in the supply chain to create transforming innovations when they simply supply components to the next company in line, getting requirements second-hand from their immediate customers while toiling in anonymity, unknown to end consumers and insulated from user reality.

> *"Going direct" is one way that companies enable their people to have direct end user contact even if they sell to other organizations along the value chain.*

Decades of research on industrial innovation shows that users are often the primary stimulus for innovation. But when technologies change dramatically, as Harvard Business School professor Clay Christensen found, customers sometimes join managers in resisting change, especially if established customers are too committed to old methods. For this reason, companies need to experiment with, and learn about, new ideas that take them beyond the desires or interests of current customers.

The more holistic the experience and the wider the view – that is, the more elements of a system that can be included in the kaleidoscope – the more likely that breakthroughs will result. Leading technology companies now recognize that they must create new commercial concepts and not simply excellent technology. They might draw from the arsenal of marketing – from brand development to great customer service – to offer more than just technology in their products; Intel, for example, helped restore America's lead in semiconductors, which had been lost to Japan, and then proceeded to leapfrog the industry by making its chips into a consumer brand (the "Intel inside").

Innovation requires courage as well as imagination. Leaders must create cultures in which experiments, questions, and challenges to the prevailing model are not just for the courageous. There is ample evidence that innovation requires multiple experiments. One study of industrial innovation showed that it took 3000 raw ideas, reflected in 300 formal proposals, winnowed down eventually to nine large development projects, to produce one commercial success. Pfizer tests over 100 leads per year in order to find one promising direction for new drug development.

Because innovation is hard to predict, may occur anywhere, and requires multiple experiments, world-class companies expect innovation all the time, everywhere. They generate activity at three levels of a pyramid:

- at the peak, a few big bets about the future, and thus the biggest investments in product, technology, or market innovation;
- in the middle, a portfolio of promising but not-yet-proven experiments, early-stage new ventures, prototypes, or other stand-alone projects;
- at the base, a large number of operationally-embedded incremental innovations, continuous improvements, and early-stage new ideas that boost immediate revenues, take out costs, increase speed, or create a customer success – but even more, suggest a promising new direction for the future.

The pyramid is not static. Influence flows in many directions: top-down, bottom-up, or horizontally across the company. The big bets influence the domain for experimentation and provide structure for the search for early-stage ideas. Modest ideas up from the bottom can accumulate into a bigger force that turns into new ideas, reaching prototype status. Projects and ideas from one part of the organization trigger new thinking and new opportunities in another part.

Thus, leaders in innovation-intensive organizations give kaleidoscopes to everyone. They empower people at all levels to search for new ideas, from constant operational improvements to dramatic breakthroughs. Time and resources can help the seeds of new ideas blossom. Small budgets – perhaps through a special seed grant fund – can help people take fast action on promising new opportunities without going through the hierarchy, bypassing a lengthy budgeting and resource allocation process. Grant funds help people pursue unexpected opportunities and incubate new initiatives without undermining local line managers. Some proposals might involve stand-alone ventures; others, projects that can be embedded within business units. The seed grant helps fund the creation of a "business plan" that would then be routed either back to the line organization for commitment to develop or could qualify for further corporate support. In addition to direct business benefits, this has the side benefit of encouraging more people to think entrepreneurially about creative ways to approach business problems and opportunities.

Making the search for innovation a part of everyone's job does not mean that people are confined to their job. Some companies encourage people to be idea scouts, looking for ideas beyond the job, the company, and the industry. I coined the term "far-afield trips" for these tours beyond conventional boundaries to encounter ideas or technologies emerging elsewhere that suggest new opportunities for the company. Creativity is stimulated by leaving familiar settings and facing the clash of perspectives and challenge to conventional wisdom that leads to breakthrough ideas. First-hand experience with power outages in developing countries led the head of a company making electricity-dependent photo identification cameras to see the huge potential for battery-operated cameras even in countries with reliable electricity. Some companies encourage tours of other companies, some take advantage of any way that people discover new possibilities – even on vacation on their own time in foreign countries where they see something they've never seen before. People within the company can also stimulate each other, especially through cross-fertilization of ideas by the contributions from people from different locations with different perspectives.

Leaders must create a culture that permits discussion of half-formed embryonic possibilities. The widely touted product-development firm IDEO holds open brainstorming sessions. Ocean Spray's regular, open, cross-level product development forums allowed a lower-level engineer at Ocean Spray to surface the idea for packaging innovations that led the beverage company to steal a march on its much-larger competitors by being the first to adopt the paper bottle. For some companies, their employees are also product users who can get involved in product development and offer important feedback regardless of position. Gillette tests its razors and blades on male employees who come to work unshaven and agree to use different products for each side of their faces. Xerox innovators involve Xerox employees (all of whom handle documents) in the search for document management solutions.

Leaders must create a culture that permits discussion of half-formed embryonic possibilities.

Product-developers have always focussed on innovation, but in the future, many others who are not called "creative" will be charged with leading innovation. There will be a new role for people to serve as "change agents" with the mandate to find and lead innovation projects within many fields and functions. And "lead sites" will take on the responsibility for developing or prototyping innovations useful in other parts of the company – field offices acting as centers for experiments on behalf of the whole. Internal new ventures focussed on a new market or new technology often create concepts that are widely applicable to the mainstream. BankBoston's First Community Bank (FCB) was designed as a bank-within-a-bank to serve neglected urban constituencies in inner cities which often had limited experience with banks; the user-friendly "First Step" savings and lending products FCB developed became desirable bank-wide offerings for any newcomer to banking.

KALEIDOSCOPE-RICH COMMUNITIES

For innovative companies, the most sought-after resource is increasingly human capital, not financial capital. Silicon Valley is awash with capital eager to fund new ventures but short of talent to run them. John Doerr, venture capitalist behind Netscape, has said that the product of Silicon Valley is not silicon but networking, and its scarcest resource is technical and managerial talent. The more desirable that talent, the more it will be sought in a world labor market – especially as professionals are educated to common world standards – facilitated by information technology. Coopers & Lybrand uses the Internet to recruit for entry level accounting and auditing jobs, including on-line assessment tools in its "Springboard" system.

Education by companies is already a $55 billion industry in the United States, and it will grow elsewhere, reflecting the need for lifelong learning. In-house education is related not to a company's size but to its market complexity and its use of new workplace practices such as team-based work, cross-functional integration, and supplier partnerships – hallmarks of world-class companies.

But leaders seeking more innovation inside their companies also have to look outside, to see whether the setting in which they operate, the communities from which they draw their talent, give them access to brainpower and to the stimulation that activates the kaleidoscopes of the mind. Excellence in primary, secondary, and higher education is one obvious characteristic of innovation-facilitating environments, but only one. Infrastructures for knowledge development and translating knowledge into commercial enterprises, supported by entrepreneurial national and local cultures, ensure that innovation thrives. Many parts of the United States exemplify the conditions associated with innovation and entrepreneurial flexibility. Silicon Valley's vitality and America's job-creating small business sector are envied by European economic development officials. American entrepreneurship involves a widely-shared belief in possibility, not inevitability (as some other cultures have it) as well as a tolerance for risk and failure. Once in danger of losing the innovative edge, America has restored its lead; the share of US patents granted to foreigners, which rose during the eighties, has declined. Since innovation-packed products and services offering high customer utility can command premium prices in world markets or stimulate demand, high levels of innovation are generally associated with higher overall wages and greater prosperity.

Regions specializing in concepts, such as Silicon Valley and the San Francisco Bay Area, Greater Boston and Eastern Massachusetts, or Greater Seattle and Puget Sound, are magnets for brainpower, which in turn is channeled into knowledge industries. The competitiveness of these regions comes from continuous innovation. They set world standards and export both knowledge and knowledge-based products that enjoy temporary monopolies and command premium prices. Greater Boston, for example, leads in innovation through educational and research institutions that attract brainpower and put it to work creating new ideas or developing the next generation of technologies; abundant support systems for entrepreneurs – sources of capital and encouragement from private and public sectors; ways to transfer promising ideas from laboratories to businesses; professional service providers (legal, banking, marketing support) familiar with industry requirements and the needs of fledgling businesses. Kaleidoscope think is further aided by dense networks within and across industries – including industry councils to informal interactions – that encourage a flow of people and ideas, facilitate alliances and partnerships, and ensure that people's imaginations are stimulated by constant exposure to new thinking.

Places in which new knowledge is valued, people learn from and teach one another, and resources are available for new ventures are more likely to keep those kaleidoscopes twisting. Such places will be world centers of innovation for the global information age. Business leaders increasingly understand that one of their new roles in the 21st century is to contribute to creating such environments in the communities in which their companies operate. World-class leaders will be cosmopolitans who avoid insularity, enjoy the challenge of confronting new and different ideas, encourage cross-fertilization and learning across boundaries, and support their people in developing and using their brainpower in pursuit of innovation.

At the turn of the 20th century, one symbol of the emerging mass manufacturing industrial era was the engineer's slide rule. A century later, we need new symbols for the global information era. I nominate the kaleidoscope – symbol of ever-changing patterns and endless new possibilities, powered by human imagination.

NOTES

CHAPTER 1

1 Huey, John and Colvin, Geoffrey (1999) "The Jack and Herb Show," *Fortune*, 11 January, p.163–166.

2 Wetlaufer, Suzy (1999) "Driving change: An interview with Ford Motor Company's Jacques Nasser," *Harvard Business Review*, March-April, p.77–88.

3 Bylinsky, Gene (1998) "How to bring out better products faster," *Fortune*, 23 November, 238[B–T].

4 http://www.insead.fr/IVC/Guide/Manager

5 Smith, Alison (1998) "Marketing global brands: The global consumer is a myth," *Financial Times*, 2 April.

6 Govindarajan, Vijay and Gupta, Anil (1998) "Global business: Turning global presence into global competitive advantage," *Mastering Global Business, Financial Times*, October.

7 Pfeffer, Jeffrey (1998) *The human equation: Building profits by putting people first*, Harvard Business School Press.

8 Reich, Robert B. (1998) "The company of the future," *Fast Company*, November, 124–150.

9 Deogun, Nikhil (1998) "Soft-drink marketers at Triarc deftly give Snapple back its 'Buzz'," *The Wall Street Journal*, 14 December, 1.

10 http://www.enron.com

11 Dillon, Pat (1998) "Innovation," *Fast Company*, December, 132–136.

CHAPTER 2

1 El Sawy, O.A. (1983) "Temporal perspective and managerial attention: A study of chief executive strategic behavior" (Ph.D. diss., Stanford University). *See also* El Sawy, O.A., (Nov 1988) "Temporal biases in strategic attention" (research paper, Department of Decision Sciences, School of Business Administration, University of Southern California).

2 *See* Kouzes, J.M. and Posner, B.Z. (1995) *The leadership challenge: How to keep getting extraordinary things done in organizations,* San Francisco: Jossey-Bass, and Kouzes, J.M and Posner, B.Z. (1993) *Credibility: How leaders gain and lose it, why people demand it*, San Francisco: Jossey-Bass. All the stories and examples of leadership in this chapter are drawn from the authors' own case research.

3 "Melissa Poe," *Caring People* [6] (Fall 1993), 66, supplemented by interview by authors with Trish Poe on 3 November 1994.

4 Blum, A. (1980) *Annapurna: A woman's place,* San Francisco: Sierra Club Books.

5 Blum, A., p.12.

6 Blum, A., p.12.

7 Arlene Blum quoted in P. Labarre, "Here's how to make it to the top," *Fast Company* (Issue 17, September 1992), p.72.

8 Kohn, A. (1986) *No contest: The case against competition,* Boston: Houghton Mifflin, p.55.

9 *Innovation Survey* (1999) London: PricewaterhouseCoopers, p.3.

10 For more information about this story and others in this section, *see* Kouzes, J.M. and Posner, B.Z. (1999) *Encouraging the heart: A leader's guide to rewarding and recognizing others,* San Francisco: Jossey-Bass.

11 Telephone interview with Jodi Taylor, Ph.D., Center for Creative Leadership, Colorado Springs, Colorado, April 1998.

12 The FIRO-B was developed by Will Schutz. It measures two dimensions of three factors. It measures the extent to which a person both *expresses* and *wants* (a) inclusion, (b) control, and (c) affection. *See* Schutz, W. (1966) *The interpersonal underworld (FIRO),* Palo Alto, CA: Science & Behavior Books. *Also see* Schutz, W. (1989) *FIRO: A three-dimensional theory of interpersonal behavior,* Mill Valley, CA: Will Schutz Associates.

CHAPTER 3

1 Schumpeter, Joseph (1911/1934) *The theory of economic development,* Cambridge, MA, Harvard University Press.

2 Hamel, Gary and Prahalad, C.K. (May–June 1990) "The core competence of the corporation," *Harvard Business Review.*

3 Chandler, Alfred D. (1962) *Strategy and structure,* Cambridge, MA, MIT Press.

4 March, James G. (1991) "Exploration and exploitation in organizational learning," *Organization Science,* Vol. 2, No. 1.

5 March, James G. and Olsen, Johan (1976) *Ambiguity and choice in organizations,* Bergen, Universitetsforlag.

6 Kao, John (1996) *Jamming,* HarperCollins Business.

7 *Fast Company,* June–July, 1998.

8 *Fortune,* 12 January 1998.

9 Kelleher, Herb (1997) "A culture of commitment," *Leader to Leader,* spring.

CHAPTER 4

1 For example, *see* Kanter, R.M. (1997) *On the frontiers of management,* Boston, MA: Harvard Business School Press; and Drucker, P.F. (1986) *The frontiers of management,* New York: Truman Talley Books.

2 Information and quotes from the individuals in this article were culled from interviews conducted as a part of my research and course development on how people learn to lead and on the evolution of business partnerships in the new technology industries. For more complete accounts, *see* the following Harvard Business School cases: "Intersoft of Argentina (A), (B), and (C)," HBS nos. 497–025, 297–026, 497–027; "Randy Haykin: The making of an entrepreneur (A)," HBS no. 498–044; "Franco Bernabè at ENI (A), (B), (C)," HBS nos. 498–034, 498–035, 498–040; "de Passe Entertainment and Creative Partners," HBS no. 494–013; "Lark International Entertainment, Ltd. (A), (B), and (C)," HBS nos. 499–023, 499–024, 499–025.

3 Gardner, H. (1993) *Creating minds,* NY: Basic Books, p.44 (his emphasis). *See*

also Csikszentmihalyi, M. (1996) *Creativity*, NY HarperCollins Publishers, and Bennis, W., Biederman, P.W. (1997) *Organizing genius*, Reading, MA: Addison-Wesley Publishing Company, Inc.

4 McCall, M. (1998) *High flyers*, Boston, MA: Harvard Business School Press.

5 For more on Franco Bernabè and the transformation of Eni, *see* Hill, L.A. and Wetlaufer, S. (1998) "Leadership when there's no one to ask," *Harvard Business Review*, July–August, 81–94.

6 Kelley R. and Caplan, J. (1993) "How Bell Labs creates star performers," *Harvard Business Review*, July–August, 128–139.

7 *See*, for example, Leonard, Dorothy, and Swap, Walter (1999) *When sparks fly: Igniting group creativity,* Boston: Harvard Business School Press.

8 Hirschhorn, L. (1992) "The new boundaries of the 'boundaryless' company," *Harvard Business Review*, May–June, 4–16.

9 *See*, for example, Murninghan, J.K. and Conlon, D.E. (1991) "The dynamics of intense work groups: A study of British string quartets," *Administrative Science Quarterly*, *36*, June, 165–186.

10 Hill, L.A. (spring 1998) "Developing the star performer," *Leader to Leader*, New York: Drucker Foundation, 30–37. For more elaborated descriptions of the paradoxes inherent in team life, *see* for example Bradford, D.L. and Cohen, A.R. (1984) *Managing for excellence: The guide to developing high performance contemporary organizations,* New York: Wiley, and Smith, K.K. and Berg, D.N. (1987) *Paradoxes of group life: Understanding conflict, paralysis, and movement in group dynamics,* San Francisco: Jossey-Bass.

11 Hill, L.A. (1991) "Beyond the myth of the perfect mentor," Harvard Business School no. 491–096.

12 Nohria, N. and Berkley, J.D. (1995) "From structure to structuring: A pragmatic perspective on organizational design," (working paper).

13 Drucker, P. (1992) "There's more than one kind of team," *Wall Street Journal*, 11 February.

14 Pisano, G. (1996) *The development factory: Unlocking the potential of process innovation,* Boston: Harvard Business School Press.

15 Hansen, M.T., Nohria, N. and Tierney, T. (1999) "What's your strategy for managing knowledge?" *Harvard Business Review*, *72* (2), March–April: 106–116. In their article, they make a distinction between personalized and codification knowledge management. Millennium's circumstances clearly demand the former.

16 Christensen, C.M. (1997) *The innovator's dilemma*, Boston, MA: Harvard Business School Press.

17 Kotter, J.P. (1990) "What leaders really do," *Harvard Business Review*, May–June: 103–111. Kotter makes a distinction between leadership and management. Leadership is about coping with change: setting direction, aligning people, and motivating and inspiring. Managing is about coping with complexity: planning and budgeting, organizing and staffing, and controlling and problem-solving.

18 Winblad, A. "Leadership secrets of a venture capitalist," *Leader to Leader*, New York: Drucker Foundation, p.184.

19 *See*, for example, Hill, L.A. (1992) *Becoming a manager*, Boston, MA: Harvard Business School Press, for a discussion of the importance of the ability to cope with the emotions and stresses of the burdens of leadership.

CHAPTER 5

1 Quinn, R.E., and Rohrbaugh, J. (1983) "A spatial model of effectiveness criteria: Towards a competing values approach to organizational analysis," *Management Science, 29*:3, 363–377.

2 Hampden-Turner, C. (1990) *Charting the corporate mind: From dilemma to strategy*, Oxford: Basil Blackwell; and Handy, C. (1994) *The empty raincoat: Making sense of the future*, London: Hutchinson.

3 Hampden-Turner, ibid.

4 Hampden-Turner, ibid.

5 Miller, D. (1990) *The Icarus paradox: How exceptional companies bring about their own downfall,* New York: Harper Business.

6 Pascale, R.T. (1990). *Managing on the edge: How successful companies use conflict to stay ahead*, London and New York: Viking.

7 Tichy, N.M., and Sherman, S. (1993) *Control your destiny or someone else will*, New York: Harper Business, p.60.

8 Eisenhardt, K.M., Kahwajy, J.L., and Bourgeois, L.J. III (1997) "How management teams can have a good fight," *Harvard Business Review* (July–August): 77–85.

9 Schein, E.H. (1998) "The family as a metaphor for culture: Some comments on the DEC story," *Journal of Management Inquiry, 7*:2: 131–132.

10 Kets de Vries, M.F.R. (1994) "Percy Barnevik and ABB," INSEAD Case no. 05/94–4308, Fontainebleau.

11 Evans, P.A.L. (1993) "Dosing the glue: Applying human resource technology to build the global organization," *Research in personnel and human resources management, Suppl.3*, Greenwich CT.: JAI Press; and Evans, P.A.L. (1992) "Management development as glue technology," *Human Resource Planning 14:4.*

12 Bartlett, C.A., and Ghoshal, S. (1990) "Matrix management: Not a structure, a frame of mind," *Harvard Business Review*, July–August: 138–145.

13 Tichy and Sherman, op. cit., p.66.

14 Collins, J.C., and Porras, J.I. (1994) *Built to last*, New York: Harper Business.

15 Kets de Vries, M.F.R., and Miller, D. (1984) *The neurotic organization: Diagnosing and changing counterproductive styles of management*, San Francisco: Jossey-Bass.

16 Kets de Vries, M.F.R. (1994), op. cit.

17 Tichy and Sherman, op. cit., p.11.

18 Rosenzweig, P., and Raillard, B. (1992) "Accor (A)," Harvard Business School case 9–393–012.

19 For further details on this tension analysis, *see* Evans, P.A.L., and Genadry, N. (1998) "A duality-based prospective for strategic human resource management," in Wright, P., Dyer, L., Boudreau, J. and Milkovich, G. (eds), *Research in personnel and human resources management: Strategic HRM in the 21st century*, Greenwich, CT: JAI Press.

20 Evans, P.A.L., and Bartolomé, F. (1979) *Must success cost so much?*, London: Grant McIntyre; New York: Basic Books.

CHAPTER 6

1 Brown, Eryn (1999) "America's most admired companies," *Fortune*, 1 March, p.70.

2 "Four pioneers reflect on leadership," (1998) *Training and Development*, July, p.38.

3 Russo, Jean-Pierre, "Operating principles," CEO report, A supplement to *Chief Executive* magazine, "Inventing new industries: A field guide to revolution without anarchy," p.21.

4 Drucker, Peter F. (1999) *"Managing oneself,"* Harvard Business School Publishing. Summary description – http://www.hbsp.harvard.edu

5 Personal interview with Edward Travaglianti, chairman and CEO, European American Bank, March 1999.

6 Personal interview with Michael A. Wellman, president, global specialty practices, Korn Ferry International, March 1999.

7 Tiersten, Sylvia (1999) "Lucent Technologies' Carly Fiorina," *Investor's Business Daily*, March 4, p.A8.

8 "Four pioneers reflect on leadership," (1998) *Training and Development*, July, p.41.

9 Row, Heath (1998) "Feeling connected to your work brings energy to the workplace," *Fast Company*, December, p.192.

10 Personal interview with Joseph Corella, systems engineering manager, Microsoft Corporation, March 1999.

11 Hallowell, Edward M. (1999) "The human moment at work," *Harvard Business Review*, January–February, p.60.

12 Hallowell, Edward M., op. cit., p.63.

13 Personal interview, March 1999.

14 Tiersten, Sylvia, op. cit.

15 Personal interview with Bernard F. Reynolds, chairman and CEO, ASI Solutions Incorporated, March 1999.

16 "Four pioneers reflect on leadership," (1998) *Training and Development*, July, p.41.

17 "Four pioneers reflect on leadership," (1998) *Training and Development*, July, p.38.

18 Personal interview with Edwin S. Marks, president, Carl Marks & Co. Inc., March 1999.

19 Personal interview with Dr James M. Shuart, president, Hofstra University, March 1999.

20 Personal interview, March 1999.

21 "Four pioneers reflect on leadership," *Training and Development*, July, p.40.

22 Personal interview, March 1999.

23 Personal interview with Bernard F. Reynolds, chairman and CEO, ASI Solutions Incorporated, March 1999.

24 Tichy, Noel M. and Cohen, Eli (1998) "The teaching organization," *Training and Development*, July, p.28.

25 Personal interview with Helene Fortunoff, secretary treasurer of Fortunoff Fine Jewelry, March 1999.

CHAPTER 7

1 Ames, Joan Evelyn (1997) *Mastery: Interviews with 30 remarkable people*, Rudra Press, Portland, Oregon.

2 Farren, Caela (1997) *Who's running your career? Creating stable work in unstable times,* Bard Press, Austin Texas.

Reference: Bennis, Warren, and Ward Biederman, Patricia (1997) *Organizing genius: The secrets of creative collaboration,* Addison-Wesley Publishing Company, Reading, MA;

Frankel, Lois P. (1997) *Overcoming your strengths: 8 reasons why successful people derail and how to get back on track,* New York, Harmony Books;

Hartwick, P.J. and Farren, Caela (1996) "Specialist or generalist? A false dichotomy: An important distinction," pp.115–132, *Future vision: Ideas, insights and strategies,* edited by Howard F. Didsbury, Jr., World Future Society, Bethesda, MD;

Peters, Thomas (1997) *The circle of innovation: You can't shrink your way to greatness,* Alfred A. Knopf, New York.

CHAPTER 8

1 Handy, C. (1994) *The empty raincoat* (2nd ed.) Great Britain: Arrow Books.

2 Howard, A. (1995) "Rethinking the psychology of work" in Howard, A. (ed.) *The changing nature of work,* San Francisco: Jossey-Bass Inc.

3 Evans, P.B., and Wurster, T.S. (1997) "Strategy and the new economics of information," *Harvard Business Review, 75*(5) 70–82.

4 Dainty, P., and Andersen, M. (1996) *The capable executive: Effective perform-ance in senior management,* Basingstoke, Macmillan.

5 Pfeffer, J. (1998) "Seven practices of highly successful organizations," *California Management Review, 40*(2) 96–124.

6 Hall, D.T. (1996) "Protean careers of the 21st century," *Academy of Management Executive, 10*(4) 8–16.

7 Hope, J., and Hope, T. (1997) *Competing in the third wave: The ten key man-agement issues of the information age,* Boston: Harvard Business School Press.

8 Tetzeli, R. (1994) "Surviving information overload," *Fortune, 130,* 26–29, 11 July.

9 Veiga, J.F., and Dechant, K. (1997) "Wired world woes: www.help" *Academy of Management Executive, 11*(3) 73–79.

10 Evans, P.B., and Wurster, T.S. (1997) "Strategy and the new economics of infor-mation," *Harvard Business Review, 75*(5) 70–82.

11 Kotter, J.P., and Heskett, J.L. (1992) *Corporate culture and performance,* New York: Macmillan.

12 Kouzes, J., and Posner, B. (1997) "Building credibility," *AIM Management,* 5–7.

13 Guyon, J. (1997) "Why is the world's most profitable company turning itself inside out?" *Fortune, 136,* 62–67, 4 August.

14 Mintzberg, H. (1994) *The rise and fall of strategic planning,* New York: Prentice Hall.

15 O'Reilly, B. (1997) "The secrets of America's most admired corporations: New ideas, new products," *Fortune,* 42–54 3 March.

16 Van de Vliet, A. (1997) "Gary Hamel," *Management Today,* 52–53 July.

17 Goleman, D. (1996) *Emotional intelligence,* London: Bloomsbury Publishing.

18 Howard, A. (1995) "Rethinking the psychology of work," in Howard A. (ed.) *The changing nature of work,* San Francisco: Jossey-Bass Inc.

19 O'Reilly, C.A. (1983) "The use of information in organizational decision making: A model and some propositions," in Staw, B.M. and Cummings, L.I. (eds) *Research in organizational behaviour* (vol. 5) Greenwich: JAI Press.

20 Davenport, T.H, and Prusak, L. (1997) *Information ecology,* New York: Oxford University Press.

21 Dainty, P., and Anderson, M. (1996) *The capable executive: Effective perform-*

ance in senior management, Basingstoke: Macmillan.

22 Senge, P. (1990) "The leader's new work: Building learning organizations," *Sloan Management Review, 32*(1) 7–23.

23 Isenberg, D.J. (1984) "How senior managers think," *Harvard Business Review, 62*(6) 80–90.

24 Drucker, P.F., Dyson, E., Handy, C., Saffo, P., and Senge, P.M. (1997) "Looking ahead: Implications of the present," *Harvard Business Review, 75*(5) 18–32.

25 Vandermerwe, S., and Vandermerwe, A. (1991) "Making strategic change happen," *European Management Journal, 9*(2) 174–181.

CHAPTER 9

1 Porter, M.E. (1980) *Competitive strategy*, New York: Free Press.

2 Simon, H.A. (1991) "Organizations and markets," *Journal of Economic Perspectives*, 5, (2): 25–44.

3 Schumpeter, J.A. (1947) *The theory of economic development*, Cambridge, MA: Harvard University Press.

4 Bartlett, C.A. and Ghoshal, S. (1995) "Rebuilding behavioral context: Turn process reengineering into people rejuvenation," *Sloan Management Review*, Fall, 11–23.

5 For a detailed theoretical argument that substantiates this point, *see* Ghoshal, S., and Moran, P. (1996) "Bad for practice: A critique for transaction cost theory," *Academy of Management Review*, January, 13–47.

6 Schumpeter, J.A. (1942) *Capitalism, socialism and democracy*, London: Unwin University Books, p.83.

7 In economic theory, this condition for market exchange is described as the "double coincidence." Its fulfillment requires what Coleman describes as "reciprocal viability" – *see* Coleman, J.S. (1990) *The foundations of social theory*, Cambridge, MA: Harvard University Press.

8 For a discussion of some commonly cited examples of such "co-ordination failures" *see* Milgrom, P.R., and Roberts, J. (1992) *Economics, organization and management*, Englewood Cliffs, NJ: Prentice-Hall.

9 To trace the theoretical development of this concept of organizational advantage, *see* Ghoshal, S., and Moran, P. (1996) "Bad for practice: A critique for transaction cost theory," *Academy of Management Review*, January, 13–47; Ghoshal, S., Moran, P., and Almeida Costa, L. (1995) "The essence of the megacorporation: Shared context, not structural hierarchy," *Journal of Institutional and Theoretical Economics*, 151(4 December) 748–759; Moran, P. and Ghoshal, S. (1999) "Markets, firms and the process of economic development," *Academy of Management Review*.

10 This is what Coleman describes as "independent viability" and "global viability" which, according to Moran and Ghoshal, characterize organizations. *See* Coleman, J.S. (1990) *The foundations of social theory*, Cambridge, MA: Harvard University Press; Moran, P., and Ghoshal, S. (1996) "Value creation by firms," in Keys, J.B. and Dosier, L.N. (eds) *Academy of Management Best Paper Proceedings*.

11 Ghoshal, S. and Bartlett, C.A. (1997) *The individualized corporation*, New York: HarperCollins.

12 This is a core argument of the theory of internal labor markets – *see* Doeringer, P.B., and Poire, M.J. (1971) *Internal labor markets and manpower analysis*, Lexington, MA: D.C. Heath and Company.

13 *See* Cappelli, P. (1995) "Rethinking employment," *British Journal of Industrial Relations*, 33(4): 563–602.

14 Leonard-Barton, D. (1992) "Core capabilities and core rigidities: A paradox in managing new product development," *Strategic Management Journal*, 13: 111–125.

15 Kanter was perhaps one of the earliest authors to argue for this new employment contract. *See* Kanter, R.M. (1989) "The new managerial word," *Harvard Business Review*, Nov–Dec: 85–92. A very similar argument has been made by Waterman, R.H., Jr., Waterman, J.A. and Collard, B.A. (1994) "Toward a career-resilient workforce," *Harvard Business Review*, July–August: 87–95.

CHAPTER 10

1 Prahalad, C.K. and Lieberthal, Kenneth (1998) "The end of corporate imperialism," *Harvard Business Review*, July–August, pp. 68–79.

CHAPTER 11

1 Hedberg, B. (1981) "How organizations learn and unlearn," in Nystrom, P.L. and Starbuck, W.H., *Handbook of organizational design: Vol. 1*. Oxford: Oxford University Press.

2 Gaarder, Jostein (1997) "Descartes," *Sophie's world: a novel about the history of philosophy*, London, Phoenix, pp.229–240.

3 Lewitt, H.J. (1986) *Corporate pathfinders: Building vision and values into organizations*, Homewood: Dow Jones-Irwin.

4 Newman, W.H. (1975) *Constructive control*, Englewood Cliffs, NJ: Prentice-Hall.

CHAPTER 12

1 French, R. and Grey, C. (eds) (1996) *Rethinking management education*, London, 1–16.

2 Giddens, A. (1994) *Beyond left and right: The future of radical politics*, Cambridge.

3 Thomas, A.B. and Anthony, P.D. (1996) "Can management education be educational?" in French, R. and Grey, C. op. cit., 22.

4 Dearden, R. on "Education and training," (1996) as quoted by Thomas A.B. and Anthony, P.D. op. cit., 23.

5 Think of Mintzberg, H. *Mintzberg on management*, New York, 1989.

6 Watson, S.R. (1993) "The place for universities in management education, in *Journal of General Management*, 19(2):23.

7 Kotter, J.P. and Heskett, J.L. (1992) *Corporate culture and performance*, New York.

8 Thomas, A.B. and Anthony, P.D. (1966) op. cit., 32.

9 Elster, J. (1983) *Sour grapes: Studies in the subversion of rationality*, Cambridge, 54.

10 Chia, R. (1997) Process philosophy and management learning: Cultivating Foresight in management education" in Burgoyne, J. and Reynolds, M. (eds) *Management learning: Integrating perspectives in theory and practice*, London, 72.

11 Chia, R. (1996) *Organizational analysis as deconstructive practice*, Berlin, 2–3.

12 Wordsworth, William, *The Prelude, Book II.*

13 Chia, R. (1997) op. cit., 76 e.v.

14 Bergson, H. (1913) *An introduction to metaphysics*, London, 44.

15 Bergson, H. op. cit.

16 Wittgenstein, L. (1992) *Tractatus logico-philosophicus* (5.6) London, 149.

17 Rorty, R. (1998) *Truth and progress: Philosophical papers III*, Cambridge.

18 Whitehead, A.N. (1929) *Process and reality*, New York.

19 Carroll, L. (1960) *Alice's Adventures in Wonderland*, New York.

20 Whitehead, A.N. (1933) op. cit., 120, as quoted by Chia in Chia, R. (1997) *op. cit*, 83.

21 Whitehead, A.N. (1929) *The aims of education*, New York, 99.

22 Goodwin, R. (1994) *How the leopard changed its spots*, New York, 169–170.

23 Audi, R. (1998) *Epistomology: A contemporary introduction in the theory of knowledge*, London, 2–5.

24 Chia, R. op. cit., 1997:87.

25 Stacey, R.D. (1996) *Strategic management and organizational dynamics*, London, 381.

26 Alvesson, M. and Willmott, H. (1992) "Critical theory and management studies: An introduction" in Alvesson, M. and Willmott, H. (eds) *Critical management studies*, London, 1.

27 Peters, B.K.G. (1997) "The past and the future," in *Opportunities and threats of European business schools in third millennium: A dean's prospective*, seminar report, 28 November, 17.

28 Vince, R. (1996) *Managing change: Reflections on equality and management learning*, Bristol.

29 Drucker, P. (1974) *Management: Tasks, responsibilities, practices*, Oxford.

30 Chia, R. and Morgan, S. (1996) Educating the philosopher-manager: De-signing the times" in *Management learning,* 27 (1) 37–64.

31 Roberts, J. "Management education and the limits of technical rationality: The conditions and consequences of management practice" in French, R. and Grey, C. (eds) (1996) op. cit., 73.

32 In 1989 in Paris, London, and Amsterdam the first conferences were organized on the quality and lack thereof of our planet.

33 Latour, B. (1993) *We have never been modern*, New York, 9.

34 *See* Essers, J. and Schreinemakers, J. (1996) "The conception of knowledge under information in knowledge management" in Schreinemakers, J. (ed.) *Knowledge management: Organization, competence and methodology*, Wrzburg, 100–103.

35 Essers, J. and Schreinemakers, J. op. cit., 102.

36 *See* Lyotard, J.F. (1979) *La condition postmoderne, rapport sur le savoir*, Paris.

37 Lyotard, J.F. (1986) *L'enthousiasme, la critique kantienne de l'histoire*, Paris.

38 Essers, J. and Schreinemakers, J. *op. cit.*, 112.

39 *See* Bauman, Z. (1997) *Postmodernity and its discontents*, New York.

CHAPTER 13

1 *Acknowledgements*: The authors would like to express their appreciation to the consortium benchmarking study participants. We would like to extend a special thanks to the partner organization representatives who have taken time out of their busy schedules to participate in this study and share their knowledge and learnings with the sponsor group. The project would never have taken place without the leadership and staff support of the American Productivity and

Quality Center (APQC) and the American Society for Training & Development (ASTD). Special advisor for the study was Jim Kouzes, chairman, the Tom Peters Group.

CHAPTER 14

1 *See The Economist*, 18 April 1992.
2 Strebel, Paul (1996) "Why do employees resist change?" *Harvard Business Review*, May/June 86.
3 *See The fifth discipline fieldbook: Strategies for building learning organizations*, Senge, Peter, Kleiner, Art, Roberts, Charlotte, Ross, Rick, Smith, Bryan, New York: Doubleday Currency (1994).
4 Several of these change initiatives are documented in "Learning histories," ethnographic studies of the complex change told from multiple perspectives. *See* the SoL web page for more information: sol-ne.org and Kleiner, A., and Roth, G. (1997) "How to make experience your company's best teacher, *Harvard Business Review*, September–October 172–177.
5 Senge, P. (1990) "The leaders" new work: Building learning organizations," *Sloan Management Review*.
6 Senge, P. (1996) "Leading learning communities: The bold, the powerful, and the invisible," in Hesselbein F., *et al, The leader of the future*, San Francisco: Jossey-Bass.
7 Senge, P., op. cit.
8 Videotaped interview (1997) "*Leadership video*" (available through Innovation Associates Inc., Waltham MA Fax: 1–781–398–8523).
9 Wenger, E. (1998) *Communities of practice: Learning, meaning, and identity*, New York: Cambridge University Press.
10 Senge, P., and Kaeufer, K. "Towards an ecology of leadership," SoL working paper.
11 All these ideas are outlined in detail in Senge, P., Kleiner, A., Roberts, C., Ross, R., Roth, G., Smith, B. (1999) *The dance of change. A fieldbook for sustaining momentum in a learning organization*, New York: Doubleday Currency.
12 Summarized from *The fifth discipline fieldbook: The dance of change: Sustaining momentum in building a learning organization*, ibid.
13 Bailyn, L. (1993) *Breaking the mold: women, men, and time in the new corporate world,* New York: Free Press.
14 Senge et al, op. cit.
15 Roth, G. and Kleiner, A. (1996) *The learning initiative at the AutoCo Epsilon Program*, 1991–1994, Center for Organizational Learning, MIT, Working Paper 18.005, Cambridge.
16 Roth, G., and Kleiner, A. op. cit.
17 Kleiner, A. (1996) *The age of heretics. Heroes, outlaws, and the forerunners of corporate change*, New York: Currency Doubleday.
18 Cooperider, D.L. and Srivastava, S. (1987) "Appreciative inquiry in organizational life," *Research in organizational change and development*, Vol 1: 129–169.
19 *See*, for example, Hamel, G. (1996) "Strategy as revolution," *Harvard Business Review*, July–Aug.
20 *See;* for example, Senge, *et al,* (1999) 444–476 for examples of creating new learning infrastructures.
21 *See* Forrester, J.W. (1971) "The counterintuitive nature of social systems,"

Technology Review, January. 52–68 (also in *The collected papers of Jay W. Forrester*, Cambridge, Mass: MIT Press, 1975); and Senge, P. (1990) *The fifth discipline*, New York: Doubleday/Currency, 58–60.

CHAPTER 15

1 On the strategic role of mass customization, *see* Pine, B.J. (1993) *Mass customization: The new frontier in business competition*, Boston MA: Harvard Business School Publishing.
2 We borrow this phrase from Giddens, A. (1991) *Modernity and self-identity*, Stanford CA: Stanford University Press.
3 Interestingly, the management literature on flexibility is concerned primarily with firm-level design and tends to address people issues from this perspective only.
4 The British sociologist Anthony Giddens has synthesized a great deal of empirical research and theory on the distinctive features and trends that characterize life in modern societies, particularly in his books *The consequences of modernity* and *modernity and self-identity*. Our thinking in the paragraphs that follow has been substantially influenced by his writing.
5 Hammonds, K., Zellner, W., and Melcher, R. (1996) "Writing a new social contract – O.K., job security is dead. What happens from here?" *Business Week*, March 11.
6 "The Daddy Trap," *Business Week*, 21 September 1998.
7 "Europe's unhappy world of work," *Financial Times*, 14 May, 1997.
8 Peters, T. (1992) *Liberation management*, New York: Alfred A. Knopf.
9 Ghoshal, S. and Bartlett, C. (1997) *The individualized corporation*, New York: Harper Business.
10 Pfeffer, J. (1998) *The human equation*, Boston MA: Harvard Business School Publishing.
11 "We want you to stay. Really," *Business Week,* 22 June 1998, pp.67–72.
12 *Financial Times,* 12/13 July 1997.
13 It is, perhaps, because people are no longer misled by this notion that empowerment has become the frequent butt of management jokes.
14 Semler, R. (1993) *Maverick*, New York: Warner Books.
15 This case is discussed in Kimberly, J. and Bouchikhi, H. (1995) "The dynamics of organizational development and change: How the past shapes the present and constrains the future," *Organization Science*, 6/1:9–18.
16 Some caution is needed here with regard to the tendency of many women and minority managers to mimic mainstream managerial attitudes and behaviors to legitimize their membership of the elite.
17 Kumar, N. (1996) "The power of trust in manufacturer-retailer relationships," *Harvard Business Review*, November–December, 92–106.
18 For more elaboration, *see* Bouchikhi, H. (1998) "Living with and building on complexity: A constructivist perspective on organizations," *Organization*, 5/2:217–232.
19 The same ISR survey reported by the *Financial Times* (14 May 1997) shows that employees in Northern European countries have the highest satisfaction scores in Europe. These countries are also the most democratized/egalitarian societies.
20 Some of these forms already exist in the form of enduring co-ordinated partnerships among independent entrepreneurs.

CHAPTER 16

1 *See*, for example, the following publications: Arzeni, Sergio and Pellegrin, Jean-Pierre (1997) "Entrepreneurship and local development," *Organisation for economic cooperation and development, the OECD Observer*, no. 204, February/March, 27–29; Birch, David L. (1987) *Job creation in America: How our smallest companies put the most people to work*, New York: Free Press; Tapscott, Don, Lowy, Alex, and Ticoll, David (eds) (1998) *Blueprint to the digital economy: Creating wealth in the era of e-business*, New York: McGraw-Hill; Williamson, Oliver E. and Winter, Sidney G. (eds) (1991) *The nature of the firm: Origins, evolution, and development*, New York: Oxford University Press; Carney, Mick (1998) "The competitiveness of networked production: The role of trust and asset specificity," *Journal of Management Studies* 35, no. 4, July, 457–479; Andrews, Philip P. and Hahn, Jerome (1998) "Transforming supply chains into value webs," *Strategy and Leadership*, July 1, 6–11; Normann, Richard and Ramirez, Rafael (1993) "From value chain to value constellation: Designing interactive strategy," *Harvard Business Review*, July/August, 65–77; Lorenzoni, Gianni and Baden-Fuller, Charles (1995) "Creating a strategic center to manage a web of partners," *California Management Review* 37, no. 3, spring, 146–163; Weiner, Michael, Nohria, Nitin, Hickman, Amanda and Smith, Huard (1997) "Value networks: The future of the US electric utility industry," *Sloan Management Review* 38, no. 4, Summer, 21–34; and Kasarda, John D., and Rondinelli, Dennis A. (1998) "Innovative infrastructure for agile manufacturers," *Sloan Management Review* 39, no. 2, Winter, 73–82.

2 Carney, Mick (1998) "The competitiveness of networked production: The role of trust and asset specificity," *Journal of Management Studies* 35, no. 4, July, 460.

3 Brandenburger, Adam M., and Nalebuff, Barry J. (1995) "The right game: Use game theory to shape strategy," *Harvard Business Review*, July/August, 57–71.

4 *See*, for example, the following publications in regard to the flattening of reporting and accountability structures: Goffee, Rob and Jones, Gareth (1998) *The character of a corporation: How your company's culture can make or break your business*, New York: HarperCollins; Hope, Jeremy and Fraser, Robin (1998) "Measuring performance in the new organisational model," *Management Accounting* (British) 76, no. 6, June, 22–23; Clemmer, Jim (1998) "Liberated performance," *Executive Excellence* 15, no. 9, September, 17; Seidmann, Abraham and Sundararajan, Arun (1997) "Competing in information-intensive services: Analysing the impact of task consolidation and employee empowerment," *Journal of Management Information Systems* 14, no. 2, Fall, 33–56; Zetka, James, R. (1998) "The technological foundations of task-coordinating structures in new work organizations," *Work and Occupations* 25, no. 3, August, 356–379; Greco, JoAnn (1998) "Designing for the 21st century," *Journal of Business Strategy* 19, no. 6, November/December, 34–37.

5 Dunning, John H. (1995) "Reappraising the eclectic paradigm in an age of alliance capitalism," *Journal of International Business Studies* 26, no. 3, third quarter, 464.

6 *See*, for example, the following publications in regard to strategic alliances and joint ventures: Anderson, Erin and Gatignon, Hubert (1986) "Modes of foreign entry: A transaction cost analysis and propositions," *Journal of International Business Studies* 17, no. 3, Fall, 1–26; Beamish, Paul W. (1987) "Joint ventures in LDCs: Partner selection and performance," *Management International Review* 27, no. 1, 23–37; Beamish, Paul W. and Banks, John C. (1987) "Equity

joint ventures and the theory of the multinational enterprise," *Journal of International Business Studies* 18, no. 2, Summer, 1–16; Davidson, W.H. and McFetridge, D.G. (1985) "Key characteristics in the choice of international technology transfer mode," *Journal of International Business Studies* 16, no. 2, Summer, 5–21; Kogut, B. (1983) "Foreign direct investment as a sequential process," in *The Multinational Corporation in the 1980s*, ed. Charles Kindleberger and Donald Audretsch, Cambridge, MA: MIT Press.

7 Yip, George S. and Coundouriotis, George A. (1991) "Diagnosing global strategy potential: The world chocolate confectionery industry," *Planning Review* 19, no. 1, January/February, 4–14.

8 *See*, for example, Fukuyama, Francis (1995) *Trust: The social virtues and the creation of prosperity*, New York: Free Press.

9 *See* http://www.sternstewart.com

10 Tapscott, Don, Lowy, Alex and Ticoll, David (eds) (1998) *Blueprint to the digital economy: Creating wealth in the era of e-business*, New York: McGraw-Hill, 19.

11 Tapscott, Don et al, op. cit., 23.

12 Chesbrough, Henry W. and Teece, David J. (1996) "When is virtual virtuous? Organizing for innovation," *Harvard Business Review*, January/February, 65.

13 Chesbrough, Henry W. and Teece, David J. op. cit., 73.

14 Seely Brown, John and Duguid, Paul (1998) "Organizing knowledge," *California Management Review* 40, no. 3, spring, 90.

15 Normann, Richard and Ramirez, Rafael (1993) "From value chain to value constellation: Designing interactive strategy," *Harvard Business Review*, July/August, 65–77.

16 *See* "Strategy and the art of reinventing value," (1993) *Harvard Business Review*, September/October, 39–51.

17 Weiner, Michael, Nohria, Nitin, Hickman, Amanda and Smith, Huard (1997) "Value networks: The future of the U.S. electric utility industry," *Sloan Management Review* 38, no. 4, Summer, 21.

18 Lorenzoni, Gianni and Baden-Fuller, Charles (1995) "Creating a strategic center to manage a web of partners," *California Management Review* 37, no. 3, Spring, 149.

19 Kasarda, John D. and Rondinelli, Dennis A. (1998) "Innovative infrastructure for agile manufacturers," *Sloan Management Review* 39, no. 2, Winter, 73–82.

CHAPTER 17

1 These quotes come from a variety of sources, mostly presentations by colleagues, including Warren Wilhelm of Global Consulting Alliance.

2 A good reference for this work is Coates, F. and Jarrett, J. and Mahaffie, J. (1990) *Future work: Seven critical forces reshaping work and the work force in North America*, San Francisco Oxford: Jossey Bass; Hesselbein, Frances, Goldsmith, Marshall, and Beckhard, Richard (eds) (1995) *The leader of the future,* San Francisco: Jossey Bass; Hesselbein, Frances, Goldsmith, Marshall, and Beckhard, Richard (eds) (1997) *The organization of the future,* San Francisco: Jossey Bass.

3 Quinn, James Brian (1992) *Intelligent enterprise*, New York: Free Press; Quinn, James Brian (1996) "Leveraging intellect," *Academy of Management Executive*, 10(3): 7–27.

4 Stewart, Thomas (1997) *Intellectual capital*, New York: Doubleday.

5 Chandler, A.D. (1977) *The visible hand: The managerial revolution in American business,* Cambridge, MA: Harvard University Press.

6 Chandler, A.D., op. cit.

7 The capability argument has been presented in Ulrich, Dave (1993) "Profiling organizational competitiveness: Cultivating capabilities," *Human Resource Planning*, 16(3):1–17; Ulrich, Dave and Lake, Dale (1990) *Organizational capability: Competing from the inside/out*, New York: Wiley.

8 Womack, James P., and Jones, Daniel (1996) *Lean thinking: Banish waste and create wealth in your corporation*. New York: Simon & Schuster.

9 Saint-Onge, Hubert (1996) "Tacit knowledge: The key to the strategic alignment of intellectual capital," *Strategy and Leadership*, March/April, 10–14.

10 Snell, Scott, Lepak, David and Youndt, Mark (1998) "Managing the architecture of intellectual capital: Implications for strategic human resource management," in Wright, Patrick, Dyer, Lee, Boudreau, John and Milkovich, George (eds), *Research in personnel and human resources management*, Greenwich, CT: JAI Press.

11 Ulrich, Dave (1998) "Intellectual capital = competence x commitment," *Sloan Management Review*, Winter, 39(2):15–26.

12 Collins, James, and Porras, Jerry (1995) *Built to last: Successful habits of visionary companies,* New York: Harper.

13 Ulrich, Dave, Zenger, Jack, Smallwood, Norm (1999) *Results based leadership,* Boston: Harvard Business School Press.

14 Wick, Cal (1993) *The learning edge: How smart managers and smart companies stay ahead*, New York: McGraw Hill.
Senge, P (1990) *The Fifth Discipline*. New York: Harper and Rowe.

15 Yeung, Arthur, Ulrich, Dave, Nason, Stephen, Von Glinow, Mary Ann (1998) *Learning capability*, New York: Oxford Press.

16 Kotter, J., and Heskett, J. (1992) *Corporate culture and performance*, New York: Free Press.

17 Ashkenas, Ron, Ulrich, Dave, Jick, Todd and Kerr, Steve (1995) *The boundaryless organization: Breaking the chains of organization structure*, Jossey-Bass.

BIBLIOGRAPHY

Ashhenas, Ron, Ulrich, Dave, Jich, Todd, and Hear, Steve (1995) *The boundaryless organization: Breaking the chains of organizational structure*, San Francisco: Jossey-Bass Publishers.

Beatty, Jack (1998) *The world according to Peter Drucker*, New York: Broadway Books.

Bennis, Warren, and Nanus, Burt (1985) *Leaders: Strategies for taking charge*, New York: Harper Business.

Bennis, Warren (1994) *On becoming a leader*, New York: Perseus Press.

Collins, James C., and Porras, Jerry I. (1994) *Built to last: Successful habits of visionary companies*, New York: Harper Business.

Conklin, David W. (1991) *Comparative economic systems: Objectives, decision modes, and the process of choice*, London: Cambridge University Press.

Davis, Stan, and Meyer, Christopher (1998) *Blur: The speed of change in the connected economy*, New York: Warner Books.

Dell, Michael (1999) *Direct from Dell: Strategies that revolutionized an industry*, New York: Harper Business.

Drucker, Peter F. (1985) *Managing in a time of great change*, New York: Penguin Group.

—— (1992) *Managing for the future: The 1990s and beyond*, New York: Dutton.

—— (1996) *The executive in action*, New York: Harper Business.

—— (1999) *The frontiers of management*, New York: Penguin Group.

Farren, Caela (1997) *Who's running your career: Creating stable work in unstable times*, Austin, Texas: Bard Press.

Gates, Bill (1999) *Business @ speed of thought: Using digital nervous system*, New York: Warner Books.

Ghoshal, Sumantra and Bartlett, Christopher A. (1997) *The individualized corporation: A fundamentally new approach to management*, New York: Harper Business.

Gibson, Rowan (1997) *Rethinking the future*, London: Nicholas Brealey Publishing Limited.

Grove, Andrew S. (1996) *Only the paranoid survive: How to exploit the crisis points that challenge every company*, New York: Currency Doubleday.

Hamel, Gary and Prahalad, C.K. (1994) *Competing for the future*, Boston: Harvard Business School Press.

Handy, Charles (1998) *The hungry spirit beyond capitalism: A quest for purpose in the modern world*, New York: Broadway Books.

Heenan, Davida and Bennis, Warren G. (1999) *Co-leaders: The power of great partnerships*, New York: John Wiley & Sons.

Hesselbein, Frances, Goldsmith, Marshall, and Beckhard, Richard (1996) *Leader of the future*, San Francisco: Jossey-Bass Publishers.

—— (1997) *Organization of the future*, San Francisco: Jossey-Bass Publishers.

Hill, Linda A. (1993) *Becoming a manager: How new managers master the challenges of leadership*, New York: Penguin.

Kanter, Rosabeth Moss (1989) *When giants learn to dance: Mastering the challenges of strategy, management, and careers in the 1990s*, New York: Simon & Schuster.

Katz, Donald (1995) *Just do it: The Nike spirit in the corporate world*, Holbrook, Massachusetts: Adams Media Corporation.

Kotter, John P. (1996) *Leading change*, Boston: Harvard Business School Press.

—— (1997) *The new rules: Eight business breakthroughs to career success in 21st century*, New York: Free Press Paperbacks.

—— (1999) *On what leaders really do*, Boston: Harvard Business School Press.

Kouzes, James M., and Posner, Barry Z. (1995) *The leadership challenge*, San Francisco: Jossey-Bass Publishers.

Levine, R. Stuart. and Crom, Michael A. (1993) *The leader in you*, New York: Simon & Schuster.

Lorange, Peter (1994) *Strategic planning process (the International Library of Management)*, Dartmouth Publishing.

Mintzberg, Henry (1994) *The rise and fall of strategic planning: Reconceiving roles for planning, plans, planners*, New York: Free Press.

Moore, James F. (1996) *The death of competition: Leadership & strategy in the age of business ecosystem*, New York: Harper Business.

Peters, Thomas, and Waterman, Robert H. (1990) *In search of excellence: Lessons from America's best-run companies*, New York: Warner Books.

Porter, Michael E. (1980) *Competitive advantage: Creating and sustaining superior performance*, New York: The Free Press.

Senge, Peter M. (1990) *The fifth discipline: The art and practice of the learning organization*, New York: Currency/Doubleday.

—— (1999) Kleiner, Art, Roberts, Charlotte, Ross, Richard, Roth, George and Smith, Bryan (1999) *The dance of change: The challenges to sustaining momentum in learning organizations*, New York: Doubleday.

Sloan, Alfred P. Jr. (1996) *My years with General Motors*, New York: Doubleday.

Stewart, Thomas A. (1997) *Intellectual capital: The wealth of organizations*, New York: Doubleday/Currency.

Vicere, Albert A., and Fulmer, Robert M. (1996) *Leadership by design: How benchmark companies sustain success through investment in continuous learning*, Boston: Harvard Business School Press.

ABOUT THE THINKERS

MOREEN ANDERSON is a consultant specializing in senior executive development. She is a senior associate of Melbourne Business School where she also conducts research and lectures in organizational behavior on the school's executive and MBA programs. The early part of her career was spent in industry working in the energy sector, followed by almost ten years in banking in the UK. She has held several posts covering such areas as human resources, corporate affairs, marketing, and strategic planning. Her research and consultancy interests have focussed on senior executives, leadership and personal development. She is co-author (with Paul Dainty) of *The capable executive*.

CHRISTOPHER A. BARTLETT is the Daewoo professor of business administration at the Harvard Business School. He is the author, co-author, or editor of six books, including (co-authored with Sumantra Ghoshal) *Managing across borders: The transnational solution* and *The individualized corporation*, both of which have been translated into more than ten languages. He has also been winner of the Igor Ansoff Award for the best new work in strategic management. Prior to joining the faculty of Harvard Business School, he was a marketing manager with Alcoa in Australia, a management consultant in McKinsey and Company's London office, and general manager at Baxter Laboratories' subsidiary company in France. Dr Bartlett is currently faculty chairman of HBS's new international executive program, Program for Global Leadership.

HAMID BOUCHIKHI is an associate professor of strategic management at Ecole Superieure des Sciences Economiques et Commerciales (Essec) in Paris, France. His research and teaching are in managerial innovation, organization theory, entrepreneurship, and evolution of executive careers. Dr Bouchikhi has collaborated with several private and public sector organizations, including Groupe Lafarge, Framatome, French-American Foundation, Philips, RATP, and Usinor.

SUBIR CHOWDHURY is the executive vice-president of the American Supplier Institute – an international consulting firm headquartered in Livonia, Michigan. He is the co-author of the best-selling quality management book *QS-9000 Pioneers*. He has been awarded the honorable U.S. Congressional Recognition, Society of Automotive Engineer's highest recognition – Henry Ford II distinguished award for excellence, Automotive Hall of Fame's young leadership and excellence award, and many international recognitions for his works and contributions. He is currently chairman of the American Society for Quality's automotive division. With world-renowned quality guru Dr. Genichi Taguchi he recently co-authored a book *Robust Engineering* (McGraw-Hill, October 1999).

DAVID CONKLIN is a professor of international strategy at the Richard Ivey School of Business, the University of Western Ontario, Canada. His research analyzes the political, economic, societal, and technological forces that impact business decision making throughout the world. Many of his publications deal with the adjustment of businesses to new trade and investment agreements. Dr Conklin consults extensively for governments and corporations, and he teaches in many countries.

PAUL DAINTY is executive general manager, strategic human resources, for Pacific Dunlop Ltd, which is a major Australian conglomerate and the seventh largest employer in Australia. He is also a professorial fellow at Melbourne Business School, Melbourne University, where before joining Pacific Dunlop he held the chair in human resource management. During the nineties, he has focussed his research activities on senior executive development, strategic leadership, and team building. Dr Dainty has published articles, monographs and several books. He was lead author of *The capable executive: Effective performance in senior management* (Macmillan, 1996), which examines the capabilities associated with effective performance at senior levels in organizations.

PAUL A.L. EVANS is a professor of organizational behavior at INSEAD, where he has for many years headed up its activities relating to human resource and organizational management (founding director of executive seminars on *Management of People* and director *of Managerial Skills for International Business*). Former board member of the Human Resource Planning Society in the USA, he is the founder of the European Human Resource Forum, a project network of 150 leading corporations. His research focusses on the intersection between leadership, human resource management, and the management of change, and he has worked as a consultant and advisor on these issues to more than 70 corporations. His books include *Must success cost so much?* (translated into eight languages), *Human resource management in international firms*, and *Transnational human resource management.*

CAELA FARREN is the author of *Who's running your career?* and a leading advocate for workers in the business world. She is the CEO of MasteryWorks Inc., Washington, D.C. She has provided workforce and career management training to many of the Fortune 500 companies and associations, including AT&T, MTV, American Express, Nissan, and BASF. Dr Farren has made several appearances on television and radio, including CNN, NBC, Associated Press Radio Network, UPI Radio Network, The Business Channel, Bloomberg Television and Radio, and many others. She has also been featured in national newspapers and magazines, including the *Los Angeles Times, Newsweek,* and *USA Today.* Dr Farren is the recipient of the prestigious 1995 Walter Storey Career Practitioner Award.

J. WIL FOPPEN is the dean, director and professor of the Rotterdam School of Management, Erasmus Graduate School of Business, the Netherlands. He was a member of the executive board of the Erasmus University, chairman of the university committee on budget and finance, and chairman of the university council. As professor of political science, he was one of the founders of the joint inter-university program in government and public administration of the University of Leiden and Erasmus University. As professor of government he initiated (in co-operation) the postgraduate European Masters in Public Administration. Dr Foppen has written and edited several books on topsports (1972), Dutch politics (1973, 1974), statistics (1975), higher education systems and policy (1989, 1991), administrative reforms in local government (1991, 1992), knowledge management and organizational learning (1996), and management learning (1998).

ROBERT M. FULMER is the W. Brooks George professor of management at the College of William and Mary. Previously he was a visiting scholar at the Center for Organizational Learning at MIT, taught organization and management at Columbia University's Graduate Business School, was responsible for worldwide management development at AlliedSignal, Inc., and was director of executive education at Emory University. He is author of four editions of *The new management* (Macmillan), and co-author in 1998 of *Executive development and organizational learning for global business* (International Business Press) and *Leadership by design* (Harvard Business School Press). He has designed and delivered leadership development initiatives in 22 countries and on six continents. Dr Fulmer is a senior fellow and special advisor to the president of the EastWest Institute, a member of International Research Advisory Board of the Strategos Institute.

SUMANTRA GHOSHAL holds the Robert P. Bauman chair in strategic leadership at the London Business School where he also serves as the director of the Aditya V. Birla India Centre. He has published eight books, over 45 articles and several award-winning case studies. *Managing across borders: The transnational solution*, co-authored with Christopher Bartlett, has been listed as one of the 50 most influential management books of this century and has been translated into nine languages. *The differentiated network: Organizing the multinational corporation for value creation*, co-authored with Nitin Nohria, won the George Terry Book Award in 1997. Dr Ghoshal's latest book, *The individualized corporation*, co-authored with Christopher Bartlett, won the Igor Ansoff Award in 1997. Described by *The Economist* as a Euroguru, Sumantra maintains teaching and consulting relationships with several American, European, and Asian companies.

MARSHALL GOLDSMITH is a founding director of Keilty, Goldsmith & Company (KGC), a consulting firm based in San Diego, California. He is a partner in the Global Consulting Alliance, and an active member of the board of governors of the Peter F. Drucker Foundation for non-profit management. He has received national recognition for co-designing one of America's innovative leadership development programs. He is co-editor of the best-selling books *The leader of the future*, *The organization of the future*, and *The community of the future*. Mr Goldsmith was ranked in the *Wall Street Journal* as one of the top ten consultants in the field of executive development.

LINDA A. HILL is the Wallace Brett Donham Professor of Business Administration in the organizational behavior area at the Harvard Business School. Her book, *Becoming a manager: Mastery of a new identity*, explores the challenges of making the transition from star producer to manager. She is also the author of *Power and influence: Getting things done in organizations*, and award-winning CD-ROM *High performance management and coaching*. Organizations with which Professor Hill has worked include Arthur Andersen, Cabot Corporation, General Electric, Bristol-Myers Squibb, IBM, Merrill Lynch, Molex International, and PricewaterhouseCoopers. Professor Hill is a member of the board of directors of Cooper Industries, the boards of trustees of the Rockefeller Foundation, Bryn Mawr College, The Children's Museum, Boston, and the board of overseers of the Beth Israel Deaconess Medical Center, Boston.

INGALILL HOLMBERG is an associate professor and director of the Centre for Advanced Studies in Leadership at the Stockholm School of Economics, Sweden. Dr Holmberg's research focusses on managerial leadership and corporate governance in different business contexts. She also runs projects on leadership and culture, and has been an advisor to the Swedish Ministry of Industry. Her latest engagement concerns the role of Swedish multinational firms in increasing the pace of knowledge creation to improve the competitiveness of Sweden as a nation.

ROSABETH MOSS KANTER holds the Class of 1960 Chair as Professor of Business Administration, Harvard Business School, Boston, Massachusetts, USA. She is an internationally known business leader, adviser to many global corporations around the world, best-selling author, prominent speaker about business strategy and change leadership in numerous countries, and advocate for effective change in public and private sectors. Among her award-winning books are *The change masters* (Simon & Schuster; Touchstone Books), *Men and women of the corporation* (Basic Books), *When giants learn to dance: Mastering the challenges of strategy, management and careers* (Simon & Schuster; Touchstone Books), *The challenge of organizational change* (Free Press), *World class: Thriving locally in the global economy* (Simon & Schuster; Touchstone Books), and *Rosabeth Moss Kanter on the frontiers of management* (Harvard Business School Press).

KATRIN H. KÄUFER is a visiting scholar at MIT Sloan School of Management and lecturer at University of Innsbruck, Austria. Her professional experience includes three years as a customer consultant at the Dresdner Bank, Germany. Her current research focusses on methods for leading profound change processes in organizations. Dr Käufer won the innovation award of the "Stiftung für Industrieforschung" for the development of the Global Studies Program. Together with Professor Galtung she founded this program in 1989–90, an integrated study program at 12 universities around the world. She has consulted with a global pharmaceutical company and a learning network of small and middle size companies.

JOHN R. KIMBERLY is Henry Bower professor in the department of management and health care systems at the Wharton School, and professor of sociology at the University of Pennsylvania. He is also the Salmon and Rameau Fellow in health care management at INSEAD in Fontainebleau, France. He works on problems of innovation, change, and industrial transformation, and their consequences for individual careers.

JAMES M. KOUZES is chairman of Tom Peters Group/Learning Systems. He has been engaged in executive education since 1969, and in September 1993 *The Wall Street Journal* cited him as one of the 12 most requested "non-university executive-education providers" to US companies. He has conducted leadership programs for hundreds of organizations, including Arthur Andersen, Boeing, Charles Schwab, Consumers Energy, Dell Computer, Honeywell, Johnson & Johnson, Levi Strauss & Co., 3M, Motorola, Pacific Telesis, Stanford University, Sun Microsystems, and the YMCA. Mr Kouzes is the co-author with Barry Z. Posner of four books on leadership, including *The leadership challenge*, and *Credibility*, both award-winners and best-sellers. Their newest collaborations are *Encouraging the heart* and *The leadership challenge planner*. They are also the co-developers of the *Leadership practices inventory*, a 360-degree assessment instrument that has been administered worldwide to over 250 000 leaders.

STUART R. LEVINE is Chairman and CEO of Stuart Levine & Associates LLC, an international consulting and training group. He was former CEO of Dale Carnegie & Associates, Inc. Stuart was awarded the 1995 Entrepreneur of the Year Award for Leadership. He is co-author of best-selling business book, *The Leader in You*. He won the 1999 Innovator of the Year award for Techno-Bridge®, leadership training for technology professionals. Mr Levine consults extensively on organizational alignment, vision, strategic planning, and change management with clients such as Microsoft Corporation, The Social Security Administration, Fort James, Young Presidents' Organization, Carl Marks Consulting Group, ARC, HMG Worldwide, and the Legal Marketing Association. Mr Levine served in the New York State Assembly. He is past Chairman of the Board of Dowling College and past Vice Chairman of North Shore University Hospital. He serves on the Board of Directors of the Olsten Corporation and European American Bank.

PETER LORANGE is the president of IMD (International Institute of Management Development) in Lausanne, Switzerland. He was president of the Norwegian School of Management (BI), and at the Wharton School, University of Pennsylvania, he was the Worster professor of international business, as well as the head of the Lauder Institute. He has also taught at the Sloan School of MIT. Dr Lorange's research interests center primarily on various aspects of strategic management, including the role of management processes and strategic alliances. He is conducting research on the strategic challenges facing academic institutions. He has written more than 100 articles and authored, co-authored, or edited 13 books. He is awaiting publication of his latest book, *The dynamic business school*.

PETER MORAN is assistant professor of strategy and international management at the London Business School. His current research focuses on how organizations and their managers can influence the ability of individuals to add value for themselves, for their organizations, and for society. His publications include *Bad for practice: A critique of the transaction cost theory* and *Markets, firms and the process of economic development*, both co-authored with Sumantra Ghoshal and appearing in the *Academy of Management Review*.

BARRY Z. POSNER is dean of the Leavey School of Business, Santa Clara University, and professor of organizational behavior. He has received several outstanding teaching and leadership awards, and has published more than 80 research and practitioner articles. He is the co-author with James M. Kouzes of four books on leadership, including the two award-winners and best-sellers *The leadership challenge* and *Credibility*. Dr Posner serves on the editorial review boards of several academic publications and on the board of directors for Public Allies-Silicon Valley and the Center for Excellence in Nonprofits. An internationally recognized expert on leadership, he has been faculty for executive development programs for such diverse companies as ARCO, Australia Post, Ciba-Geigy, Gymboree, Hewlett-Packard, Kaiser Permanente Health Care, Motorola, Pacific Telesis, Silicon Graphics, TRW, and the United Way.

C.K. PRAHALAD is Harvey C. Fruehauf professor of business administration and professor of corporate strategy and international business at the University of Michigan's Graduate School of Business Administration. Together with Professor Gary Hamel, his work has helped to redefine what it means to be strategic, by looking beyond the current ideas on business transformation to the more visionary concept of industry transformation. As a consultant, Dr Prahalad has worked with many multinational companies, including Eastman Kodak, AT&T, Cargill, Philips, Colgate-Palmolive, Motorola, Marriott, Oracle, and Whirlpool. Two of the Harvard Business Review articles he co-authored with Gary Hamel won McKinsey prizes. He is co-author with Hamel of best-selling business book *Competing for the future*, and with Yves Doz of a pioneering book on multinationals, *The multinational mission*.

JONAS RIDDERSTRÅLE is an assistant professor at the Stockholm School of Economics, Sweden and works at the Institute of International Business and the Centre for Advanced Studies in Leadership. Dr Ridderstråle has been involved in research, teaching and consulting in the fields of international management, the future firm, and leadership styles in the information age. In 1997 he published his latest book, *Global Innovation*, soon to be followed by *Funky business*. Dr Ridderstråle is a highly appreciated speaker with frequent engagements all over the world.

PETER M. SENGE is a senior lecturer at the Massachusetts Institute of Technology. He is the author of the widely acclaimed best-selling book *The fifth discipline: The art and practice of the learning organization* and, with his colleagues Charlotte Roberts, Rick Ross, Bryan Smith and Art Kleiner, co-author of *The fifth discipline fieldbook: Strategies and tools for building a learning organization*. He is also the co-author of *The dance of change*. Dr Senge has lectured extensively throughout the world, translating the abstract ideas of systems theory into tools for better under-standing of economic and organizational change. His work articulates a cornerstone position of human values in the workplace; namely, that vision, pur-pose, alignment, and systems thinking are essential if organizations are to realize their potentials. He has worked with leaders in business, education, health care and government.

LAWRENCE TAPP is the dean of the Richard Ivey School of Business, the University of Western Ontario, Canada. His reputation as an innovator and catalyst of change stands him in good stead as he prepares to lead Ivey into the next millennium. In 1985, he initiated and led the world's largest leveraged buy-out outside the USA that created the Lawson Mardon Group Limited. His interest in post-secondary education is reflected in his long service on the McMaster University Board of Governors (1985–95). Between 1993 and 1995 he served as an adjunct professor in the faculty of management at the University of Toronto, earning "top professor" ratings from the MBA and EMBA students. He also served as chairman of the University of Toronto Faculty of Management Advisory Board from 1992–95.

DAVE ULRICH is a professor of business administration at the University of Michigan Business School. He is the author of *Human resource champions: The next agenda for adding value and delivering results*, and co-author of *Organizational capabil-ity*, and *The boundaryless organization. Business Week* hailed him as one of the world's top ten educators in management and the number one educator in human resources. Dr Ulrich has received the Pericles Pro Meritus Award for outstanding contribution to the field of human resources, and has consulted with over half of the Fortune 500.

INDEX